*The Poetics of Difference*

THE NEW BLACK STUDIES SERIES

Edited by Darlene Clark Hine
and Dwight A. McBride

*A list of books in the series appears
at the end of this book.*

# The Poetics of Difference

## Queer Feminist Forms in the African Diaspora

MECCA JAMILAH SULLIVAN

**UNIVERSITY OF ILLINOIS PRESS**
Urbana, Chicago, and Springfield

© 2021 by Mecca Jamilah Sullivan

Manufactured in the United States of America
1 2 3 4 5 C P 5 4 3 2 1
∞ This book is printed on acid-free paper.

Library of Congress Cataloging-in-Publication Data
Names: Sullivan, Mecca Jamilah, author.
Title: The poetics of difference: queer feminist forms
    in the African diaspora / Mecca Jamilah Sullivan.
Description: Urbana: University of Illinois Press, 2021.
    | Series: The new Black studies series | Includes
    bibliographical references and index. | Identifiers:
    LCCN 2021006472 (print) | LCCN 2021006473
    (ebook) | ISBN 9780252043963 (cloth ; acid-free
    paper) | ISBN 9780252086038 (paperback; acid-free
    paper) | ISBN 9780252052897 (ebook)
Subjects: LCSH: African literature (English)—Black
    authors—History and criticism. | African literature
    (English)—Women authors—History and
    criticism. | American literature—African American
    authors—History and criticism. | American
    literature—Women authors—History and criticism.
    | Literature, Experimental—20th century—History
    and criticism. | Identity (Philosophical concept) in
    literature. | African diaspora in literature. | Women,
    Black, in literature. | Feminism and literature. |
    Queer theory.
Classification: LCC PR9340 .S85 2021 (print) | LCC
    PR9340 (ebook) | DDC 820.9/928708996—dc23
LC record available at https://lccn.loc.gov/2021006472
LC ebook record available at https://lccn.loc.gov/
    2021006473

# Contents

# Acknowledgments

*Well . . . that's different.*
This is the loving way Black women in my life let me know I'm up to something strange, unusual, somewhat new. The phrase carries weight—not quite judgment, but critique. And yet, it often also carries tenderness, as though the words are meant to remind the hearer that she is cared for, in spite of the difference, and because of it.

Many people have loved, cheered, cared for, and critiqued me through this project. I have to thank, first, my mother, Dr. Martha A. Sullivan ("big Mecca"), whose tremendous example sets the scope of my vision; my father, James P. Sullivan, whose poet soul is truly special; and my little brother, Malik, style icon, with whom I first began to imagine a practice of black/queer care.

My deepest gratitude to the University of Illinois Press, especially to Dawn Durante, whose vision and attentive eye have made this project what it is, and Alison K. Syring Bassford, who led the book to full fruition. Huge thanks to Laurie Prendergast for helping me through the process with immeasurable generosity and heart, in the midst of a global pandemic.

I am ever grateful to my teachers and mentors: Thadious Davis, your generosity even at the earliest stages of this project has been remarkable. Herman Beavers, Heather Love, and Salamishah Tillett, this book would not be possible without you. My thanks to the great Cheryl Wall, whose presence was a light I'm honored to have known. Jennifer DeVere Brody, Evie Shockley, Alexis De-Veaux, Darryl Pinckney, Samuel Delany, John H. Bracey, Andrea Hairston, Paula Krebs, Barbara Savage, Ginetta Candelario, Ania Loomba, E. Frances White, Ellen Eisenman, Ann Ferguson, Brenda Allen, Amy Kissell, Anne Rosenthal, and Ginger Leigh, thank you for supporting the kinds of thinking that have led me here, and teaching me how to make it all work. Deepest gratitude to Kevin

Quashie, with whom I have learned and laughed so much over all these years, each moment a gift.

Many thanks to my fabulous colleagues at Bryn Mawr College and in the Tri-College Consortium, whose intellectual engagement and support have brought much joy to this process. Thanks especially to E-House and its regulars, including Linda-Susan Beard, Kate Thomas, Bethany Schneider, Jennifer Harford-Vargas, Jamie K. Taylor, Colby Gordon, Chloe Flower, Michael Tratner, Dan Torday, Gail Hemmeter, Betsy Litsinger, Matthew Ruben, Jen Callaghan, Bryn Thompson, and the homie Airea D. Matthews. I am also grateful to the Africana Studies Program, the Gender and Sexuality Studies Program, the Latin American, Iberian, and Latina/o Studies Program at Bryn Mawr, as well as the Tri-Co Philly Program. I can't think of a warmer, more vibrant intellectual home in which to have developed these ideas. Thanks also to the department of English at the University of Pennsylvania and the department of Women, Gender, Sexuality Studies at UMass for making this project fuller and better.

I am grateful for the support of the following fellowships and organizations, without which this project would not have been possible. Deepest thanks to the Institute for Citizens and Scholars/ Woodrow Wilson Career Enhancement Fellowship, the Office of the Provost's and the Faculty Research Grants Program at Bryn Mawr College, the Postdoctoral Fellowship in Black Feminism at Duke University, the Postdoctoral Fellowship in African Diaspora Literature at Rutgers University, the Gaius Charles Bolin fellowship at Williams College, the Mellon Foundation, the Social Sciences Research Council, the Faculty Fellowship at the Five College Center for the International Study of the Americas, the Barnard College Center for Research on Women, the Modern Language Association, and the National Women's Studies Association, whose support has been invaluable.

I've been fortunate to spend time with many incredible minds in these academic streets. Thank you to everyone who has helped shape this project with their questions, feedback, and collaborative musings: GerShun Avilez, Tsitsi Jaji, Sarah Mantilla Griffin, Isabel Geathers, Julius Fleming, Savannah Shange, Tanisha C. Ford, Brandon Woods, Tshepo Masango-Cherry, Nicole Meyers-Turner, Kirsten Leng, Abbie Boggs, Meta DuEwa Jones, Aldon Lynn Nielson, La Marr Jurelle Bruce, Rhon Manigault-Bryant, James Manigault-Bryant, Rashida Braggs, Cae Joseph Messena, and Marlon M. Bailey, thank you for your imprints on this book. Shout out to *The Feminist Wire* for giving me new ways to touch community in the early stages of this project, and the Philadelphia Burlesque Academy for keeping it moving. LH Stallings, Marlon Moore, Angelique Nixon, Treva Lindsey, and Marlo David, thank you for your brilliance and the crazy good times. Darius Bost, I learn more about thought and humanity every time I talk to you. C. Riley Snorton, my truest homie, thank you for being a rider. Started from the bottom; to the AC we go.

Thank you to my day-ones: Effie Richardson, Nina Sharma, Erica Locke, Nicole Shawan Junior, Connie Utada, Kamilah Aisha Moon, Kieu Smith, Keisha Warner, Lecynia Marie Swire, Hanifah Walidah, you have helped me see this through. None of this would be without you. Cheryl Clarke, cher poète, I'm tickled to call you my friend. Jeanette Aycock, there are no words for my love and gratitude. No hill for a stepper, indeed!

Thank you to my heart-loves, my mind-guides: Toni, Audre, Ntozake, whose voices help me clear my own. And thank you to my students, who remind me why it matters.

*The Poetics of Difference*

# Black Queer Feminist Poetics

## *Rereading the Intersection*

> *Being women together was not enough. We were different.*
> *Being gay-girls together was not enough. We were different.*
> *Being Black together was not enough. We were different.*
> *Being Black women together was not enough. We were*
> *different. Being Black dykes together was not enough.*
> *We were different. . . .*
>
> It was a while before we came to realize that our place was
> the very house of difference. . . .
>
> —Audre Lorde, *Zami* (1982)

Setting out to tell a version of her life story in her 1982 narrative, *Zami*, Audre Lorde finds the genre conventions of autobiography, memoir, and mythology to be insufficient. To address this problem, Lorde creates what she terms a "biomythography," a heterogeneous genre borrowing elements of each of those narrative forms, but also incorporating song lyrics, poetry, lists, letters, and several other types of writing. Rather than reformulate the story of her "becoming" to fit any single genre rubric, Lorde invents a composite genre to accommodate her understanding of herself and her social experience. *Zami* follows the narrator/protagonist's coming of age as the lesbian daughter of Grenadian immigrants in New York. At the close of the text, she expresses the ultimate failure of her efforts to situate herself in communities defined by racial, gender, and sexual alterity. Even in combination, each of the identities these communities claim—"black," "woman," and "dyke"—is "not enough" to describe Lorde's understanding of her self and her difference.

Throughout her expansive oeuvre, which includes poems, essays, and speeches along with *Zami*, *The Cancer Journals*—Lorde's other full-length autobiographical prose work—and *Need*, a mixed-genre performance poetry "chorale," Lorde lists her various identifications with an anagrammatic quality of mixture and repetition. Along with her race, gender, and sexuality, Lorde repeatedly invokes difference through her age, class, ethnicity, fatness, creative interests, reproductive status, relationship status, health status, and disability in varying list-like configurations, refusing to offer any one set of differences a stable pride of place.[1] For Lorde, as *Zami*'s narrative suggests, it is difference itself that reconciles the experiences of blackness, womanhood, sexuality, and this broader expanse of other alterities. Difference defines her subject position, and the invented genre of the "biomythography" emerges as the only possible "place" in which that difference is fully legible.

Lorde's conclusion that identifications based on finite combinations of race, gender, and sexuality would leave crucial aspects of her subjectivity missing articulates a long-standing problematic in black women's identity theorizing. In positioning an unnamed but ubiquitous experience of difference as a point of departure for poetic praxis, Lorde anticipates challenges to prominent late-twentieth-century models of intersectionality. Coined in 1989 by legal studies scholar Kimberlé Crenshaw to describe the specific simultaneous impacts of racism and sexism on black women's legal, civic, and sociopolitical experience, the term "intersectionality" has since been taken up in academic, activist, and cultural discourses as a signifier of multiple difference ("Demarginalizing the Intersection" 140; "Kimberlé Crenshaw on Intersectionality"). In these discourses, the intersection has served as a way of naming the simultaneous, concurrent, and mutually imbricating functions of several power structures (including racism, sexism, classism, heterosexism, homophobia, cissexism, transphobia, ableism, and Eurocentrism) as well as the sociopolitical locations of subjects and communities impacted by multiple forms of oppression. This broadening of intersectionality's contexts and meanings has also led to debates about its usefulness in contemporary discourse, and a struggle to define its value as a language for describing difference.[2] Lorde's vision of the "biomythography" highlights the crucial role of the literary imagination in intersectionality theorizing. In creating the genre of the biomythography as a discursive site for inhabiting multiple difference, Lorde suggests that an effective language of black feminist difference requires not only the sort of sociopolitical specificity that both intersectionality and its critics strive for, but also a radical artistic and creative vision that can express experiences of multiplicity, complexity, and simultaneity in ways that normative English prose cannot reach.

Lorde's poetics, even in this short passage mentioned above, instantiate her artistic theory of multiple difference. By breaking form from the prose narrative that precedes the passage—a narrative in which she describes her search for community as a young woman in 1950s New York City—Lorde provokes a break in readerly experience as well, asking her reader to open to the destabilization, fragmentation, and multiplicity her narrator describes. The anaphoric repetition of "being . . . together was not enough" replicates the insufficiency of individual, discrete identity categories such as race, gender, and sexuality as viable criteria for black feminist belonging, and highlights the failure of standard English prose to provide language for that failure. By italicizing this prosepoetic section and setting it off from the rest of the text, Lorde asks the reader to contend with rupture in the whitespace, and to experience difference as an interpretive obstacle on the material plane of the text. She requires us to navigate language differently—to stop, read, and reread for her meaning: even when identity seems definitive, for black women, difference persists.

Here, Lorde leads us in a queer reading of blackwoman difference in two important ways: she opens for the reader the multiple nonnormative "outsider" positions through which she moves; she also prompts the reader to develop queer reading practices, ways of reading that both apprehend and destabilize the workings of power continuously within and between words, phrases, lines, and sentences. Repetitions, parallels, and parities are constantly invoked and constantly fail, giving way to the triumph of difference over the coherence, and thus forming the fragmented, shifting, unlocatable, and incompletable narrative center of what Lorde insistently reminds us is a black lesbian life. Lorde positions black lesbian living as both lexicon and narrative frame for a queer theory of difference: in *Zami*, black lesbian life is both story and character, text and typography, and it asks us to learn to read the theory and glean its meanings both within and between the lines.

Following Lorde's logic, I take up *difference* both as a means of naming the specific forms of otherness by which black women have been barred from power and life in Western colonial logics (for example, race, gender, class, sexuality, nationality, and [dis]ability), and as a means of articulating the capaciousness and complexity of black women's subjectivities, which defy normative logics of language and categorization. These nuances, I argue, are often found in the disruptive and anti-normative aesthetics of black feminist cultural production—a realm of aesthetic practice that is constantly linked with black women's nonnormative erotics.

Using this model of difference, I read intersectionality as a queer creative practice that produces formally subversive, genre-bending creative expression and necessitates queer reading strategies for interpreting difference in black feminist life. Rereading *Zami* for Lorde's poetics requires that we envision intersectionality not as a strategy primarily useful for charting conceptual or even political interrelationships between identificatory categories, but as part of a black feminist literary tradition in which the expression of psychic and bodily experiences of difference interrogate power and wage anti-oppressive critique. Reading *Zami's* queer poetics invites us, in other words, to resituate intersectionality within its proto-discourses in black women's expressive culture and humanistic thought.

*The Poetics of Difference* takes up this project, charting the black queer feminist contexts and creative strategies with which artists, writers, and performers have shaped intersectionality theorizing. Recent debates on black feminism and intersectionality from historical and social science perspectives have named the challenges of theorizing multiple forms of difference in ways that acknowledge the indeterminacy of gender and race, the complexities of nation and class, and the multiple meanings of sexuality. Yet black women's literary cultures have long theorized these complexities—though often in languages, spaces, genres, and forms that Western academic scholarship has yet to fully embrace.

Literary scholars such as Elizabeth Alexander, Mae G. Henderson, Karla F. C. Holloway, Dale E. Peterson, Samantha Pinto, and Dorothy J. Hale have charted crucial links between black women's subversive narrative strategies and their subjective multiplicities, opening space for an extended theory of a black feminist poetics.[3] Likewise, the works of scholars including Nadia Ellis and Omise'eke Natasha Tinsley have charted important paths in exploring the queer sexualities of African diaspora women's literary cultures and questioning the elision of black women's creative and narrative theorizing. In *Ezili's Mirrors: Imagining Black Queer Genders*, Tinsley illuminates how Western academic hegemonies of knowledge and language facilitate these elisions. She decenters the framing concepts of queer studies and instead looks to Caribbean narrative cultures—and specifically to the gender-subversive and sexually subversive Caribbean mythological figure Ezili—as an "other vocabulary" of gender and sexuality (10). By initiating, as Tinsley puts it, "a discussion of black Atlantic genders and sexualities not primarily through queer studies, but rather within a lineage of black feminisms: a lineage which pushes me to ask what it would sound like if scholars were to speak of Ezili the way we speak, say, of Judith Butler," Tinsley invites us to activate the critical interventions of queer and feminist diasporic narrative cultures and let them guide our own theorizing (11). Moreover, by framing both these elisions and the modes by which to address them as a matter of language and lexical retooling, Tinsley joins these other scholars in opening space for specific interrogations of how subversions of literary form, language, and creative expression facilitate black women's queer feminist theorizing.

As these theorists suggest, radical black feminist expression occurs in several spaces, touching the literary page but also extending beyond it to other expressive realms, including music, visual art, theater, dance, and other modes of performance. In each of these forms, black feminist artists engage in disruptive aesthetic practices, often deploying interruptive uses of language to critique and reimagine constructions of black womanhood in their given mediums. In addition, Lorde's insistence on framing her search for collective self-definition through spatial metaphors of bodily location ("our place was the very house of difference") emphasizes the specific role of embodiment in black feminist poetics. Following these logics, I advance a theory of "poetics" that comprises aesthetic, artistic, and formal choices in range of creative genres often connected to—but not limited to—those forms widely recognized as "literary." The vision of black feminist poetics proposed here rejects generic, disciplinary, and philosophical frameworks that impose fixed distinctions between the realms of (literary) voice and (expressive/sentient/somatic) body. Instead, I offer a model of poetics that accommodates multiple forms of linguistic and bodily expression. Further, I argue that it is precisely by disrupting the discrete categories of the "literary" and the "bodily" that black feminist artists often make their queerest poetic interventions.

*The Poetics of Difference* seeks to enter the unexplored spaces of black women's queer creative theorizing. It seeks to learn its languages, to read the textures of its forms. In so doing, *The Poetics of Difference* aims to signal the space beyond both fixed notions of the intersection and its erasure in academic discourse. I gesture instead to a space of queer imagination where black women constantly proliferate new languages to speak the many names of difference.

## The Faultlines of Intersectional Theorizing

> The synthesis of these oppressions creates the conditions
> of our lives . . . Even our Black women's style of talking/
> testifying in Black language about what we have experienced
> has a resonance that is both cultural and political.
> —Combahee River Collective, "Black Feminist Statement" (1977)

Reading black women's poetics of difference offers important interventions into key theories of intersectionality, highlighting the theory's pre-discourses in literary studies and emphasizing the place of embodiment and diaspora in black feminist theorizations of multiple difference. Since the term's coining by Crenshaw in 1989, the concept of *intersectionality* has largely been understood as a late-twentieth-century product of US social science and critical race discourses, mobilized by queer studies, postcolonial studies, and other academic fields, and later emerging in social justice and activist discourse. This narrative of intersectionality's meanings and legacies elides the contributions of black women poets, novelists, performers, artists, and rhetoricians across the diaspora who have, for centuries, theorized linked racial and gender politics in their work.

In the decades before Crenshaw coined the term, the 1970s and early 1980s gave rise to robust conversations about difference between and among feminists, particularly around questions of race, class, gender, and sexual expression. The solidification of a self-designated women of color feminist discourse and the discursive development of the sex wars debates in the United States took shape largely through grassroots feminist literary publishing venues, many of which circulated poetry, fiction, visual art, and other creative works alongside critical essays, refusing to make empirical distinctions between the two. The importance of literary and mixed-genre journals like *Conditions*, *Sinister Wisdom*, *Amazon Quarterly*, *Big Mama Rag*, *On Our Backs*, *Off Our Backs*, and publishers like Cleis Press, The Crossing Press, Naiad Press, Diana Press, Shameless Hussy Press, Kitchen Table: Women of Color Press, and others demonstrates the crucial role of literary culture in charting both black feminist thought in general and discourses around racism, classism, gender norming, and sexual stigma within feminist discourse. Likewise, gatherings like the 1982 Scholar and Feminist Conference "Toward A Politics of Sexuality" (at which Hortense Spillers presented her important essay "Interstices: A Drama of Small Words," whose arguments are crucial to this study) staged robust critical feminist conversations on sex and power within academic and nonacademic spaces. This history reveals how black feminism's key interventions regarding difference circulate through 1970s and 1980s literary culture, and how they inform what we now understand as "intersectional analysis" through innovative models of publishing, genre subversion, and creative theorizing.[4]

Even in intersectionality's recognized prototexts, important emphases on literary culture and expression have gone underexplored. In the Combahee River Collective's canonical 1977 Black Feminist Statement, a known prototext for intersectionality theorizing, the Collective critiqued what they termed the "interlocking," "manifold and simultaneous oppressions" faced by black women, including "racial, sexual, heterosexual, and class oppression," and offered an "integrated analysis and practice" for understanding and combating these linked structures (210). For the Collective, this practice was necessarily rooted in narrative—in expressing and understanding the "undeniably . . . personal genesis for Black Feminism, that is, the political realization that comes from the seemingly personal experiences of individual Black women's lives." This involved not only direct action and political coalition among black women, but also "talk[ing] about our feelings" and "look[ing] more deeply into our own experiences and, from that sharing and growing consciousness . . . build[ing] a politics that will change our lives." (210–212). For the collective, this political power of self-expression is inseparable from creative subversions of language, and from the innovative "style[s] of talking/testifying" that black women develop (213).

Alice Walker's extended definition of "womanist" throughout *In Search of Our Mothers' Gardens* (1983) also centers creative cultural expression as key in black feminist theorizing. Walker's womanist is a woman who both "loves other women, sexually and/or nonsexually," and who "[a]ppreciates and prefers women's culture. . . . Loves music. Loves dance. Loves the moon. *Loves* the Spirit. Loves love and food and roundness. Loves struggle. *Loves* the Folk. Loves herself. *Regardless*" (vii). That same-sex sexuality is central in both Walker's and the Combahee River Collective's manifestos is not coincidental. For them, as for Lorde, theorizing black feminist praxis beyond race and gender—in this case, a praxis that combats heterosexism and acknowledges queer desire as central aspects of its mission—requires the breadth of storytelling and the nuance of creative expression.

Late-twentieth-century models of "intersectionality," however, tended to privilege categories of "race, gender, and class" or "race, gender, and sexuality," often at the expense of nation, gender expression, embodiment, and several other differences. This intersectional mapping of difference has drawn critique from a number of theorists, including Jennifer Christine Nash, Jasbir Puar, and others, who have argued that "intersectionality" is an inadequate optic for understanding the performative and processual dynamics of identity within a contemporary global context. These critiques largely question the plausibility of a useful theory of difference that insists upon a consistent focus on black women, even as languages of race and gender (including "blackness" and "womanhood") shift and expand in contemporary understanding. Puar has argued that, for example, within the field of feminist studies, "the insistent consolidation of intersectionality as a dominant heuristic may well be driven by anxieties about maintaining the 'integrity' of a discrete black feminist genealogy, one that might actually obfuscate how intersectionality is thought of and functions differently in different strands of black feminist and [non-black] women of color feminist thought" (52). Nash critiques recent popular misreadings of intersectionality, particularly those that dismiss the recent swell of interest in intersectionality as an organizing framework for undergraduate student activism and other efforts to make change within academia. Ultimately, however, Nash argues that intersectionality theorizing has steeped black feminists in a form of "defensiveness," in which the project of correcting popular misreadings, historicizing intersectionality's obscured black feminist intellectual foundations, and reiterating its connections to black women "conscript black feminism into a largely protective posture, leaving black feminists mired in policing intersectionality's usages, demanding that intersectionality remain located within black feminism and reasserting intersectionality's 'true' origins in black feminist texts" (*Black Feminism Reimagined* 12–13).[5]

Yet, black women's poetics of difference demonstrates that the work of articulating intersectionality's meanings for black womanhood is less a matter of "policing" discourse than an effort to correct flagrant misreadings, underreadings, and outright dismissals of black women's subjective complexity over generations. This dismissal of black women's intersectional experience runs hand-in-hand with the dismissal of black women's art and its theoretical nuances. Even as scholars recognize the theoretical contributions of figures such as Lorde, Walker, June Jordan, Cheryl Clarke, Ghanaian writer Ama Ata Aidoo, and members of the Combahee River Collective as crucial to intersectionality discourse, these writers' simultaneous positioning as both critical theorists and creative writers has been largely unacknowledged; the impact of their art on their theories of difference has yet to be explored. Re-situating intersectionality within its geneses in black women's storytelling traditions reveals a broad range of rich, underexplored theories of difference offered by black women and highlights the extent to which black women's creative and formal innovations have always been political acts.

The problem of proliferating difference that Lorde's "biomythography" articulates is the problem of the "interstice"—what Hortense Spillers calls "the missing word" of black women's difference "which allows us to speak about and . . . which enables us to speak at all" ("Interstices" 156). *The Poetics of Difference* extends "intersectional" frameworks to consider these variegated "interstices" of black women's difference as a central focus of black feminist poetics. I explore the location of the interstice in concert with Spillers's vision of the "nuantial," which describes a nexus of black women's sexual and subjective complexity written *out* of the blackwoman body at the moment of colonial contact. For Spillers, "[w]inning the right to the *nuantial* . . . goes with the territory of subjecthood, which must be earned for some; it is also proximate to 'sexuality.' In order to name black women in the sexual, the investigator is obligated to back all the way up to that suspenseful chapter in the unfolding of subjecthood, which begins for Africanity in the West *not* with a body . . . but with what that body was meant to *mean* via the powerful grammars of capture." ("Peter's Pans" 14; emphasis in original). The nuantial signals those disallowed nodes of complexity, contradiction, difference, and agential sexual desire denied black women in the violent processes of diaspora. If the interstice names the "missing" discursive presence that allows black women to "speak about [our sexuality] . . . and that which allows us to speak at all," the nuantial describes the infinite complexities of desire, subjectivity, and blackwoman being rendered silent at the discursive location of the interstice (Spillers 26, 156).

I deploy these visions of nuantial expression and interstitial location to explore conceptions of blackwoman difference that, like Lorde's, resist static, hierarchical spatial frameworks and acknowledge difference's innumerable contact zones. I use the term *blackwoman* to invoke an adjective-form descriptor of aspects of black womanhood that does not rely on the potentially cisnormative, transphobic, body-normative, and conceptually imprecise languages of "black female" experience and subjectivity. As a fat black queer cisgender woman with economic security born in the United States, it is my aim to think difference complexly, to examine relentlessly the multiple, sometimes conflicting, relationships to power that shape my perspective, and to reach for language that does the same. The interstice and the nuantial serve as linked metaphors for the shifting and infinitely complex web of intertwining differences through which structuralist and post-structuralist notions of social being and subjecthood are defined.[6] Taking up Spillers's notions of the interstice and the nuantial together here reveals how black queer feminist poetics (both those created by queer artists and those that require queer reading strategies) shift the locus of subjecthood into a black queer feminist space, in which the nonnormative "interstices" of racial and gender othering are animated by the "nuantial" silencings of sexual hegemony such that the project of effectively speaking (or writing, rapping, singing, painting, or otherwise projecting) against the full scopes of both racial and gender oppression is inherently queer. Moreover, the nuance of the interstice shows how these black/queer speech acts require the creation of queer forms on the part of writers and the acquisition of queer reading strategies by their readers.[7]

As a term constructed specifically to address the erasure and obfuscation of black women's sexuality, the interstice expands intersectionality's founding definitions by imagining sexual difference not as a "secondary" component of black women's experience (as it figures in Crenshaw's foundational model of the theory) but as a crucial starting point for more capacious—and thus more precise—interrogations of black women's alterity.[8] The spatial metaphoric functions of the interstice allow us to imagine the shifting through-lines and contact zones between the *intersection* and the *interior*—the spaces and pathways of communication that join and distinguish organized social identities and structures such as race, gender, sexuality, nation, and class with experiences such as pleasure, desire, vulnerability, and fantasy, which, though more subjective and less readily organized into recognizable languages of identity, are deeply engaged with both social categorization and with the processes by which identities are produced, mobilized, and reified by structures of power and oppression.

Reading through the interstice allows for a diasporic black queer feminist critique of identity, in which "queerness" indexes not only sexual difference but also anticolonial, antiracist, antielitist, anti-patriarchal, and anti-normative identification in the African diaspora through antinormative erotics. The term *African diaspora* refers to the presence and multidirectional circulations of African-descended people and cultures throughout the globe; I use the terms *Afrodiasporic* and *diasporic* as adjective forms to describe people, cultures, and histories of or relating to the African diaspora. While multiple theories of diaspora exist (several of which are explored in this introduction and in chapter 3), one aim of many contemporary African diaspora theorists is to develop language for productively naming historical, cultural, and political connections between African-descended people across the globe while also acknowledging the often widely different political, historical, cultural, and material circumstances that shape life in various diaspora locales.[9] For Spillers and others, these differences of diaspora experience are inseparable from gender and sexual difference; as Spillers demonstrates, it is the violent colonial and patriarchal processes of diaspora that nullify black women's "nuantial" erotic subjectivities and that relegate their language to the unspoken "interstices" of dominant narrative ("Peter's Pans: Eating in the Diaspora" 14).

Queer models of difference as imagined by black women artists offer an important language for articulating these interstices and nuances of diaspora. Recognizing the impossibility of coherent visions of "womanhood," "queerness," or racial "blackness" across diasporic space, *The Poetics of Difference* instead considers how creative sites of artistic expression and imagination envision nuanced, dynamic, diasporic collectivities and wage anti-normative critique at multiple sites. This notion of queer Afrodiasporic poetics extends Cathy Cohen's proposition that we take "queerness" seriously as a raced, gendered, and classed formulation that holds the potential not only to articulate nonnormative sexual alterity, but also to facilitate coalitions between anti-homophobic, antiracist, antielitist, and other "anti-normative" movements and ways of thinking (22). Just as Cohen, writing in 1997, brings a black feminist/intersectional perspective to bear on queer theorizing, I use this black feminist model of queerness to complicate contemporary intersectionality theorizing, pushing intersectionality studies to engage more fully the far reaches of Afrodiasporic womanhood that breathe in the queer, creative spaces of the interstice.

The paradigm of the interstice also supplies a black feminist analytic for articulating the place of linguistic and literary expression in black feminist critique. As both "that which allows [black women] to speak about" simultaneous experiences of difference *and* that which enables black women "to speak at all," the interstice calls attention to the ways in which black women's subjectivity is silenced in numerous social discourses across diasporic space. Encountering African diaspora women's literature through the interstice highlights a long-standing condition in which, in conversations about the complexity of human subjective experience, black women have been left "awaiting *their* verb" (Spillers "Interstices" 153; emphasis in original).

By writing themselves through the interstice, Lorde and the other African diaspora women writers and artists gathered here resist static, finite models of intersectionality, foregrounding the interdependence of race, gender, sexuality, and class and linking these to more abstract, anti-hierarchical, *black/queer* notions of illimitable difference.[10] Leslie McCall states in her 2005 essay, "The Complexity of Intersectionality," that "[t]he terms complex, complexity, and complexities appear frequently and are central in key texts on intersectionality, although no text focuses on complexity as such" (1772 n2). These writers offer a corrective to the fault line of contemporary intersectionality theorizing—its inability, as yet, to offer practicable methodologies and languages for explicitly examining the multiplicity of black women's identity differences without organizing those differences into hierarchies of importance. *The Poetics of Difference* addresses this absence, positioning identity difference as both a hermeneutic for literary analysis and an object of study in African diaspora feminist literature. The writers and artists gathered here develop poetic strategies that impel readers to contend with several concurrent modes of form and genre, asking for an attentiveness to a complex rubric of difference as requisite for engaging their texts. I focus on the works of contemporary Anglophone writers and language-based artists including Lorde, Ntozake Shange, Aidoo and Dionne Brand, Suzan-Lori Parks, Toni Morrison, Akilah Oliver, Achy Obejas, Bessie Head, Krudxs Cubensi, and others. I argue that Afrodiasporic women and nonbinary writers of the late twentieth and early twenty-first centuries have reframed identity around radical models of difference by subverting conventions of genre and form.[11] Following Lorde, Krudxs Cubensi, and others, I use the term "women" to include a range of genders and identities, including nonbinary, trans, and other genders aligned with self-articulated visions of black womanhood. "Women" means all those who have identified as women, often alongside other gender identifications."

In their poetic practice, these writers insist, as Lorde does, on figuring black womanhood as both a social location shaped by linked oppressions, and a set of subjective experiences as rich, contradictory, nuanced, and volatile as human life itself. They write through and past the intersection to access the inarticulable nexus of difference that separates type from subject, object from being, semiotic fantasy from breathing human life. Through radical acts of imagination, these artists and writers use language and literature to create new possibilities for identity—possibilities that, when taken seriously, allow us to imagine more capacious, more livable lives for black women and black queer people.

## Toward a Poetics of Difference

> I have written all of these works from my perspective as a black woman, which I believe is no less representative of humanity than any other point of view.
> —Harryette Mullen, *Recyclopedia* (2006)[12]

The tactic of voicing difference through genre subversion is a prominent characteristic of African diaspora women's writing in the last half-century, though few critics have explored these strategies. The period between the late 1960s and the 1980s saw a proliferation of genre-bending black women's texts that continue to inform black women's literary praxis in the present moment.[13] This period marks the overlap of the American Civil Rights and Black Power movements, the height of twentieth-century African decolonization, the solidification of a concentrated Black Arts Movement in the United States that disproportionately emphasized the work of male writers,[14] and the emergence and intensification of interrogations of race within second-wave feminism. This period also saw the popularization of Pan-African, Afrocentrist, and Afrodiasporic consciousnesses among black people in the Americas, Africa, Europe, and the Caribbean, which had significant effects on black cultural expression in several diaspora locales.[15]

The confluence of these factors—the popularization of an Afrodiasporic consciousness in several national contexts, the solidification of the Black Arts Movement in the United States and its masculinist focus, and the interplay of anticolonial, Civil Rights, and Black Power perspectives in the fight for feminist interrogations of race—prompted a move toward new artistic modes among black women writers underexplored in contemporary scholarship. Ntozake Shange names the social and political need for such creative innovation in the US context in her 1978 essay, "takin a solo/ a poetic possibility/ a poetic imperative." Interrogating cultural criticism and literature that privileges monolithic notions of "representation" over creative expression, Shange observes: "if you are . . . female & black in the u.s.a/ . . . you have one solitary voice/ though you number 3 million/ no nuance exists for you/ you have been sequestered in the monolith/ the common denominator as persona" (*Nappy Edges* 3). This condition forces the sacrifice of black women's "singularity" in favor of a false racial authenticity, and produces a cultural crisis in which blacks, "as a people . . . have so claimed 'the word'/ . . . we don't even pay attention to who is speakin" (9, 3).[16]

While Shange frames her argument against the rhetorics of racial representation in the context of the Black Arts Movement in the United States, the pervasive transnational black consciousness of her own work and her focus on the expansiveness of black women's "singularity" indicate the diasporic reach of her critique.[17] This "singularity" not only points to the intersection of distinct identity categories and experiences within black cultural production, but also signals the less-recognized nuances of black subjectivity, what Shange calls the "richness of [the black artist's] person," as reflected in the turns and textures of creative voice. As Shange observes, this nuance resonates through poetic strategies, and occurs explicitly as a "difference/in syntax, imagery, rhythm and theme" (10).[18]

Black women writers from the late 1960s onward have used insurrectional formal modes and subversive formulations of genre to emphasize this difference through their writings. While some critics cite Gwendolyn Brooks's 1953 prose novel, *Maud Martha*, as a pivotal text in the emergence of a twentieth-century black American feminist ideology and aesthetic, I instead read her 1968 poetic novella *In the Mecca* as a foundation of contemporary black feminist subversive poetics.[19] *In the Mecca* inaugurates a legacy of explicit, critical explorations of blackness through black women and girl protagonists, and incorporates diasporic frameworks and critiques of gender and sexuality to explore multiple facets of black intra-racial difference through a multi-genre form. Texts such as Lorde's "biomythography," *Zami* Shange's "choreopoem" *for colored girls who have considered suicide/when the rainbow is enuf* (first performed in 1974 and published in 1975), and Aidoo's "prosepoem" novella *Our Sister Killjoy* (1977) mark a concentration of black women writers and artists who challenge ideas about black womanhood by pushing the limits of genre. These texts also open space for several other forms of less explicit generic and formal subversion and emphasize new theorizations of blackwoman difference that engage with these innovative texts of the 1960s, '70s, and '80s—extending, exploring, and remixing their logics in the present moment.

These writers and artists, I argue, develop what I term a *poetics of difference*—a set of subversive aesthetic strategies that uses multiplicities of form and genre to respond to global discourses of antiracism, decolonization, feminism, and anti-heterosexism that circulate and overlap in the late twentieth and twenty-first centuries. These forms function as both artistic innovations and theoretical interventions into how social difference and identity are imagined. By mobilizing multiple voices, genres, media, and aesthetic modes simultaneously, contemporary diasporic feminist experimental writers and artists train readers to navigate multiple forms of difference in the formal properties of their texts and reveal the radical queernesses of both black feminist subjectivity and black feminist formal innovation in the African diaspora.

I read these strategies as falling within two overarching formal modes: (1) the development and naming of new, hybrid, black feminist genres and (2) the subversive reformulation of recognizable genres to interrogate black women's experiences of difference. The foundational genre-bending texts of Lorde, Shange, and Aidoo in the 1970s and 1980s bear important links to recent examples of black women's experimentalism and reveal the political stakes of contemporary black feminist form. Placing these earlier works in conversation with more recent experimental gestures—such as those by black American lesbian poet Akilah Oliver, queer South African visual activist Zanele Muholi, Cuban lesbian hip-hop group Krudxs Cubensi (aka Las Krudas), Trinbagonian Canadian lesbian poet Dionne Brand,[20] and others—allows us to see the theoretical and political stakes of black women's experimental poetics more fully.

Black women's poetics of difference have their effects not only through the products of creative praxis—that is, through the production of artistic artifacts that echo the aesthetics of black queer feminist experience—but also on the interpretive methodologies that they require of their readers. These poetics call for the development of what I name an "interstitial hermeneutics"—an interpretive strategy that requires readers to navigate difference in the material, intellectual, and affective dynamics of the reading experience. Through these strategies, readers must make several contacts with textual difference: in the acquisition of new, unfamiliar languages, in the suspension and rerouting of expectations of genre, and in the unexpected movement between media and expressive forms. Here, formal subversion re-figures the text as a site of the interstice. Through the interstice, the poetics of difference thus enable both creative and interpretive engagement with what Spillers terms the "missing word" of blackwoman difference.

The process of navigating difference produces different effects for different readers. For those familiar with the particular differences in question, interstitial hermeneutics echo and affirm these experiences on a formal level, simulating the sense of "place" and belonging that Lorde's biomythic praxis, for example, creates. For others, grappling with black women's difference on a formal level requires them to take note of interstitial experience and to engage this experience in order to glean meaning from the text. Like any interpretive challenge, this can produce a range of effects, from frustration to discomfort to exclusion to isolation and relative powerlessness, each of which also attends black women's lived experiences of difference. Interstitial hermeneutics thus replicate on a formal level a range of psychic experiences in which, as Fred Moten suggests, the meanings of blackness are

> given to us only in and by way of a kind of failure or inadequacy—or, perhaps more precisely, by way of a history of exclusion, serial expulsion, presence's ongoing taking of leave—so that the non-attainment of meaning or ontology, of source or origin, is the only way to approach the thing in its informal (enformed/enforming, as opposed to formless), material totality? Perhaps this would be cause for black optimism or, at least, some black operations. (182)

Interstitial hermeneutics perform such "operations," working through readerly experiences of exclusion and non-apprehension to destabilize the meanings and power configurations of blackness not as a hegemonic tool for racialization, but from a perspective of interstitial possibility in which racial blackness is inseparable from innumerable other forms of black difference. By pushing readers to develop new and nuantial ways of reading black feminist texts, black queer feminist poetics proposes new "forms" of blackness—or, more specifically, new methods for imagining existing and future forms of blackness—that create their own meanings, narratives, and registers of presence (and absence) and that need not make themselves legible exclusively within the histories of expulsion and exclusion through which blackness is otherwise read. These poetics make use of the inapprehensible and presence-less character of blackness and supply it with the illimitable contours of the black/queer nuantial. The forms they create as a result task readers with making up blackness anew in their own imaginations.

As Lorde's biomythics suggest, this project of reformulating readerly encounters with blackness through interstitial hermeneutics is constantly attentive not only to race, class, gender, and sexuality as identity and experience but also to the interdependence of racism, classism, sexism, homophobia, and numerous related structures and practices of hegemonic othering. The nuance of interstitial hermeneutics demands what Carole Boyce Davies calls a "certain literacy, critical analysis and cultural critique in the recognition of coded words" that render the complexities of interstitial subjectivity through literary form (*Moving beyond Boundaries* 9). Rather than deploy the conventional literacies through which English-language readers are trained to approach single-genre, monolinguistic, and form-conforming texts, these writers' poetic strategies require readers to *experience* difference as they shift among various genres, languages, textual modes, and narrative structures. By training readers in an interstitial hermeneutics, these writers and artists introduce a politically engaged literary praxis that functions both through black women's *speaking*—the subversive claiming and reclaiming of silenced modes of expression for which black feminist theorists have continually argued—and through a rigorous *hearing and listening*, a distinct and attentive effort on the part of the reader to understand and engage what black women have to say.

By privileging difference in their formal structures and interpretive effects, these writers and artists also offer new models of anti-normative identification underexplored in contemporary literary studies, queer studies, Africana studies, postcolonial studies, and feminist discourses. They forward models of identity that extend beyond what Lorde calls "single-issue" frameworks (such as masculinist "antiracist" action) and complicate even dual frameworks (such as "lesbian feminist" discourses that fail to interrogate race). These writers thus forge links between civil rights, Black Power, and anticolonial ideologies and movements on behalf of "women, other peoples of Color, gays, the handicapped, . . . [and] all disenfranchised peoples of . . . society" ("Learning from the '60s" 138). By reproducing the interconnectedness of oppressions as experiences of form, they destabilize the power of those who can logically claim the power of "normalcy"—which, as Lorde and others have pointed out, is a negligible if not nonexistent group.[21] Further, these writers undermine a "longstanding social situation in which those of us who stand outside that power often identify one way in which we are different . . . forgetting other distortions around difference, some of which we ourselves may be practicing" (Lorde "Age, Race, Class and Sex" 116).

In demanding this self-interrogation of their readers, black women's poetics of difference also make space for important re-interrogations of both blackness and the category of the human. Although, as L. H. Stallings argues, "aspirations for a progressive society and imagined futuristic models of being posthuman remain linked to a form of humanism that cannot make legible" the fullness of black life and difference, black women's poetics of difference remind us that other humanisms have always been possible and, in fact, necessary (*Funk the Erotic* 123). In a global environment in which blackness is violently denied the basic rights of the very humanity some black scholarship seeks to push past, these writers ask us to pause, to return to the human, and to reimagine it in and through black women's queer creative terms.

*The Poetics of Difference* explores that reimagining in order to examine what silenced subjectivities black queer feminist forms articulate. These writers and artists bring Lorde's queer "biomythics" to bear on what Sylvia Wynter later terms *bio-mythois*, a possibility of the human in which both "bio" (the biological) and "mythos" (the storytelling-symbolic) form "the knowledge of the human conceptualized in the direction of a hybridity . . . therefore *bios* and *mythoi*. And notice! . . . *humanness* is no longer a noun. Being human is a praxis!" (Wynter in McKittrick, *Sylvia Wynter*, 22–23; emphasis in original). With their poetics, these writers and artists engage, critique, and re-create praxes of story and skin, inventing black/queer feminist humannesses that not only accommodate difference, but insist upon it, and take their shape around it. Invoking humanistic praxis and interpretation, they suggest, as Mullen does, that not only can black women be human, but that, more importantly if "the human," is to retain any use in a liberatory future that retains coherent linguistic links to our political present and past, it must look like, sound like, and *be* blackwoman, with all the nuance and complexity that entails.

## Theorizing Experiments in Difference

> . . . [P]eople of color have always theorized—but in forms quite different from the Western form of abstract logic. And I am inclined to say that our theorizing (and I intentionally use the verb rather than the noun) is often in narrative forms, in the stories we create, in riddles and proverbs, in the play with language. . . . How else have we managed to survive with such spiritedness the assault on our bodies, social institutions, countries, our very humanity?
> —Barbara Christian, "The Race for Theory" (1989)

Black feminist and critical race scholarship have consistently emphasized voice and linguistic expression as a means of survival. From the eighteenth- and nineteenth-century publication of African, African American, and Caribbean slave narratives through the contemporary moment, black intellectual traditions have been deeply entwined with black literatures and have thematized access to, and effective use of, language as sources of power. These models of voicing as power are often attended by a productive inversion, in which silence is framed as powerlessness. Audre Lorde, Barbara Christian, Evelynn Hammonds, and Wahneema Lubiano all stress this function of silence and silencing as agents of oppression against black women and situate the voice as a primary tool for organizing against racist, sexist, and classist power structures.[22]

More recently, Kevin Quashie has moved to trouble this binary by theorizing quiet as a radical mode of human sovereignty in black cultural expression (6). Quashie suggests that "quiet" is an access point to realms of black being vital for black life, survival, and pleasure. Quiet *is a pathway toward* and *a locus of* interiority, intimacy, and imagination; it is also a poetic approach that renders black subjects as "human beings whose everyday acts are not countenanced exclusively by resistance . . . [and] whose living is sovereign" (99). Quiet is thus less about public silence than it is about the many expressivities of black interiority: "Quiet is often used interchangeably with silence or stillness, but the notion of quiet [here] is neither motionless nor without sound. Quiet, instead, is a metaphor for the full range of one's inner life—one's desires, ambitions, hungers, vulnerabilities, fears" (6). These nuances of interiority shape the contours of blackwoman voicing. As Evie Shockley (following Mae G. Henderson) observes, "[t]o survive and thrive . . . black women have had to learn to speak dialogically in ways that can be heard by our 'others,' both through similarity and across difference" (*Renegade Poetics* 18). Considering Afrodiasporic women's poetics of difference expands this notion by positioning nuantial difference as black women writers' most consequential interarticulatory similarity. Put another way, reading for black women's poetics of difference urges us to consider that black womanhood's most crucial similarity is the illimitability of difference itself.

These theories invite us to explore further the particular tones, timbres, and strategic arrangements of black feminist voicing in literary and artistic expression. Ato Quayson observes that vocal and linguistic "heterogeneity" are defining qualities of African diaspora literature; to understand diasporic writing, Quayson states, is to "read for the signs of multivocality and disjuncture that lie within it" ("Incessant Particularities" 130). Black feminist analytics enable and complicate such reading. Critical race theory and feminist standpoint theory's emphases on "storytelling" and "perspectivism" in struggles for civic justice reiterate this point and reveal the political stakes of black feminist form (Collins *Black Feminist Thought* 270; Delgado 53). Collins argues for a "black feminist standpoint" from which black women's perspectives "serve as one specific social location for examining points of connection among multiple epistemologies." Itself an extension and critique of larger feminist discussions of standpoint theory in the 1980s and 1990s, Collins's formulation articulates the radical and anti-normative possibilities of black women's storytelling, and the potential black women's storytelling holds for forwarding anti-normative politics consistent with Cohen's black feminist framing of the queer.[23]

Models of "voice," "story," "narrative," and "perspective" abound in social and political theorizing, yet have been held at an odd distance from the specific creative, literary, and poetic strategies that those terms also reference. For black women writers, each of these serves as both a political tool and a creative device. Subverting formal conventions in each of these areas is a move toward undermining intersecting structures of power. Several recent thinkers have offered provocative explorations of black and transnational poetics, opening ample space for a sustained discussion of black queer feminist poetics. GerShun Avilez's *Radical Aesthetics and Modern Black Nationalism* (2016), Carter Mathes's *Imagine the Sound: Experimental African American Literature after Civil Rights* (2015), Anthony Reed's *Freedom Time: The Poetics and Politics of Black Experimental Writing* (2014), Meta DuEwa Jones's *The Muse Is Music: Jazz Poetry from the Harlem Renaissance to Spoken Word* (2012), and Evie Shockley's *Renegade Poetics: Black Aesthetics and Formal Innovation in African American Poetry* (2011) all reflect an exciting surge in scholarly conversations on black poetics and experimentalism. This dialogue has coincided with rich conversations on transnational and diasporic literary aesthetics, which include Jerome C. Branch's *The Poetics and Politics of Diaspora: Transatlantic Musings* (2015) and Jahan Ramzani's *A Transnational Poetics* (2014), as well as important contemporary studies of African diaspora feminist literature, including Samantha Pinto's *Difficult Diasporas: The Transnational Feminist Aesthetic of the Black Atlantic* (2013) and Cheryl Higashida's *Black Internationalist Feminism: Women Writers of the Black Left 1945–1995* (2011).

Contemporary work in African Diaspora sound studies, in particular, opens space for rich discussions of voice and embodiment in queer and feminist Afrodiasporic poetics. In *Phonographies: Grooves in Sonic Afro-Modernity* (2008), Alexander Weheliye explores the centrality of sonic expression to theories of Afrodiasporic difference, positioning black sonic cultures as "the principal modality in which Afro-diasporic cultures have been articulated" and as a crucial lens into "the cultural political, economic, and epistemological complexities" that attend the global circulation of black cultures and the racial imaginaries that circulation provokes in modernity and beyond (5). Tsitsi Ella Jaji's 2014 *Africa in Stereo: Modernism, Music, and Pan-African Solidarity* likewise explores the sonic aesthetics of Afrodiasporic identity, "modernity," and multiple circuits of diasporic exchange through the circulation of diasporic music (212).

Tina Campt's notion of "listening to images" is particularly helpful in developing a diasporic interstitial hermeneutic. Campt develops a partly synaesthetic interpretive method in which visual images of African diaspora experience can be read through the sonic, which "can be listened to, and, in equally powerful ways . . . can be felt" (6). By theorizing this listening as "a profoundly haptic form of sensory contact" that functions both through listening and feeling, Campt highlights the bodily and affective dimensions of interstitial hermeneutics, and invites us to explore how queernesses of both creative "form" and bodily experience shape diasporic blackness. Together, these models of sonic diaspora—along with models of black sonic experience forwarded by Quashie and others—open space for inquiry into the queer resonances of sound and voice in black feminist cultural expression on the Afrodiasporic stage.

This turn toward a serious exploration of black aesthetics and poetics signals an interest among many contemporary literary scholars in exploring the politics of black poetic form and investigating the links between black aesthetics and contemporary black social life. Yet, despite the breadth and prominence of this conversation, few critics have explored in-depth the relationships between black women's poetic subversion and black feminist intersectionality, and none has done so in a full-length study. These works, alongside crucial explorations of black women's poetics by Alexander, Hale, Henderson, Holloway, Peterson, and Pinto open space for an extended theory of a black feminist poetics that centers queerness in its conceptions of difference.

*The Poetics of Difference* enters this space, extending recent work on Afrodiasporic poetics and placing it in conversation with black queer and feminist texts and methodologies to reveal more fully the political stakes of black women's creative theorizations of difference. As Barbara Christian has famously argued, black theoretical life—and black women's theorizing in particular—occurs, among other places, in nuances of and imaginative engagements with language. To take black women's theoretical contributions seriously, then, we must learn to read for the subversiveness of these nuances—for the politics of black women's linguistic "play" (68).

Constructing a theory of black feminist poetics requires an interdisciplinary—and, in fact, a *black/queer*—approach to black poetic form. It challenges us to think creatively about the overlapping meanings of form and difference in various discursive spaces, and to tap into a range of methodologies—such as those of performance studies, sexuality studies, diaspora studies, and hip-hop studies—not often mobilized in engagements with of black poetics. It also requires that we bring literary critical conceptions of aesthetic blackness into direct engagement with black queer feminist perspectives on difference.

*The Poetics of Difference* thus expands on what Pinto terms a "critical engagement with aesthetics, as not just a form but the form of politics, [which] moves us into the systemic analysis of how gender and race operate" in the African diaspora (3). I extend this race- and gender-based exploration of form to consider the place of sexuality—and of queerness in particular—in literary reflections on diasporic identity and politics. And, where Shockley, Mathes, and Reed offer nuanced readings of African American poetics and politics in the post–civil rights United States, I use an intersectional, transnational feminist lens to draw connections between these forms and those emerging during and after decolonization in various other sites of the African diaspora—including Cuba, Ghana, Botswana, and South Africa—focusing on their interventions into discourses on gender and sexuality. By making these connections through a transnational feminist hermeneutic focused on women's texts, I expand the predominantly male-centered archive these earlier studies tend to engage and begin a discussion on queerness and nonnormative sexuality currently absent from black poetics discourses' identity critiques.

Crafting a theory of black feminist poetics also reanimates and reframes long-standing methodological debates in studies of black women's literature and culture. One such conversation remains central to this study: Mae G. Henderson's and Dorothy Hale's conflict, in the late 1980s, around the place of European formalist languages in black feminist criticism. Henderson's use of Bakhtinian theory in "Speaking in Tongues," sparks a debate crucial to investigations of the poetics of difference and interstitial hermeneutics. In a response to Henderson in her essay, "Bakhtin in African-American Literary Theory," Hale challenges Henderson's methodology, arguing that Russian formalist theory is unsuited for use in reading black literature, largely because it reduces issues of social context and experience to language; for Hale, Bakhtin's social formalism "encourages him to portray the people who use language as strangely immaterial, or rather materialized in and through language" (447). Yet some of these languages have proved useful to contemporary black feminist poets as well. Poet Harryette Mullen highlights the usefulness of Russian formalist terminology in poetic theorizations of difference, referring to her 1995 poetry collection *Muse and Drudge* as "a heteroglossia for collaborative reading," in which the presence of multiple speakers and vocal registers allows readers to engage "the flavor of difference in language" beyond normative English (xi).

Following Henderson, Mullen, and others, I use some Russian formalist terminology to push beyond the limited social framework of Western critical analysis and to consider textual and literary heterogeneity alongside questions of black women's anti-normative subjectivity. The terms *heteroglossia, polyglossia, hybridity*, and *dialogism* are particularly useful to this study. In Bakhtin's formulation, heteroglossia signals a novelistic mode in which "[a]uthorial speech, the speeches of narrators, inserted genres, [and] the speech of characters . . . permit a multiplicity of social voices and wide variety of their links and interrelationships" to be reflected within a given text (262). This formulation is useful in exploring the appearance of multiple distinct narrative voices in African diaspora women's prose works and the social significance of those pluralities; I also use this term to refer to multivocalities in black women's poetic and dramatic works, as well as to the heterogeneous genres that some Afrodiasporic women writers invent. Similarly, Bakhtin's use of "polyglossia" to describe the presence of multiple distinct "national languages" and/or multiple "social . . . dialects" in novelistic prose is helpful in describing black women writers' creation of shared spoken idioms to rearticulate national and diasporic identity (12).

I use these terms not to displace black women's theoretical contributions, but rather to supplement them, and to signal some of the particular formal discourses from which black women theorists have been excluded, despite their active engagement with questions of subjectivity and aesthetics. Like Christian,

I am concerned with both the creativity of black women's social thought and the intellectual value of our creative praxis, without which these discourses are woefully incomplete.

## The Queer Poetics of Afrodiasporic "Blackness"

". . . [B]eing queer is not a costume
or appearance but rather skin deep."
—Zanele Muholi, visual activist [24]

Black women writers' poetic theories of identity reimagine black womanhood, but they also open space for more expansive models of Afrodiasporic "blackness." In the works of the African, Caribbean, Caribbean-descended, and black American writers and artists I consider, forwarding difference-based theories of identity throws constructions of race into question, inviting us to consider new models of global blackness. As Kamari Clarke and Deborah Thomas point out, in contemporary Afrodiaspora, "blackness does not just index race; it also indexes gender, class, ethnicity, sexuality, religion, labor, nationality, transnationality, and politics" in specific ways and toward the production of specific social meanings bound by time and place (*Globalization and Race* 4). In these writers' imaginaries, "blackness" is not defined only (or even primarily) by race and nation, but by the multiple, queer presences of difference that mark black women's lives.

I argue that among the functions of black women's poetics of difference is the development of what I term "diasporas of difference"—mappings of transnational identification, political engagement, and diasporic space that center nuantial models of difference constantly engaged with gender and sexual antinormativity. Diasporas of difference resist claims to a single coherent global blackness and trouble narratives of diaspora that position "blackness" as a genderless and heteronormative signifier of transnational connection. Instead, they reimagine global space and transnational connection according to the nuantial—that is, according to the subversive expression of interstices of gender, sexual, socioeconomic, bodily, and other experiences of alterity. In these frameworks, the connective tissue of diaspora is black feminist difference itself.

As lesbian South African photographer and visual activist Zanele Muholi suggests, it is not simply race that black skin signals. Queerness—and the multiplicity of gendered, bodily, and social experiences it encompasses—is also "skin deep." For women in the diaspora, blackness is defined in these multiple differences of the interstice, and black bodies are sites on which these differences are written and read. Writing diaspora through the queerness of the interstice, these artists and writers turn away from "single-issue" diasporic frameworks, and instead forward modes of transnational identity and collective belonging defined by black women's difference. They develop a queer aesthetics located on and in the "skin" of blackness and imagine diasporic blackness as a site shaped by the queer.

Attention to black women writers' queer poetics makes this point a material fact of the reading process. On the terrains of their pages, stages, mounted prints, and video screens, the writers and artists I explore create models of diaspora that highlight blackness as a capacious set of constructs that appear in several different social, political, and historical contexts, and constantly signal several forms of difference. These visions of diaspora emphasize the ways in which, even as a racial indicator, "blackness" is itself a polysemous category variegated by national, ethnic, and gendered contexts. They intervene in contemporary discourses on diaspora to posit an infinitely complex identification with racialized *and other* differences as a through line of Afrodiasporic identity. These works show that Afrodiaspora is as complex and dynamic as black genders and sexualities themselves.

Reading diaspora through a black queer feminist perspective articulates this range of differences. As a trope signaling a broad range of differences and a term that is, itself, defined by difference,[25] queerness, like diaspora, is an ideal tool for exploring the relationships of identification and othering among various identificatory groups and global locales. Generally deployed to hail the forced and unwilling migrations and dislocations of queer people as a result of social, political, economic, and spiritual/religious effects of homophobic violence and disenfranchisement, "queer diasporas" offer an important set of possibilities for imagining spatial movements and cross-boundary identifications forged by multiple difference. Anne-Marie Fortier argues, "By embracing queer and/or diaspora, theories of identity turn" away from hierarchizations of identity and "toward contingency, indeterminacy, power, and conflict" within global and transnational identificatory groupings (183). Rinaldo Walcott, in his groundbreaking essay "Outside in Black Studies: Reading from a Queer Place in the Diaspora," extends this thinking, illuminating the ways in which "diaspora, by its very nature, its circumstances, is queer" (97). Rather than support or veil the hierarchical logic of vertical or "internal"/"external" models of diasporic multiplicity, queer diaspora brings the core notion of interlocking difference to bear on discourses of transnational identification.

Gayatri Gopinath's formulation of queer diaspora is also helpful in this context. Reading diaspora through a queer framework, Gopinath suggests, "productively exploits the analogous relation between nation and diaspora on one hand, and between heterosexuality and queerness on the other: in other words, queerness is to heterosexuality as the diaspora is to the nation" (*Impossible Desires* 11). While Gopinath's focus is a South Asian diaspora instantiated by imperialist impositions of British understandings of social and civic organization on South Asian communities, her vision of queer identification as a synecdoche for diasporic expansiveness is useful in mapping what I term black women's diasporas of difference.

The interplay of difference and diaspora takes on a specific complexity in the context of Afrodiaspora, where the categories of both "nation" and "race" are contested, and where "queerness" (in its conceptual meaning of "difference") must address the polysemousness of black identifications as well. Particularly in the "new" political, economic, and social contexts of diasporic movement from the late twentieth century onward, the presence of African and Afro-Caribbean immigrants and black Latinx communities demands a conception of Afrodiaspora that destabilizes what Africana Studies scholar Jill Humphries terms "the superordinate racial category of 'black'" both in multiethnic spaces like the United States and within global discourses more broadly (275, 276). In an effort to weave the defining differences of "diaspora" with an equally complex model of blackness and Africanity across nations, Sandra Jackson-Opoku offers the term "transDiaspora" to describe "an intersecting current of ideas that attempts to braid borderlands of nation, language, culture and community" in both "old" and "new" [African] diaspora experiences (477).

While these formulations are extremely helpful in acknowledging the various diasporas in which black subjects participate across the globe, none of them reaches so far as to map a concept of diaspora that both escapes hierarchical vertical frameworks of difference *and* acknowledges the specific identifications of race, nation, gender, sexuality, ethnicity, language, and more that remain crucial in African diaspora women's experiences. And while each of these theories gestures toward "culture" as a site on which diasporic identification is worked out, the potential implications of a multi-diasporic identitarian framework for black poetics and literary forms remain to be explored. Walcott, for example, illuminates the ways in which both queer and diaspora analytical frameworks require a hermeneutic strategy—what he calls "diaspora reading practice"—attentive to multiple difference (90). Similarly, Joseph McLaren refers to what he calls a "genre of diaspora representation" that depicts black American characters "returning" to Africa, while Susan Stanford Friedman uses the notion of a "poetics of dislocation" to describe diasporic subjects' need to document their transnational and transcultural experiences in writing (McLaren 423; Friedman 205).

Each of these theories reveals provocative connections between diasporic experience and literary production, yet no full study has taken up the task of illuminating the dynamics of specific poetic strategies arising from queer and feminist experiences of diaspora. Reading for black women's poetics of difference expands these conceptions of diasporic cultural production. Through their invented languages, heteroglossic structures, and genre amalgamations, I argue that the writers and artists gathered here enact queer projects of black feminist worldmaking, forwarding new models of diasporic identification and community defined by the illimitability of black women's difference.

## Black Queer Feminist Forms of Difference

The chapters that follow explore black women's poetics of difference in four key forms: (1) the use of subversive poetics to construct black queer feminist historiographies in poetry and coming-of-age fiction; (2) the construction of queer modes of bodily articulation in mixed-genre works; (3) the development of black queer feminist models of diaspora through embodied language forms in poetry, performance, and hip-hop; and (4) the invention of interstitial spoken languages for complicating models of black women's sexuality across a range of genres, including fiction, dramatic writing, and black queer feminist hip-hop. The first two chapters are an exploration of the "nuantial" creative practices of black queer feminist writers and artists while the last two chapters can be imagined as an investigation of the "nuantial" hermeneutics and nuanced reading strategies enabled by a broader range of black feminist writers and artists (queer and not); I employ a queer method of reading throughout, reiterating the strategy of a black queer feminist interstitial hermeneutics by example.

Chapter 1, "Biomythic Times: Voice, Genre, and the Invention of Black/Queer History," considers the place of the poetics of difference in charting black queer feminist historical lineages. Borrowing from Lorde's formulation of the "biomythography"—a composite genre to accommodate her understanding of herself and her social experience—I argue that her poetics of difference enable a "biomythic historiography" essential to contemporary African diaspora queer feminist literary praxis. I use Lorde's formal and political interventions in *Zami* to read Trinidadian-Canadian poet and novelist Dionne Brand's *In Another Place, Not Here* (1996), as well as her Griffin Prize–winning long poem *Ossuaries*. I read Lorde's and Brand's works alongside Cuban-born novelist, poet, and translator Achy Obejas's *Memory Mambo* (1996) to show how these writers use multiple narrative strategies and shifting narrators/speaking voices to critique dominant models of history and genealogy and to situate their characters within specifically queer lineages of their own design.

In each of these texts, narrators and characters bring multiple voices and perspectives into their own voice in order to highlight queerness as crucial to their self-construction; they use queerness as a basis for forging intergenerational ancestries and lineages between black women, thus creating queer histories absent from the historical record. I argue that these shifting narrator/speakers' storytelling strategies invoke queer Afrodiasporic epistemologies that undermine Western models of time and subjectivity and reveal the ways in which Afrodiasporic relationality itself might be read as queer. I use the term "black/queer" to suggest the shared significatory functions of the terms "black" and "queer" as indicators of nonnormativity, and the ways in which the two are discursively inseparable in black queer women's experience. Black/queer gestures toward an identity and aesthetic rooted not only in racial and sexual alterity, but in experiences of disempowerment on the grounds of gender, class, and diasporic location as well as the interstitial experience of difference that Lorde's biomythics signal. Finally, I consider briefly how the poetic dimensions and cross-genre circulations of the #SayHerName media movement, popularized in 2015, extend and complicate these legacies in digital media, making space for new archives of black life that center black women, black queer people, and black trans and nonbinary people in contemporary narratives of black futurity and survival.

In the next two chapters, I consider how such a black queer feminist poetics of difference allows writers and artists to reimagine erotic embodiment, language, and diaspora. Chapter 2, "'walkin on the edges of the galaxy': Queer Choreopoetic Thought in the African Diaspora," explores how the poetics of difference yields imaginative constructions of embodied voicing that make space for nuanced articulations of black women's embodiment and center sexual subjectivity and queer erotic desire. I argue that formal and conceptual fusions of textuality and corporeality are a prominent (though underexplored) strategy among queer women writers and artists of the African diaspora. I term this strategy *choreopoetic thinking*, borrowing from Ntozake Shange's invention of the *choreopoem* in *for colored girls who have considered suicide/when the rainbow is enuf*, in which Shange melds dance and lyric forms to articulate black women's erotic and subjective experience. I examine the particular usefulness of the choreopoem and similar invented genres for queer women's literary and performance cultures of the African diaspora, considering the question: *what's queer about the choreopoem form?*

I read both the well-known stage version of *for colored girls* and the less frequently explored poetry collection version of the text, placing them alongside recent works by black queer and feminist artists who either use the genre of choreopoem directly or offer new generic designations that link with the choreopoem's logics of embodied voice. This includes Haitian American lesbian writer Lenelle Moïse's 2002 choreopoem, "Cornered in the Dark," queer South African photographer Zanele Muholi's 2011 mixed-genre "visual fusion," *what do you see when you look at us?*, and "Evil Beautiful Sunshine," a narrative burlesque performance piece by Chicava HoneyChild Tate, creative producer of the queer-affirming performance collective Brown Girls Burlesque. Exploring these texts through queer and feminist theories of voice and body—particularly through black lesbian poet Akilah Oliver's notion of "flesh memory"—I argue that choreopoetic thought reorders connections between body and voice, offering a poetics of difference that allows black queer and feminist artists to challenge limiting narratives of blackwoman embodiment, and to tell new stories of bodily experience rooted in pleasure, desire, and freedom.

Chapter 3, "Feeling Colors and Seeing Speech: Body/Language and Black Women's Diasporas of Difference," extends this exploration of embodied voice to consider its impacts on black feminist models of diaspora. I examine radical amalgamations of body and voice as a modality of the poetics of difference in black women artists' engagements with diaspora and transnational identification. I focus my analysis on lesser-known performance works by Shange, alongside the work of black Trinbagonian Canadian poet M. NourbeSe Philip and queer Cuban hip-hop group Krudxs Cubensi (also known as Las Krudxs). Reading these texts alongside prominent theories of black transnational identification and recent conceptions of feminist diaspora, I argue that these artists' formal meldings of body and voice articulate a project of black queer feminist worldmaking that render visible the complexities of global blackness and thus forge space for more expansive models of Afrodiaspora.

These artists develop what I term a *body/language*—a poetic strategy that links the body to spoken/written language systems in order to complicate how black diasporic gender is read. I argue that bringing textual linguistic systems onto the terrain of the body allows diasporic feminist writers and artists to imagine modes of identification in which corporeal markers of "blackness" (such as skin) are rendered inseparable from the illimitable subjective nuances of voice and narrative. By holding the racialized body in tension with the voices and stories that issue from it, these artists construct a blackness that is constantly complicated by gender, nation, sexuality, and other forms of difference, including fatness and nonnormative embodiment. I argue that, through body/language, these writers use the expressive technologies of the body to reject models of diaspora that prioritize finite "blackness" as a coherent joining identification; instead, they offer a poetics of difference that redefines Afrodiaspora according to queer, nuantial models of difference that privilege nonnormative modes of feeling, pleasure, and desire.

In Chapter 4, "'Languages of Love,' 'TALK' of Sex: Interstitial Idioms of Body and Desire," I extend my exploration of poetic polyglossias to examine the invention of shared, spoken languages in contemporary black women's texts. I argue that through this modality of the poetics of difference, black women writers develop what I term interstitial languages: shared, spoken idioms invented by authors and characters to contest dominant discourses about black women's sexuality and to express otherwise inarticulable linkages among sexuality, race, class, sexuality, and nation in Afrodiasporic women's experiences. I focus my analysis on American playwright Suzan-Lori Parks's *In the Blood* (1999) and *Fucking A* (2001); South African–Botswanan writer Bessie Head's short story, "Life" (1989); Ghanaian writer Ama Ata Aidoo's prosepoem novella, *Our Sister*

*Killjoy* (1977); and American writer Toni Morrison's novel, *Love* (2003). Examining these texts alongside contemporary feminist linguistic scholarship and African diaspora cultural criticism on the politics of language, I argue that by inventing unfamiliar linguistic systems in already heterogeneous texts, Parks, Head, Aidoo, and Morrison foreground for readers and viewers the multiple differences that define black women's identities and signal the innumerable ways in which those identities can be articulated through literature. In closing, I turn to the presence of "interstitial idioms" in contemporary women's hip-hop across the diaspora. Considering the works of American rapper Missy Elliott, I explore how invented languages subvert discourses of sexuality, embodiment, and desire, and make space for new forms of intimacy and erotic connection.

Through their poetic engagements with difference, the writers, artists, and performers gathered here introduce models of subjective multiplicity that may be useful to several groups, but that are firmly rooted in black women's experiences. By writing their identifications through the interstice, these artists acknowledge difference as an expansive ground on which several aspects of identity are constructed and given meaning. Yet, through their poetics of difference, they also emphasize that for African diaspora women subjects, the broad terrain of difference is everywhere corrugated by the commingling impacts of enslavement, colonization, state-sanctioned desubjectivation and sexual objectification, and social and systemic patriarchies and racisms—experiences that endure over several generations and do not translate into dominant discourses without imaginative uses of language.

The living history of the interstice produces a psychic situation in which black women's interstitial positionalities make it impossible *not* to think, live, and write from multiple perspectives.[26] Black women artists' poetics of difference thus do not represent instantiations of a universal or universalizable experience of multiple difference, even as they offer crucial information about difference and human life. Instead, these writers and artists introduce a specific set of creative approaches to an expansive confluence of hegemonies—approaches generated by black women, for whom creatively navigating illimitable difference is a constant fact of interstitial life.

By rendering simultaneous experiences of difference at the level of form, these artists' poetics of difference not only call into question the coherence and discreteness of feminist studies, Africana studies, and queer studies discourses, but also make important interventions in current conversations within each of these fields. Because the poetics of difference reconstruct the scope of human experience as they impact black women's lives, they complicate recent scholarly explorations of history, gender, the body, and communal, national, and transnational belonging as tools of identification. Reading each of these identifiers through the poetics of difference illuminates the ways in which black women writers and artists have conceived of and crafted complex models of difference; it also illustrates how the literary subjectivities they produce introduce fuller interpretations of blackwoman—and human—experience. Attention to black feminist discourse as a humanist enterprise demonstrates how the grounds on which black women's identities are written, read, and contested are constantly shaped by difference and by structural and linguistic silencings. This humanistic approach also has important implications for theories of black posthumanism. My investment in "the human" centers the creative voices and material lives of the black women artists I study, many of whom, like Mullen, see humanness as a malleable lexicon through which to speak (and speak for) the continuance of black women's lives. This humanist poetics signals the possibilities of Wynter's "bio-mythois," through which, as McKittrick suggests, "humanness might be newly conceptualized . . . to reanimate and thus more fully realize the co-relational poetics-aesthetics of our scientific selves" (*Sylvia Wynter: On Being Human as Praxis* 8). The "co-relational poetics-aesthetics" of Wynter's "bio-mythois" find literary instantiation in Lorde's biomythography, and in the other subversive forms gathered here. These forms demonstrate how black women writers have mobilized formal and poetic difference as a tool for rethinking human difference, its sociopolitical meanings, and its complex relations to bodily life. On the one hand, "difference" defines human subjectivity at the most basic level by disaggregating self from other; on the other hand, the illimitability of "difference"—the vast and unending field of self/other constructions—is, arguably, the idea that most consistently vexes identity theorizing, a conceptual faultline that consistently results in hierarchical categorizations of identity and lists of social alterities that are inevitably incomplete. This failure to articulate the complexity of human difference invariably excludes black women from the realm of the human—a realm that often determines life and death in black and queer communities. While several scholars have compellingly argued against privileging "the human" as a useful category for imagining liberatory black futures,[27] I am interested in how the artistic modalities of bio-mythois/ biomythics allow us not to *prove* black humanity, but to reimagine the human according to black queer feminist difference in a way that enables us to link our futures to the languages and experiences that have shaped our pasts and presents. These artistic forms call on us to acknowledge the persistent presence of hegemonic notions of "humanness" in systems of oppression and to access the interpretive nuance and radical potential of poetics and *humanistic* engagement to trouble normative visions of subjectivity and being within and beyond academic discourse. I view this as a crucial step in any theoretical movement toward a liberatory black future.

Reading Afrodiasporic women's poetics of difference through a queer and anti-normative lens throws these many forms of difference into relief. Such an interpretive strategy exposes the ways in which black women writers and artists reconfigure silence as polyvocal speech and remap restrictive "boundaries" of power as lines for drawing new cartographies of blackwoman possibility. These writers undermine those ideological systems that appropriate difference to arbitrate humanity by welcoming some into a sphere of sanctioned complexity and contradiction while confining others to tight geographies of image, trope, and type. By voicing the differences among and between black womanhoods, the writers and artists gathered here challenge contemporary scholarship to redefine the human, shaping it according to bodies and lives dominant language has yet to imagine.

The works gathered here span and respond to crises of power and oppression that quite literally threaten the lives of black women and black queer people. In doing so, they imagine new possibilities for black queer and feminist futurity. Narrating lives shaped in part by intertwined crises—from the ongoing global HIV/AIDS epidemic, to the everpresence of domestic violence and sexual assault, to mortal crises of medical and economic disenfranchisement, to the state-sanctioned murders of black queer and trans people throughout the diaspora and more—these artists write through decades of lethal violence against the discursive erasure of their own deaths, and toward new visions of living. These artists are writing for our survival, our freedom, and our futures, not only as black people, not only as women, but as inscrutable forces of skin *and* story whose and inner lives and collective worlds are shaped by the complexities of raced and gendered being, and infinitely more.

# CHAPTER ONE

# Biomythic Times

## *Voice, Genre, and the Invention of Black/Queer History*

In those years my life had become increasingly a
bridge and field of women. Zami. Zami. A Carriacou
name for women who work together as friends and
lovers. We carry our traditions with us. Buying boxes
of Red Cross Salt and a fresh corn straw broom for my
new apartment . . . new job, new house, new living the
old in a new way. Recreating in words the women who
helped give me substance.
—Audre Lorde, *Zami*

In Audre Lorde's hybrid autobiographical text, *Zami: A New Spelling of My Name* (1987), the term "Zami" serves three key functions. As a "new spelling" of Lorde's name, it is an act of self-definition in which Lorde stakes linguistic claim over her identity. Later in the text, we learn that "Zami" is a Carriacou (the language of Lorde's mother's homeland) plural noun naming women's same-sex labor, affection, and desire, offering linguistic proof of queer historical presences in her mother's homeland. Finally, it is the titular marker for Lorde's genre invention, the "biomythography" through which Lorde tells a partially fictionalized, multi-genre, intertextual narrative of her coming-of-age as a black queer woman, and of her many-tiered search for self and belonging. By invoking these three simultaneous functions of "Zami" (as self-naming, as genre, and as proof of a black queer history), Lorde retools the term to link processes of self-definition, genre innovation, historical self-location, and coming-of-age.[1] "Zami" thus serves not only as a "new spelling" of Lorde's name, but a new way of writing black queer processes of being, belonging, and becoming. It names the creative act through which Lorde joins personal and collective histories to make space for black queer women's futurity.

As both a literary text and a genre-building concept, *Zami* illuminates the role of the nuantial in literary evocations of black/queer temporality. Engaging Lorde's biomythics in *Zami* demonstrates the contours and functions of black queer feminist reading strategy and offers a useful interpretive frame for reading difference in other genre-subversive texts. Lorde's particular "recreating" of personal and collective black/queer histories in the text also links to key black/queer historiographic methods crucial to several queer Afrodiasporic texts. As in several black/queer diasporic texts, in *Zami* the text itself is the method; the biomythography serves as both an example of the historiographies black/queer experience necessitates and an interpretive frame for reading black/queer stories.

This chapter explores the interplay of formal invention, history, and black queer womanhood in Afrodiasporic women's literary culture. Lorde's imperative to "liv[e] the old in a new way" queers perspectives on history common to many Afrodiasporic cultures and critical traditions, including, for example, the axiom that "you have to know where you come from to know where you're going."[2] Lorde questions the viability of empirical distinctions between past, present, and future, and instead suggests a fluidity and interdependence among these and other timespaces. By linking images of her imagined Grenadian homeland to her climactic definition of "Zami" as a term for specifically same-sex modes of belonging, sexual relationality, and selfhood, Lorde positions queerness as central among the "traditions" that diaspora people must carry with them as they create new futures and redefines "tradition[al]" valuations of the past on her own queer terms (*Zami* 26). It is not only her ethnic or personal history ("where she comes from") that Lorde must "know" in order to move into her future; she must also create evidence of a shared cultural past textured by the nuantial interstices of gender and sexual difference—a black/queer/woman diasporic history—and carry that evidence with her if she is to survive. Queering history in *Zami*, Lorde uses her poetics of difference to create what I term a *biomythic historiography*—a creative reimagining of historical narrative and historicity that asserts black queer presence by creating and documenting black queer pasts, with the specific aim of affirming and enabling black queer futures. Biomythic historiography upsets normative models of historiography—which most contemporary Western thought frames as animated by teleology, linearity, and a hegemonic focus on verifiable event. It also offers new models of historicity that emphasize the simultaneity and mutual constitution of timespaces and the creative manipulation of those timespaces as crucial for black/queer being. In this sense, the creative construction of these histories by black queer women writers is, in itself, a radical act. As Matt Richardson points out, "to claim such an assemblage of creative interpretations of the self is also dangerous in its dizzying audacity and flagrant noncompliance with the terms of our dehumanization" (*The Queer Limit of Black Memory* 9).

This "flagrant noncompliance" with dominant narratives of black queer life requires similarly spectacular departures from standard narrative form, genre, and temporality. Lorde and other black/queer writers destabilize readerly expectations—particularly of narrative voice and narrative time—in order to convey the multisubjectivity and multidirectionality of black/queer historical narrative. As Michelle Wright notes in *Physics of Blackness*, understanding the meanings of blackness requires attention to "the phenomenology of blackness—that is, *when* and *where* it is being imagined, defined, and performed" (3). Wright argues that we look to nonlinear "epiphenomenal time" as the constant "'now' through which the past, present, and future are always interpreted" without direct causal relation to stable pasts. In this disengagement from linear time, blackness's meanings shift and expand according to how they are expressed and read, and 'in what locations, both figurative and literal'" (ibid.). Yet as the example of *Zami* suggests, these multi-temporal iterations of blackness are not only "figurative and literal" but also *literary*. Just as Lorde's biomythographic narrator creates a timespace in which she can "new liv[e] the old in a new way," centering her queerness and multiple other differences in her vision of black/queer diasporic history, so do several other queer writers of the African diaspora intervene in epiphenomenal time specifically to invent black/queer histories. I use the term "black/queer history" here to signal the mutual and multidirectional imbrication of "black" and "queer" historical narratives, and to reference the subversive creative practices by which black queer writers and artists (re)create those intersecting histories by centering the nuantial in their poetics. For many queer writers of the African diaspora, blackness and queerness are not separate identificatory markers; rather, they are contiguous signifiers of a difference that defines temporal and social experience. In their worlds, there cannot be black history without several forms of queerness, and there cannot be black queer survival without several concurrent black histories.

As *Zami* shows, biomythic historiography functions as a heterogeneous praxis that destabilizes dominant expectations of both the genres in which histories are constructed and the subjects whose stories are told. Just as Lorde's text uses several poetic, narrative, and temporal forms to chart a shared nuantial history of black/queer life, the coming-of-age fictions of Trinbagonian Canadian writer Dionne Brand and Cuban American writer Achy Obejas demonstrate how biomythic historiographies incorporate elements of documented history, personal narrative, shared communal lore, and individual erotic fantasy in reimagining individual and collective queer pasts. They enact upon the archive the function of Hortense Spillers's model of the interstice, writing the "missing words" of black/queer presence on accepted historical narratives ("Interstices" 156). They thus activate the queer potential of the "silence in the archive" of black history's traumas which, as Saidiya Hartman notes, elides the contradictions and complexities of black women's experiences of diasporic life ("Venus in Two Acts" 4). Hartman's vision of the archive provides important language for how this silence becomes creative practice: by "Listening to the unsaid, translating misconstrued words, and refashioning disfigured lives," these writers (and often characters themselves) create histories that situate both individual and collective in temporal scapes that endure into futurity (3). Lorde's choice not to include the prefix "auto" in the genre designation of the "biomythography"—and her decision to code the imagined elements of the story in the context of "myth" rather than "fiction"—point to the collective and intergenerational resonances that make up the scope of *Zami*, even as the term also serves as "a new spelling" of the author's own name.

The genre of the "biomythography" taps the epic temporal resonances of mythology while also leaving open the possibility of narrative distance and depersonalization inherent in the biographic form. It thus traverses timespaces, bringing the present in constant contact with past and future, and uses the ostensibly individual voice of the narrator to speak in and from multiple modes and perspectives, as do several polyvocal diasporic oral traditions of mythology. Like *Zami*, black women's biomythic historiographies are as much "biographies" of partly invented historical black/queer communities as they are individual stories of coming-of-age and survival. These historiographies are valuable precisely *because* they are partly imagined, even as their sustaining effects are urgently real.

The biomythographic works of Lorde, Obejas, and Brand are part of a rich, underexplored lineage of poetic innovation and historiographic fantasy in queer diasporic literary culture. There is a significant and underexplored archive of queer texts of the African diaspora that use multiplicities of voice and genre to render black/queer histories that highlight the multiplicity of black/queer subjects by disturbing distinctions between self and other and between present and the past. These include: African American critic, memoirist, and science fiction writer Samuel Delany's memoir, *The Motion of Light in Water* (1988); African American fiction writer and critic Randall Kenan's short story collection, *Let the Dead Bury Their Dead* (1992); Afro-German fiction writer Olumide Popoola's novella, *This Is Not about Sadness* (2010); African American poet Kamilah Aisha Moon's biomythographic poetry collection, *She Has a Name* (2014); African American novelist and poet Sapphire's, *Push* (1996); Jamaican novelist Michelle Cliff's, *No Telephone to Heaven* (1986); African American filmmaker Isaac Julien's iconic *Looking for Langston* (1989); and Liberian American screenwriter and video artist Cheryl Dunye's film, *The Watermelon Woman* (1996). These authors and texts lay a foundation for what Essex Hemphill calls a black queer "language . . . esthetic," tuned specifically for expressing shared black queer experience stricken from dominant social narratives (*Brother to Brother* xxiv). Historiography, for these authors, is not an effort to retrieve or document the past, but a self-conscious and explicit act of creativity. They reveal historiography as a creative, processual invention of lineages, ancestors, kinship tales, and personal narratives through which the present is sustained and the future is made possible.

Biomythic historiographies engage the poetics of the nuantial in two key ways: (1) they construct black/queer ancestral lineages through acts of vocal subversion and imaginative temporality and (2) they develop heterogeneous point-of-view strategies to disturb normative, genre-specific constructions of narrative time and subjectivity. I begin with an examination of Trinbagonian Canadian lesbian poet and novelist Dionne Brand's novel *In Another Place, Not Here* (1996) and her long poem, *Ossuaries* (2010), in which Brand's narrators and speakers subvert the formal conventions of the realist social novel to chart what I term "genealogies of singularity"—black/queer ancestries created by imagining figures of both historical and folkloric pasts in terms of their relationships to multiple difference and by creating erotic and political identificatory links with those figures.

I then turn to Cuban American journalist, poet, novelist, and translator Achy Obejas's novel *Memory Mambo* (1996), an Afrolatina lesbian coming-of-age story characterized by what I term "syndetic bildung"—a fictional device in which coming-of-age trajectories require heteroglossic narrative structures and intimate engagements with imagined pasts. Syndetic bildung subverts white, Western bildungsroman ideals of individualism and static futurity and replaces them with the objective of mutual identification through a black/queer difference located in the past. In Brand's work, biomythic historiography occurs as black/queer historiography, in which the interstices of self-identified blackness and queerness allow and demand new poetic historiographic praxis for Brand's women protagonists. In Obejas's novel, this biomythic praxis takes the form of queer Afrolatina historiography, a term I use to acknowledge the specific dynamics of blackness in Latinx Afrodiasporic communities, and the particular ways in which race is contested within Obejas's text. In both historiographic structures, it is the effort to create and identify through the past that propels black/queer narratives forward.

These historiographies highlight the queer and feminist possibilities of futurity in Afrodiasporic literature, and challenge the turn in queer studies to antisocial and anti-futurist discourses, in which queer subjectivity is thought to be defined and made meaningful by its oppositional relation to social connectedness and futurity.[3] White twentieth- and twenty-first-century theories of queer identity and temporality such as those offered by Julia Kristeva (1982), Leo Bersani (1985), Michael Warner (1999), Lee Edelman (2004), Heather Love (2007), and others have examined the usefulness of abjection, stigma, and anti-futurism for constructing radical queer identifications. Edelman's theory of abject anti-futurism meets a particularly direct challenge in Brand's work. Edelman critiques what he terms "reproductive futurism," through which (Western) social discourses seek to obscure queerness by positioning heterosexual reproduction as the arbiter of personhood. To reject this schema, Edelman suggests that queer subjects must embrace an "ascription of negativity" in which "the queer comes to figure the bar to every realization of futurity, the resistance, internal to the social, to every social structure or form." Edelman places his model of queer abjection in direct opposition with crucial black feminist discourses of hope and survival, arguing that one major responsibility of contemporary queerness is "to refuse the insistence of hope itself as affirmation" (*No Future* 4).[4]

For queer people in the African diaspora, I argue that abjection only functions as a valuable political frame when it is deployed, as in Darieck Scott's usage, as a way of articulating the psychic and social impacts of racism, homophobia, and other systems of hegemonic normativity on black queer subjects (15).[5] In Kristeva's foundational definition of the term, abjection might potentially signal the "loathing" and "radical . . . exclu[sions]" visited on black queer identities for its refusal to "respect borders, positions, rules" (*Powers of Horror* 2, 4). Yet identification through retrospective "abjection" fails to account for black women's and black queer people's historical efforts against oppression, as it denies the energy, hope, and visioning required simply to endure in a world in which, as Lorde famously puts it, "we were never meant to survive" (*The Collected Poems of Audre Lorde*). In suggesting that queer theory and queer subjects align their radical ideologies against futurity, this scholarship denies the persistence and violence of racism, sexism, classism, and other hegemonic structures that queer Afrodiasporic women subjects constantly face, and through which they must continually engage the past, present, and future.

In inventing history to make black queer women's continuance possible, Lorde's, Brand's, and Obejas's work demands answers to the questions recent queer discourses of anti-futurism bury in rhetoric: Who has the luxury of valuing abjection? Who can afford *not* to dream of the future? Their work positions the affective registers of *gay shame* as inextricable from the political imperatives of *black pride* and black feminist survival, troubling logics that look to abject sites of "the past" as a haven for identities barred from normative ideas of "the future" by dismantling distinctions between the two.[6]

Reading the works of Lorde, Brand, and Obejas through the technologies of a nuantial black/queer feminist poetics highlights these writers' efforts to create the impossible futures that much of white queer studies dismisses. Their narrators and speakers issue a vehement challenge to anti-futurist logics, locating them within the strain of "single-issue" thinking that black feminism has historically worked to dismantle. Invoking black feminist imperatives of radical self-recovery, they reject the "ascription of negativity" that Edelman celebrates, in which "the queer comes to figure the bar to every realization of futurity, the resistance, internal to the social, to every social structure or form" (4, 5). Further, approaching time from nonlinear Afrodiasporic frameworks, these writers refuse to reject the future as "mere repetition . . . just as lethal as the past" or to eschew narrative histories in which the "dream of self-realization" occurs through "the impossible place of an Imaginary past" (31, 10). By unsettling distinctions between past, present, and future for the purposes of black/queer hope and affirmation, Lorde, Brand, and Obejas reject white anti-futurist models of queerness that find their authenticity in death, and in which, as Edelman argues, "what is queerest about us, queerest within us, and queerest despite us is this . . . to insist that the future stop here" (31). Instead, they use their poetics of difference to illuminate the multiple linkages between past and present, self and other, injury and hope, so that their futures may be possible.

These futures highlight the queer and feminist potentials of Afrofuturism. By imagining diasporic futures predicated on nonnormative conceptions of time and subjectivity, biomythic historiographies are deeply engaged with models of queer Afrofuturism as forwarded, for example, by literary scholar Amandine H. Faucheux, in which the term describes both the works of queer-identified Afrofuturist writers and "illuminates the functions of racial and sexual metaphors in speculative contexts in general," allowing for "an intersectional approach" to tensions of racial, gender, and sexual power that emerges in speculative and fantasy writing ("Race and Sexuality" 565). They also engage Susana Morris's vision of "Afrofuturist feminism," which she defines as "a literary tradition in which people of African descent and transgressive, feminist practices born of or from across the Afrodiaspora are key to a progressive future" (153). While many scholars understand Afrofuturist texts as those that depict such futures directly within their narratives (that is, those set at least partially in imagined futures), the writers gathered here use multi-temporal biomythic historiographies to highlight those futures' urgent importance within familiar timescapes and to reveal their inextricable links to invented, imagined historiographic pasts.

Biomythic historiography also offers a much needed black queer feminist response to some of the central questions of Afropessimism put forth by Jared Sexton, Frank Wilderson, and others. Sexton, for example, considers "whether a politics, which is also to say an aesthetics, that affirms (social) life can avoid the thanatological dead end if it does not will its own (social) death" (16). For Sexton and others, state, social, and historical structures of antiblackness preclude black life within known social worlds and produce a situation in which "black life is *lived* in social *death*," that is, outside of recognized/recognizable configurations of sociality, and, instead "underground, in outer space" (29). Yet Afropessimist discourses have continually failed to take up black feminist temporalities, which emphasize collectivity, simultaneity, futurity, and survival.

As an aesthetic deeply rooted and actively engaged in black queer and feminist political aims—and black feminist visions of collectivity in particular—biomythic historiography challenges Afropessimist logics. By investing in both past and future as feats of collaborative imagination rather than singular matters of temporal fact, biomythic historiography positions history and futurity as creative responses to both the social death of enslavement and colonization, and to the fantasy of freedom to come. In these historiographies, black/queer life is made possible precisely through real and necessary socialities that operate both on the bodily plane *and* in the "outer space" of the collective black/queer feminist imagination.

Considered together, *In Another Place, Ossuaries*, and *Memory Mambo* offer a queer feminist view of diasporic lineage that reshapes historical narratives of migration and belonging around black queer women's nuantial subjectivity. Brand and Obejas develop what Omise'eke Natasha Tinsley terms a "queer, unconventional, imaginative archive," creating and documenting lineage of black queer women ancestors, both through the imaginative acts of their protagonists and through authorial poetics of voice (*Ezili's Mirrors* 193). In each case, the past is an "imagined" creative artifact, important precisely because it sustains the present and enables the future (Edelman 10). Brand's manipulations of poetic and narrative form and Obejas's subversions of the bildungsroman genre allow each writer to develop historiographic modes in which both characters and authors rewrite history to include black/queer presences. In the invention of these histories, heterogeneous voices, shifting perspectives, and reconfigured genres expose the interstices of black womanhood and enable an imaginative vision of black queer timescales tilted to futurity and tuned for survival.

## Collaging Diasporic Histories of Difference: Dionne Brand's *In Another Place Not Here* and *Ossuaries*

On the island of "Nowhere," identity, lineage, and belonging are consummately queer. In the cultural logic of the fictional Caribbean setting of Dionne Brand's 1996 novel, *In Another Place, Not Here*, phenotypes, anatomies, and bloodlines bear far less genealogical meaning than the nuanced ticks, impulses, and desires that differentiate individual subjectivities and mark them, in various ways, as queer. Difference, in the novel, inaugurates anti-normative modes of belonging, threaded through "the very weave" of Nowhere's history, as well as through Brand's narrative strategy (39). In Brand's works, "belonging [i]s not singular," yet the echoes of belonging are *constituted by* singularity—that is, by those nuances of identity that challenge monolithic notions of blackness and define black women's subjectivities and creative voices according to difference (3, 9). Brand introduces textual worlds in which singularity, difference, and a broadly figured queerness shape Afrodiasporic women's identities and form the basis for new means of history-making propelled by creative invention and expressed through queer poetic forms (40). Brand's 2010 long poem, *Ossuaries*, illustrates the impact of identification through difference on poetic constructions of history in her work. Disavowing imperial models of belonging that deny the heterogeneity of Afrodiasporic women's identity and experience, Brand's protagonists create forms of cross-temporal belonging rooted in black women's intersectionality and diasporic fragmentation.

*In Another Place* follows the relationship between Elizette, a black lesbian cane worker living on an un-named Caribbean island on the verge of decolonization, and Verlia, a college-age emigrant who returns from Canada at the novel's opening to organize for revolution. Brand introduces three major narrative voices in the novel: Elizette's first-person narration, which presents the novel's first section, "Elizette, Beckoned"; an omniscient third-person narrator, who tells Verlia's story in the second section, "Verlia, Flying"; and Verlia's first-person voice presented through her journal entries toward the close of the novel. Through this multi-vocal expression of blackwoman identity, Brand's narrators explore both personal histories of coming-of-age in diaspora, and communal histories of the island from enslavement onward, examining the place of black women's sexuality and multiple forms of queerness in each of these narratives.

*Ossuaries* continues this project of historicizing blackwoman difference through poetic form. Named for "receptacle[s] . . . for the bones of the dead; [t]hat in which relics of the dead past are preserved" and "mental or spiritual charnel house[s]," the long poem tells the story of Yasmine, an American-born black activist who reflects on her political work and past loves from an unnamed "underground" space of self-exile, telling her story through both first- and third-person points of view ("Ossuary"). While Brand does not explicitly identify Yasmine as queer or lesbian, Brand constructs her identity and understands her history through what she terms "solitary perfectable strangeness," a keen sense of difference that both includes and extends beyond the standard "theories/ of plurals" that dominant feminist and black nationalist rhetorics address (15). This "strangeness" conjures a poetic strategy of estrangement in which the poem's fifteen sections move through two concurrent speaking voices: a third-person "she" who follows Yasmine through the even-numbered sections and a first-person "I" from whose perspective the odd-numbered sections are presented. In both *In Another Place* and *Ossuaries*, Brand's poetics use voice to unsettle history, situating it as a product of Afrodiasporic queer women's imaginations and a tool for structuring black queer women's futurity.

In *In Another Place,* Brand uses Verlia's character and a shifting third-person narration to dramatize the self-conscious creative construction of black/queer women's history. Verlia's story, like the first-person speaker of *Ossuaries*, acts as a synecdoche for the text's larger narrative voice, explaining both the importance of creative historiography and the aesthetic means by which black queer histories are crafted. As an immigrant in Toronto, Verlia embodies a number of alterities; in addition to her lesbian identity and the marginal ethnic, national, and class positions she inhabits, the personal history she has received from communal lore holds that she "was supposed to be a boy but came out a girl" (132). This complex of difference is linked intimately to her investment in political history, which provides the narrative material for her historicization of her queerness.

Before moving to Toronto, Verlia lives in Sudbury, Canada, with an aunt and uncle who insist on proving themselves as "harmless" and "just like white people," much like the black "sellouts" against whom Verlia constructs her political identity (140–142, 177). In addition to their assimilationist and accommodationist politics, Verlia's Aunt Idrisse and unnamed uncle[7] also represent the dangers of heteronormative models of black history and lineage. Their home in Sudbury, to Verlia, represents the hegemony of heteronormativity, and the dangers of denying intra-racial difference in order to efface blackness itself:

> In Sudbury, if they conform to some part of the puzzle, they are convinced that they will be rewarded with acceptance. Ordinariness. Man, woman, husband, wife, couple, parents, Black. They are counting on the first six words. They think that her addition will fill out some of the rest, somehow, she senses, make them white in this white town. . . . It does not matter that in this town they will remain odd, they will never be noticed as fully there. (141)

Verlia is expected to reify the couple's "[o]rdinariness" by solidifying their place within the symbolic order, in which legibility within patriarchal, heterosexual family structures constitutes normalcy and legitimates both individual subjectivity and shared kinship ties (Lévi-Strauss 259, 478–497). Her black queer woman body is ironically positioned as an antidote to the "odd[ness]" and sexual deviance that, as Michelle Wright notes, is always already attributed to black bodies (143). Yet Verlia's rejection of the symbolic order—and of an identity based on reproductive gender and sexuality—takes on particular importance in light of her family's island ties, and her later interest in nationalist politics. Within the postcolonial and nationalist contexts of Brand's native Trinidad, M. Jacqui Alexander argues, "Not just (any) *body* can be a citizen any more, for some *bodies* have been marked by the state as non-procreative, in pursuit of sex only for pleasure, a sex that is non-productive of babies and of no economic gain. Having refused the heterosexual imperative of citizenship, these bodies, according to the state, pose a profound threat to the very survival of the nation"

("Not Just [Any] Body" 6). By refusing to participate in heteronormative kinship even as the offspring around which that lineage coheres, Verlia asserts not only her own identity as a queer woman but also her refusal to acquiesce to the heteronormative models of lineage that shape both citizenship and dominant nationalist politics. Given the extent to which "the nationalist state mediates the massive entry of transnational capital within national orders, but blames sexual decadence (lesbian and gay sex and prostitution) for the dissolution of the nation," Verlia's choice to remove herself from heteronormative lineage marks an act of self-rehistoricization in which she fashions her body as a tool for the construction of new lineages to which both pleasure and radical anti-normative politics are central (Alexander 6, 7).

Verlia engages in this re-historicization by crafting a difference-based genealogy of her own. Directed to "make something of herself" by her aunt and uncle, Verlia assembles images of iconic political and social figures including Adam Clayton Powell Jr., Rosa Parks, Chairman Mao Zedong, Nina Simone, Mahatma Gandhi, James Brown, Otis Redding, Jean-Jacques Dessalines, and Fidel Castro in a shoebox, constructing an aspirational scrapbook of "the things that she needed to know" to make herself "a new person" (Brand *In Another Place* 161, 159, 169). Arranged not according to any shared ethnic, racial, national, or even temporal linkage, but rather according to the "feeling" of political empowerment each provides, the clippings become creative media for Verlia's black queer history.[8] In separating herself from heteronormative kinships and lineages, she collages icons of multiple anti-normative struggles to constitute what she deems "her new past." Here, she enacts a creative historiography, creating for herself the kind of imaginative archive Hartman suggests is necessary for full evocations of black women's diasporic experience (3, 4). Yet through this act of creative historiography, Verlia also locates herself and her history firmly outside of the symbolic order, constructing herself as a "new" queer woman for whom "[b]its of newspaper are her history, words her family" (Brand *In Another Place* 165). Her rejection of normative kinship structures (that is, her refusal to play the role of the Symbolic "Child" against which Edelman rails) does not preclude her future but *enables* it.[9] She needs this invented archive of the past precisely to create the "new person" she must become as a black queer woman moving through time and space. She thus brings black queer feminist worldviews to bear on normative visions of kinship and historicity, a move that highlights the normative underpinnings of white queer anti-futurist critiques.

Verlia's self-awareness in her creative historiographic efforts in *In Another Place* is facilitated in part by the presence of the semi-omniscient third-person narrator who situates her story within its temporal and historical context; in *Ossuaries*, however, Brand paradoxically offers her first-person speaker even greater awareness of and control over the poem's historiographic project. The speaker hails herself as "I, the slippery pronoun, the ambivalent, glistening/ long sheath of the alphabet flares beyond her reach," and later laments: "If only I had something to tell you, from here/ some good thing that would weather/ the atmospheres of the last thirty years" (9, 103).[10] Brand's first-person Yasmine establishes herself as an emblem of poetic subversion and an arbiter of both Yasmine's story and the form of its telling. This speaker is not simply an *older* version of Yasmine, but a concurrent consciousness removed not so much by lived years as by the "atmospheres" of time-space. She speaks not only from the distance of hindsight, but also, crucially, from a psychic and epistemological "other place, not here," where she reflects on, relates, and reconstructs Yasmine's "strange" history.

Narrating Yasmine's story from these shifting temporal scapes, the two speakers of *Ossuaries* are able to both articulate and to contextualize the queer, creative, historiographic process Yasmine undertakes. At the close of "Ossuary V," the first-person speaker expresses Yasmine's anxieties about the viability and legibility of her own "strange" history in first person, wondering: "will my bones glitter beyond these ages, / will they burn beyond these photographs'/ crude economy? (51). Then, shifting to Yasmine's third-person consciousness in the following section, the speaker describes "this genealogy she's made by hand, this good silk lace, / Engels plaited to Bird, Claudia Jones edgestitched / to Monk, Rosa Luxemburg braids Coltrane" (52). Just as Verlia, in *In Another Place*, cathects to her collaged genealogical figures in hopes that their radicalism will "recur" in and beyond her, Yasmine's pantheon of anti-normative activists and philosophers "reshape[s] time itself," allowing her to understand the social dynamics of her history in the present, and to imagine her own story "glitter[ing] beyond these ages" (161, 53, 51).

Critics have noted the importance of Brand's reconstructions of history to contemporary black queer theory. Borrowing from M. Jacqui Alexander's notion of "expansive memory," Matt Richardson argues that Brand and other important diasporic lesbian writers develop "expansive historiographies" that "comment on and reimagine the past but without concern for historical verisimilitude. Expansive historiographic texts are not bound by the thick description and period detail that historical fiction demands" (*The Queer Limit of Black Memory* 12). Close attention to Brand's poetics—and her narrative description in particular—suggest that, for Brand, linguistic detail works not against but toward the expansion of historiography, allowing for multiple layers of subjective meaning and nuance that *aid in*, rather than limit, the historicization of black queer difference.

By crafting their genealogies through icons of multiple differences (that is, the distinct but overlapping imperatives of antiracist, feminist, black nationalist, and socialist figures) and multiple expressive cultural forms (including jazz, blues, and gospel music), Brand's characters construct trans-temporal identifications consistent and conversant with Shange's model of "singularity." Shange introduces the term in her 1991 essay "takin' a solo/ a poetic possibility/ a poetic imperative," calling for blackwoman literary voices that resist the "monolith" of racial representation and instead express "the singularity of [black] persons/ our spaces" (3, 9). Shange's "singularity" signals the far reaches of difference and articulates "queerness" in its fullest form; it points not only to the intersection of distinct identity categories within black subjectivity, but it also signals the more minute nuances of black subjectivity, what she calls the "richness of our persons," as reflected in the turns and textures of voice.

Both Verlia and Yasmine apply this model of "singularity" to their history-making and use it to develop genealogies through that link them to singularities and queernesses of the past. Yasmine's "lace" of lineage, like Verlia's genealogical clippings, evokes Michel Foucault's understanding of the material through which genealogies are constructed. Foucault's genealogies, like Verlia's and Yasmine's collages, operate "on a field of tangled and confused parchments, on documents that have scratched over and recopied many times," demanding the imaginative use of a "vast accumulation of source materials" (*Foucault* "Nietzsche, Genealogy, History" 139–140). Moreover, genealogy, in Foucault's formulation,

> must record the *singularity* of events outside of any monotonous finality; it must seek them in the most unpromising places, in what we tend to feel is without history—*in sentiments, love, conscience, instincts*; it must be sensitive to their recurrence, not in order to trace the curve of their evolution, but to isolate the different scenes in which they are engaged in different roles. . . . *Genealogy does not oppose itself to history . . . it opposes itself to the search for "origins."* (140, emphasis added)

While Foucault's notion of "singularity" is in a different register from Shange's (emphasizing discreteness of time and space over those of subjective or identitarian "nuance"), the centrality of unrecognized "sentiments, love, conscience, [and] instincts" to both illustrates the importance of difference to the construction of human relationships across time. Brand's genealogies engage these dual singularities; they link "singular" anti-normative historical figures and events according to the subjective queernesses and "singularities" that motivate them. Her characters use poetic historiographies to create a model of history in which people of the present are defined not by the samenesses of race, gender, or bloodline, for example, but by the nonnormativities and differences they share with people of the past.

This queer linkage of past, present, and future serves as a shared identificatory practice in Brand's texts, connecting various historical moments and various diaspora locales through Brand's poetics of difference. The first-person speaker of *Ossuaries* relates Yasmine's identification with difference through the painter

Jacob Lawrence's 1947 painting "Shipping Out" (part of his "War Series"), which visually connects black military involvement in World War II to the Middle Passage. In the painting, the contorted bodies of black soldiers are depicted stacked horizontally in narrow sleeping quarters as lighter, shadowy figures holding rifles occupy the foreground of the image. Viewing this painting, the first-person Yasmine remarks: "who could not see this like the passage's continuum," and observes the images' "ships, newly dressed/ [as] if we could return through this war" (81, 82). This impossibility of "return," evocative of Brent Edwards's model of Afrodiasporic experience, is a failure of static, linear history and the artifice of imagined "border[s] . . . between then and now" (82). It is this imaginary temporal rift that Yasmine's two narrators bridge. The narrators graft a subjectivity split in two by concurrent histories of colonialism, elitism, racism, sexism, and other normative oppressions, offering the "hope" of a "convergent mimesis" against "the diatonic . . . ragged plumage of our disappearances" (89).

The cultural logic of Nowhere, within *In Another Place*, casts a corresponding doubt on the fixity of identity and links it to the nonnormative modalities of lineage that characterize Afrodiasporic experience. Elizette's first-person narration describes the attitudes Nowhere's first-generation slaves held toward human relationships of ownership and belonging. For them, she reveals, places and people

> didn't need description or writing down. Certainly not owning. And belonging? They were past it. *It was not wide enough, not gap enough, not distance enough. Not rip enough, belonging.* Belonging was too small, too small for their magnificent rage. They had surpassed the pettiness of their oppressors who measured origins speaking of a great patriarch and property marked out by violence. (42, emphasis added)

This rejection of "belonging" is both a rejection of the violent colonial, imperialist, patriarchal, and capitalist social economies through which black people and women are continually denied subjectivity, and a reformulation of lineage in Afrodiaspora. By framing the intersubjective connections "belonging" aims to capture in terms of "gap[s]" and "rip[s]," Elizette introduces the possibility of an opposing, anti-normative genealogy that expands Edwards's and Paul Gilroy's understandings of difference-based Afrodiasporic identity to include specifically black queer women's perspectives. Nowhere's relational structure accounts simultaneously for the destruction of African social structures and relationships enacted through colonization and enslavement, for the violent "rip[ping]" and rendings of black bodies during and after colonial contact, and for the "internal" "gap[s]" and differences within black identities; yet it articulates these identifications through figures whose voices must be understood in the context of their black womanhood (Gilroy *The Black Atlantic* 32; Edwards *The Practice of Diaspora* 64).

As a plot device, Brand's genealogies narrativize Edwards's notion of Afrodiasporic *décalage* (Edwards's term for exposing overlapping differences of black diasporic experience through language) and reorients it around black womanhood. Brand's genealogies position the "gaps," "discrepancies," "diversities," and "internal" differences that form "the very weave of [black Diasporic] culture," as central to diasporic blackwoman identity (64). Yasmine's and Verlia's efforts to articulate a historicized cross-temporal identity of black womanhood illustrates the larger instabilities of Afrodiasporic identification that *décalage* signals, and gestures toward the potential of narrative strategy for creating black queer historiographic modes. In Nowhere, as in diaspora, "[n]obody . . . can remember when they wasn't here"—a condition that ultimately leads inhabitants to accept "the ultimate purposelessness of recalling" (8, 25). Yet, as the third-person narrator of *In Another Place* states, everyone in this situation "lived in the past or had no past but a present that was filled, peopled with the past" (44). Brand's narrator, like her characters, reimagines the "gaps" of diaspora not as *losses* of history, but as queernesses in themselves, and as opportunities to create queer Afrodiasporic women's survival.

## Erotic Narration and Black/Queer Historiography

Historical connectedness through difference is a fundamental principal of the social schemas of *In Another Place* and *Ossuaries*, and this sense of difference as a queer means of cross-temporal connection reverberates in narrative encounters with the erotic in both texts. Inside *In Another Place*, the communal memory of Nowhere is structured largely around the history and mythology of the island's foremother, Adela, who serves as an urtext of identity and multiple difference in the island's community. Adela is an embodiment of queerness-as-difference. She is a woman, a slave, an African, and an obeah healer. She also wills herself blind to avoid having to look closely at her place of captivity (signaling a further difference of physical ability) and, though she gives birth to eight children, she refuses to "mother" them, performing a subversive rejection of symbolic kinship similar to that which Verlia performs generations later (Brand 19).

Adela serves as an emblem of difference through narrative décalage, foregrounding the heterogeneities of black identity—including racial and gender alterity, along with differences of spiritual ideology, (dis)ability, embodiment, and a nonnormative relation to dominant structures of kinship and reproduction. Adela serves—both on the island of Nowhere and within the text of *In Another Place* itself—as a black queer woman ancestor. As Richardson points out, "[t]he Black queer ancestor is an unimaginable figure in mainstream dia-sporic memory. That she does not exist is a fiction of domination, an effect of trauma that has made her illegible even in alternative archives. To speak of her, one has to be creative and seize the means of archival production while pointing to her absence in written history and in memory. Black lesbian writing, then, is a practice of historical commentary, a trespass against demands of evidence, finding recourse and voice through the creation of imaginative counternarra-tives and embodied practices" (14).

Adela's ever-presence constantly effects such an imaginative trespass, shap-ing the narrative of *In Another Place* by uniting Brand's three distinct narrative voices and exposing the heterogeneities and tensions within each. Elizette's first-person narrative often includes direct addresses to Adela, and Verlia's first-person voice seems, in many ways, to channel Adela, voicing the anger, nationalism, and longing for home that characterize the lore around Adela, and thus positioning Verlia as an additional heir to Adela's "'true true' name"—the name given to her before her capture, representative of the loss of her nuanced subjectivity in enslavement (20). Finally, the relatively omniscient third-person narrative may be read as that of Adela herself, gathering the thoughts, dreams, preoccupations, and actions of her biological and nonbiological descendants and incorporating them into a single narrative, all while maintaining markers of their discrete voices, separate interiorities, and "'true true' selves."

Brand's queering of narrative voice according to black women's difference al-lows for black queer histories created not only by the *characters* (as in Yasmine's and Verlia's collaged genealogies), but also by the narrative itself. Elizette's first-person narration within *In Another Place* illuminates such a process. Where Verlia and the first-person speaker of *Ossuaries* construct their histories of difference by collaging historical icons of anti-normativity and incorporating publicly available historical narratives into their own formations of self, Eli-zette makes her queer history through a series of intimate engagements with a queer matriarchal figure using Adela's voice. As a child, Elizette is abandoned under a tree near the home of a neglectful and emotionally distant woman (and a biological descendant of Adela's) who takes her in. Barred from biologi-cal and affective identificatory ties, Elizette determines that the "samaan tree [is her] mother," and begins her quest for a personal history. Her obsession with historical elusiveness is accelerated by the voice of the caretaker, whom, upon Elizette's appearance, inquires about both Elizette's lineage and identity by asking, "Who is you now? Where you come out?" two questions to which Elizette responds with a single answer: "Me en't know" (40, 31). Elizette looks to the story of Adela in much the same way as Verlia and Yasmine look to global political icons, using scraps of Adela's story to piece together an understanding of herself, and to locate that multifaceted self within a shared history (24). Yet whereas Verlia's and Yasmine's genealogies of singularity are rooted in shared affective and ideological identifications, Elizette's search for difference-based ancestry is largely erotic and enables her to understand her own queer desire.

As an adult, Elizette reflects on her choice to leave her abusive heterosexual marriage and pursue a relationship with Verlia, musing: "it have plenty woman waiting their whole blessed life for that [kind of man] and what make me turn woman and leave it I don't know but it come. Bad spirit they say, bad or blessed, it come." (4). Framing the history of her same-sex desire in terms of "spirit," Elizette invokes the island's queer diasporic genealogies. Just as, because of the identificatory rifts enslavement visits on the island, kinship can't "be sent in blood no longer," and instead "would have to come from spirit," Elizette's queer sexual identity takes on a lineage rooted not to biology or social experience, but to a subjective nuance of erotic inclination and bodily impulse, potentially inherited from a nonbiological forbear (*In Another Place* 32). Here, instinct and desire are as crucial as blood and body in defining identity. By determining that an unidentified "spirit" confers her queer desire, Elizette turns the genealogical lens of Nowhere inward to better understand her sexuality, searching herself for reverberations of an identificatory tie that can connect her to a black queer woman past.

The process of re-membering a queer Afrodiasporic past occurs through intimate, erotic narrative engagements with emblems of multiple difference already endowed with historicity. For Elizette, this figure is Adela. As an emblem of this singularity, Adela structures not only the way identity and lineage are imagined, but also how they are expressed through acts of voice. Confronted with a new home that "could not yield to her grief," Elizette's third-person narration recalls that Adela determines "that this place was not nowhere and is so she call it. Nowhere. She say nothing here have no name. She never name none of her children, nor the man she had was to sleep with and she never answer to the name they give she which was Adela" (18). Adela engages in what L. H. Stallings terms a black female "trickster trope mechanism of unnaming," to access an "empowering liminality that can interrupt the logic of Western gender" (*Mutha Is Half a Word* 13). By using this strategy to rewrite the island's historical narrative, Adela enacts what Anthony Reed terms "unsaying," which "pushes the text to the point of its unintelligibility, alerting us anew to the mechanisms by which writing ordinarily conveys meaning" (*Freedom Time* 37). Adela's unnaming dismantles the logic of chattel slavery (in which the master's name reifies their ownership of enslaved bodies) and signals her rejection of Western historiographies based solely on verifiable memory, both of which would force her to imagine the moment of enslavement as central to the story of her life.

Adela's rejection of Western topography enables the anti-normative structures of identification that reconfigure historical relationships on the island, and open space for queer transhistorical connections that occur through narrative voice. As a result of her unnaming, the people of Nowhere come to view proper names in opposition to "'true true' names" which articulate "the heart" of things, places, and people, and point to specificities of "spirit," like the "spirit" to which Elizette attributes her queer desire (18). The concept of the "'true true' name" is introduced through Elizette's first-person narration as she describes her own introduction to Adela's story:

> I get to find out that Adela forget she "'true true' name" and she tongue before she leave this earth. I think deep about how a place name Nowhere could make sense and I discover that Adela had to make her mind empty to conceive it. The place she miss must have been full and living and take every corner in she mind so when she reach, there was no more room for here. . . . Cool cool it leave she, so cool. It leave like breeze, dark with more wanderings, dark with destination and dark with she life. . . . Her heart just shut. It shut for rain, it shut for light, it shut for water and the rest of what we follow. (20–22)

Here, Elizette's first-person narration complements Adela's radical un-voicing. Brand's narration presents Elizette's account of Adela's story in a persistent present tense to signal the ongoing elusiveness of the grammars of historicity for the island's inhabitants. Even scenes framed initially in the preterit tense—such as Elizette's accounts of Adela's "forg[otten]" name and her "miss[ed]" home—take on the present verb tense intermittently, becoming present-tense stories of "forget[ting]" and "miss[ing]," as dialect echoes the fractured histories of diaspora (Brand 20–22). In turning to the first-person collective pronoun "we," Brand's narration articulates a subjective continuity between Adela, the contemporary inhabitants of Nowhere, and the narrators of the novel.

Noting the "void[s]" of language, identity, and history that Adela leaves on the island, Elizette undertakes a parallel process of *re-naming*, working to "make up . . . names for Adela' things" and to "keep them in [her] head for Adela" (Brand 20). She names the plants, places, fruits, and people Adela has refused to name, determining that if she says "these names for Adela it might bring back she memory of herself and she true name. And perhaps [she] also would not feel lonely for something [she doesn't] remember" (24). Elizette's yearning to "bring back" Adela's memory of her "true true" self parallels her search for the "spirit" that defines her own queer desire (4). Elizette's creative renaming works alongside Adela's insurrectional unnaming; like Adela, she reformulates language to assert her subjectivity and take agency in the larger historical narrative of the island.[11] Elizette's historiography links her to the "spirit" of Adela, providing her with the self-constructed history she needs in order to pursue queer pleasure. Through the figure of Adela, Elizette reconstructs both her personal and national histories in hopes that knowing "where [she] come out" will help her better understand "who [she] is" (31).

The erotic timbres of such history-making processes are echoed through the voices of Brand's characters and narrators. The sensuousness of poetic historiography becomes explicit in *Ossuaries*, in which both the first-person and third-person speakers anthropomorphize linguistic forms and present both story-telling and story-hearing as bodily experiences. In describing herself as "I, the slippery pronoun, the ambivalent, glistening/long sheath of the alphabet," the first-person speaker frames her own first-person pronoun "I" as a split signifier (signaling both Yasmine's retrospective and acting perspectives), and as itself a body, whose physical characteristics and sensory appeals hold themselves and their histories "beyond [the third-person Yasmine's] reach" (22). This "slippery" signifier allows for what Gloria Wekker terms "a reading of a multiplicitous self; a self that is multilayered, complex, integrating various instantiations of 'I.' . . . This complex 'I' is not the fragmented self postulated under postmodernity and should not be equated with it" (*The Politics of Passion* 2). Rather, it speaks to the nuantial "multiplicity" of Caribbean women's subjectivities, allowing them to refer to themselves and their experience in both creole and colonial languages, as well as "in singular and plural terms, in feminine and masculine terms, and in terms of third-person constructions" (Wekker 2, 3). Like Elizette's attempt to internalize Adela's story of queerness-as-difference, this withholding of narrative in *Ossuaries* is defined by the erotic; the speaker's account of "strange" history, like the silenced "underground" narratives of socialist activism in which Yasmine steeps, is both seductively bold and elusively "hidden," evocative of both "a lover's clasp of/ violent syntax and the beginning syllabi of verblessness" (20).

Indeed, for Elizette, this linguistic quest for queer history occasions her first encounters with erotic intimacy and prompts the first stirrings of queer desire she experiences in the novel. While her caretaker is vehemently opposed to intimacy and expresses distaste at the thought of "loving," she maintains a compulsive desire to speak to Elizette, both about her own history and about the island's larger shared histories that begin with Adela. In response to her competing desires for self-isolation and connection through voice, the caretaker forces Elizette to face the wall as she tells her stories, to which Elizette listens intently for mention of Adela (32). The third-person narrator describes Elizette's listening experience in highly sensual and erotic terms:

> She could feel the story crawl over her shoulders and up her neck, she could feel it like something brown and sweet making the hair at her neck tremble. . . . She cut out the way the woman wrung out the words, as if wringing a dress dry, her voice would stretch and squeeze. She was glad she faced the wall. She did not want to see her mouth dry as a dress waist. She caught her words, as soon as they were thrown, taking the dress waist and soaking it in water again, drenching it in the dampness of Moriah . . . filling it out to the full bloom of Adela, each time the story came towards her standing against the wall. She never tired; she caught it over and over again, filled it billowy and wet. (33)

Elizette transposes her fantasies of Adela onto her caretaker. The caretaker's lips (through which Adela's story issues) become emblems not only of history, but also of same-sex erotic desire and of Elizette's construction of her own sexuality. Elizette's first-person description of this experience invokes the narrative functions of the erotic, which, as Lorde suggests, is palpable in "the way [the] body stretches to music and opens into response, harkening to its deepest rhythms, so every level upon which [one] sense[s] also opens to the erotically satisfying experience" ("Uses of the Erotic" 56). Denied visual contact with the speaker, Elizette is able to revel in the "rhythms," and "music" of her voice, and to "feel," as she says, that voice's sensual and erogenous contact with her body. She embraces this foreclosure of the visual in favor of the vocal in her poetic historiography; even in the fantasies she constructs while listening, she prefers not "to *see*" her caretaker's voice—symbolized in what we might view as the partly yonic[12] image of a dress waist wringing dry—but rather to *hear* it, and to "drench" the sound in a "dampness" evocative simultaneously of sexual arousal and of domestic labor, both of which are crucial to Elizette's womanhood.[13]

Elizette's "ca[tching]" and "cut[ting]" of this historical narrative, like Verlia's "clipping" and Yasmine's "edgestitch[ing]" of icons of difference to construct their own queer genealogies, echo throughout Brand's third-person narration. The repetition of "she could feel" and the phrase "she caught it over and over" call the reader's attention not only to the act of storytelling, but to Elizette's sensory, corporeal experience of hearing and listening. The narrative's alliterative phrasing and the repetition of sibilant consonants (as in "something brown and sweet," and "her voice would stretch and squeeze") underscore Brand's deployment of water imagery in the sensual expression of black queer women's stories. Here, the narration makes palpable both the flow of Adela's history and the rush of the caretaker's voice, echoing the "deep . . . rhythms" of Lorde's erotics, and including the reader in Elizette's erotic experience of queer historiography.

This erotic historiography has direct political ramifications, dramatizing erotic listening practices crucial to Brand's larger project of destabilizing hegemonic and normative white histories.[14] Throughout *In Another Place*, Brand's poetics of difference allows Elizette to absorb and reconfigure normative narratives to arrange a story of black/queer history that affirms her intersecting identities, elucidates her queer desires, and allows her to advocate for both, placing her nuantial subjectivity within an imagined future that constantly engages the collective past.[15] By infusing her caretaker's voice with her own creative construction of Adela's history, Elizette is able to construct for herself the homoerotic fantasy that empowers her to leave her abusive husband and pursue a life with Verlia.[16]

Brand's poetics of difference in *Ossuaries* extends this historiographic work, locating her poetic speakers in a black/queer history of difference, and thus articulating the explicitly political potentials of biomythic historiography. While the first-person Yasmine warns that "verbs are a tragedy, a bleeding cliffside, explosions/ I'm better off without," the third-person speaker dissents, insisting on the crucial role of artistic language in addressing histories of oppression. Describing Yasmine's psychic flights of fancy in her "strange" underground, the third-person speaker describes her yearning

> to undo, to undo and undo and undo this infinitive
> of arrears, their fissile mornings,
> their fragile, fragile symmetries of gain and loss
> this is how she wakes each day of each underground year,
> confessions late and half-hearted pour from her sleeping
> mouth, beginning in the year of her disappearances. (14, 21, 22)

Yasmine's "confessions" not only express regrets about her personal past, but also articulate the complex and overlapping schemas of political "gains and losses" through which black queer women's histories in Diaspora are charted. Black queer women's history, for Yasmine, is as "fissile" as her own split voice and is as incompatible with static notions of victor and vanquished as it is with fictional "borders" between self and other or present and past (*Ossuaries* 82). Sitting at a bar, she muses:

> . . . I wish for permanence
> then cast it off as dullness, stupidity
> then wish again for certainty to be
>
> in life, sitting at a bar,
> cigars hanging from my fingers, I'd tip
> the waitress half the cost of everything
>
> to inhabit whole. (*Ossuaries* 107)

Narrative's propensity for rupture is a source of frustration for Yasmine, but it also invites her to imagine queer convergences of both history and self. Imagining a "whole" that can accommodate both impermanence and certainty, and positioning it as a space she might inhabit, Yasmine configures *herself* as an ossuary, the embodied persistence of the "strange" past; and a fantasy of black/queer, cross-temporal "whole[ness]."

This fantasy of queer "wholeness" finds narrative fulfillment in Elizette's erotic historiography within *In Another Place*. Listening to her caretaker's renderings of history, Elizette wants "the woman to talk about Adela, *like Adela would talk*" (35, emphasis added). Rather than wanting to *see* Adela's reappearance in her (as in the "spitting spitting image" through which the island tends to recognize belonging), Elizette's primary desire is for an aural intimacy in which, through her own interstitial listening and nuantial speech, she can both re-create history and experience her own black/queer subjectivity at once (Brand *In Another Place*

40). In rehearing and retelling the story of Adela's departure from Nowhere, Elizette and her caretaker enact a slippage of focalization that reflects the novel's larger poetics of difference and activates its biomythic historiography. Elizette narrates the caretaker's telling of Adela's story, folding each of the novel's three narrators into a chorus of queer identity, history and voice:

> "Better she than me. Yes. Leave is all I . . . she could think of. All the marks on she . . . me is for thinking of leaving. Each time she . . . I see leaving I . . . you could not stop it. As if my hand was out of control or heading for where it ought to be, as easy as if it was coming to rest at my . . . she side. Leave I . . . she ought to be a woman her dress tail disappearing toward the dense rain forest of Tamana going to my life, she *marronage* [ . . . ] Her mouth taste the cool charm of a stone past and I determine to stop this imperfect persistence of flesh jostling the air. Now this time I . . . she dreamless, she . . . I done imagining. Leave is all I could think to do. My hand don't follow me, every piece of she mind have a mind by itself. I . . . she say is so things is." (36, ellipses in original)

In retelling Adela's "marronage," Elizette's first-person narrative ventriloquizes the speech of her caretaker, whose own voice is sporadically subsumed by that of Adela, itself in a continual process of splitting as she and her singularity self diverge. As Adela's voice sheds the identity imposed upon her through enslavement, the narrator's speech quakes under the weight of her departure into her "'true true' self" and pre-enslavement past. "Every piece" of Adela finds expression through language as her black, blind, African, Caribbean, woman, and queerly matriarchal selves escape the pain of their present enslavement in favor of "the cool charm of a stone past." Here, the pronouns "I" and "she" become as polysemous and "slippery" as the blackwoman subjectivities they hail. Like the historiographic and historicized voices of Yasmine in *Ossuaries*, the voices of Elizette, Adela, and the caretaker who connects them merge in these pronouns, reconstituting the words such that they reflect all of these women's voices and perspectives, as well as the many queernesses of each.

Brand's poetics of difference throughout *In Another Place* and *Ossuaries* not only locates her black queer protagonists in a history of difference, but also challenges the reader to deconstruct binaries of past and present, self and other, in engaging the text. In turning to the second-person "you" ("you could not stop it"), the heteroglossic narrator of *In Another Place* hails the infinitely heterogeneous presences of Brand's readership, both implicating them in the histories of enslavement, racism, misogynist violence that prompt Adela's disappearance and inviting them to participate in the subversive, affirming, black queer self-exploration through which Elizette responds.

In the final dictum "is so things is," Brand's narrators speak black queer women's histories into the present tense, issuing a decisive critique of ideologies and histories that seek to exclude them. As Elizette's, Verlia's, and Yasmine's narratives show, the invention of black / queer history is a complex creative process in which distinctions between self and other, past and present, memory and myth are thrown into question. Brand's narrators collaborate to correct what the logic of Nowhere holds as colonization's most destructive violence against the black queer woman subject: the refusal of its languages to express her identity and "yield to her grief" (*In Another Place* 18). Brand's poetics of difference, then, is not only subversive, but is also healing. It inserts into recent discourses of queerness a black feminist ethic of hope, a commitment to the practice of faith in possibility, and to the healing potential of black women's creative imaginations. This practice allows queer women of the African diaspora to understand themselves in the context of a past that persists in the present and ensures that their stories will continue as long as there are voices to tell them.

## Syndetic Bildung and Queer Afrolatina History: Achy Obejas's *Memory Mambo*

If Brand's poetics of difference within *In Another Place* works to historicize diasporic women's queernesses through narrative voice, Achy Obejas's *Memory Mambo* explores the failure of such a project and its implications for novelistic genres, as well as for queer diasporic futurities. Published and set in 1996, Achy Obejas's *Memory Mambo* tells the story of Juani Casas, a young Cuban American lesbian coming of age in a working-class Latinx enclave of Chicago. Like Verlia and Elizette, Juani struggles to understand and accept her interstitial identity through a search for history. Yet where Verlia and Elizette are both able to construct themselves by collaging various black/queer historical narratives, Juani's search for a historically located queer self does not find such completion. Obejas's narrative dramatizes a series of linguistic inaccessibilites and communicative failures that prevent the queer diasporic subject from "mak[ing] something of herself," as Brand's characters might (Brand 159). Without access to the narrative material through which to create queer history, alienation and isolation haunt Juani throughout *Memory Mambo*, thwarting her own process of becoming, and revealing the temporal and vocal poetics of a specifically queer Afrodiasporic bildungsroman form.

Like *In Another Place*, Obejas's novel traces its protagonist's struggle for identity, which is closely linked to her search for a history. Just as Verlia and Elizette work to define their interstitial selves and locate those selves within the history of Nowhere, Juani longs to construct a version of the mythical past of Cuba in which her queerness is reflected. Juani's struggle to articulate an Afrodiasporic queer history has a marked effect on *Memory Mambo*'s narrative, both impacting

Juani's narrative voice and subverting major conventions of the bildungsroman as a genre.[17] Tracing Juani's efforts to negotiate her multiple differences, Obejas reconfigures the novel of becoming. She forwards a queer Afrolatina coming-of-age process in which growth, futurity, and self-discovery require intimate engagement with the past. In illustrating the centrality of historiography to queer diasporic becoming, Obejas subverts both formal and thematic conventions of the bildungsroman, challenging distinctions between self and other, as well as between past, present, and future. Like Brand and Lorde, Obejas disturbs the linear temporalities and causal narratives of time that, as Wright argues, distort dominant readings of diasporic experience (*Physics of Blackness* 3). In *Memory Mambo*, Obejas demonstrates how these disturbances of time and subject also queer the diasporic bildungsroman form.

For queer women in the African diaspora, coming-of-age requires both negotiating multiple intersecting identifications and locating the interstitial self within a similarly heterogeneous historical context. Obejas's characters use creative historiographies to explore nuantial visions of Afrolatinidad, considering their own complex subject positions in opposition to "white" standards while also illustrating how Afrolatina identity intersects with various national, sexual, ethnic, and gender identities and the histories they reflect. Without completing these two intertwined processes—the negotiation of her own multiple differences and the historicization of her queer Afrolatina identity—Juani's narrative of becoming cannot find completion.

I use the term "queer Afrolatina" to signal the multiplicities inherent in Afro-diasporic Latinx women's identities and the links those subjectivities bear both to "queer" sexual identifications and to the multiple differences that "queerness" can address. Miriam Jiménez Román and Juan Flores define Afrolatinidad as "an expression of long-term transnational relations and of the world events that generated and were in turn affected by particular global social movements" that create ethnic and racial identifications among "people of African descent in Mexico, Central and South America, and the Spanish-speaking Caribbean, and by extension those of African descent in the United States whose origins are in Latin America and the Caribbean" (*The Afrolatin@ Reader* 1).

The duality of Afrolatinidad is key to understanding Obejas's characters and the past and present interstice through which they emerge. Afrolatinidad emphasizes the African ancestry of many Latinx and Latin-American people and the extent to which "Latinidad and blackness are not mutually exclusive" and also acknowledges the complex workings of race within Latinx communities (10). In the gendered structures of Spanish language, "Afrolatina" identity specifically signals women-centered Afrodiasporic experiences of Latinidad.[18] These identities are constantly in explicit or indirect conversation with discourses of blackness and race, even as they complicate the binaristic schemas of black and white identity that have historically characterized understandings of race in diaspora locales such as the United States. Obejas centers this complexity within Juani's narrative; her mother, Xiomara, is a woman with "café con leche" skin consumed with a desire to erase her own African ancestry. As Juani observes, "my mother will do anything to deny her real lineage . . . the whole legend around Las Casas positions the question of race between white and Indian, consigning most of the issue of blackness to silence" (32, 33)." In an effort to enact this silencing, Xiomara marries a "pale" man (Juani's father) in hopes of lightening the family line; her children's bodies, however, betray these efforts, leaving her to criticize her children's "kinky hair and full lips," and "propensity for darkness after any exposure to the sun" (34). This failed effort to silence and erase African lineage and blackness defines the family history and shapes Juani's search for her own identity, as well as her efforts to imagine a collective past.

Obejas is explicit about drawing connections between Afrolatina subjectivities and heterogeneous histories at the level of voice. *Memory Mambo* is narrated from an ostensibly consistent first-person point-of-view located within Juani's consciousness. Still, Juani's interstitial subjectivity has a fragmenting and complicating effect on her first-person narration. Early in the novel, she states: "sometimes other lives lived right alongside mine interrupt, barge in on my senses, and I no longer know if I really lived through an experience or just heard about it so many times, or so convincingly, that I believed it for myself— *became the lens through which it was captured, retold, and shaped*" (9; emphasis added). Juani identifies her narrative presence as a "lens" through which her family's stories of exile and emigration, women's struggles with patriarchy and abuse, and her own story of young queer love are told. Though she herself is a twenty-four-year-old lesbian woman living in Chicago, the histories she relates over the course of the novel express a range of gender, sexual, national, and other identities, including those of her middle-aged, heterosexual mother, her heterosexual male Cuban American siblings and cousins, and her relatives of various ages and gender and sexual identifications who remain in Cuba—each of whose voices, Juani suggests, is present in her own.

Juani's description of her multi-vocal perspective reflects the crucial role of biomythic historiography in constructing queer Afrolatina identity. Juani establishes her narrative voice as one that filters multiple subjectivities and multiple differences, fusing them into a first-person narrative and thus "ret[elling]" collective history such that it reflects a multiplicity of identities. Though she claims this multiplicity as central to her identity and her narrative voice, the heterogeneity of her narrative "lens" is a source of much frustration for Juani. While she acknowledges that history must be "retold and shaped" through her own voice, she is also plagued by a yearning for an objective vision of history, or an understanding, as she puts it, of "what *really* happened" (14).[19] Obejas thus fits Juani with a series of linked objectives: if her quest for subversive queer self-voicing is to be fulfilled, she must negotiate the multiplicity of her identity, accept the impossibility of a "real" history, and take on the task of creating her own.

Juani's conception of herself as a lens for apprehending history mirrors the function of what Faedra Chatard Carpenter calls the "archivist" of queer historiographies. As Carpenter suggests, "history is fashioned and its documentation is inevitably filtered through the lens of the archivist who—unwittingly or consciously—impresses himself or herself upon the record" (325). By assuming this role, Juani supplies the subjective, affective, and erotic nuance that, as Hartman points out, is missing in archival records of women's Afrodiasporic experience (4). As the "archivist" of a queer Afrolatina history, Juani both gathers her personal and family histories *and* enacts, on the plot level, the coming-of-age narrative *Memory Mambo* traces. These two archival practices—of storytelling and plot action—take on in a series of important metaphorical parallels. Juani's actions, choices, and conflicts—her rifts with her family members, her efforts to understand her sexuality, and, most prominently, her relationship and violent breakup with her girlfriend, Gina—all deepen her contact with her nuantial identity. These plot conflicts also catalyze her to attempt to historicize that identity, an effort that undermines the conventions of Western coming-of-age fictional narrative.

Juani's search to claim and historicize queer diasporic multiplicity demands poetic strategies and narrative modes that extend beyond the temporal and subjective logics often used to define the white Western bildungsroman As a genre designation, the bildungsroman is an unstable rubric, used to describe several different kinds of narratives that reflect themes of growth, identity, and "becoming." As Sondra O'Neale points out, "aspects of Bildung" are central to many black women's novels, even as they depart from "traditional Bildungsroman patterns" of limited temporal scope and consistent engagement with family ("Race, Sex, and Self" 26, 27). Rita Felski considers this breach with family a crucial aspect of the postmodern women's bildungsroman, in which "the emancipation of the protagonist is located above all in a changed consciousness [through which] the heroine comes to redefine herself as an acting subject," rather than a product of male fantasy. For Felski, this freedom is "[u]sually realized on the narrative level through an act of separation from familial and sexual ties" (133). Yet in Afrodiasporic/queer women's coming-of-age novels, narrative autonomy, psychic "emancipation" and rejection of family are not so easily equated. *Memory Mambo* departs from Western bildungsroman formulations of "progress" by positioning a return to history and a *reconstruction* of family narratives as crucial to individual growth.

Franco Moretti's assessment of the modern bildungsroman form in *The Way of the World: The Bildungsroman in European Culture* offers insight into the normative assumptions involved in Western conceptions of coming-of-age fiction. For Moretti, "youth is . . . modernity's 'essence,' the sign of a world that seeks its meaning in the *future*, rather than in the past" (556, emphasis in original). Moretti identifies two dominant themes of the bildungsroman—mobility and interiority. Both of these, he argues, emerge as a result of the freedom and opportunity ushered in by industrialization, a phenomenon through which "the world of work changes at an incredible and incessant pace, [and] the colorless and uneventful socialization of 'old' youth becomes increasingly implausible" (555).[20] Moretti's models of "modernity" and "youth" privilege a white, Western, educated, male subjectivity, presupposing a Western bourgeois culture as the origin of youth. Such models exclude black women, for whom modernity and modernization do not usher in an unmixed "incredible and incessant" rush of new labor opportunities. For Afrodiasporic women, lack of access to civic and social power, capital, and various levels of freedom render both the "colorless" security of premodern youth and the "colorful" possibilities of emergent white male "freedom" are not only "implausible," but impossible.

Both Felski's and Moretti's conceptions of the bildungsroman fall short of addressing the specificities of Afrodiasporic/queer women's coming-of-age. While Moretti's bildungsroman positions internal change and social identity development as mutually exclusive foci of two distinct bildungsroman types,[21] Felski's model of the women's coming-of-age novel relies on the sustained support of "a broader female community" to effect women and girl protagonists' liberation (138).[22]

Juani's trajectory in *Memory Mambo* highlights the hetero- and anglo-normative limits of these models. Obejas introduces a model of "becoming" in which transformation and social self-contextualization are mutually constitutive, and in which liberation fails not because of an inadequate presence of woman-centered community, but because of her inability to construct a specifically queer Afrolatina familial identification across temporal lines.

For first-generation queer women in the United States, attempts to develop and cement an identity "aided by the friendship of other women" are often complicated and fraught, particularly in environments where the nuantial differences of sexuality, ethnicity, gender expression, national and racial identification, and political ideology do not constitute shared experience (Felski 139). While Juani has access to a community of queer Latinas, Juani's self-contextualization is not alongside these peers' identifications, but against them. The tensions among interstitial identities within Juani's friendship group are clearest in her relationship with Juani's lover, Gina, a "self-hating queer" who believes that "being a public lesbian [would] somehow distract . . . from her *puertorriqueñismo*" (Obejas 78). Gina invokes racial allegiance to disavow her queerness. She dismisses Juani's interest in claiming a queer identity as ethnically motivated racial treason, remarking: "that's so white, this whole business of sexual identity. But you Cubans, you think you're white" (ibid.). This in-group rejection of her Afrolatina queerness directly contrasts Juani's understanding of her narrative multisubjectivity and places her within an identificatory dilemma in which, as she states, "my lesbianism is not the cause of my alienation, but it's part of it" (79).

By simultaneously fulfilling Juani's queer desire and rejecting her queer identity on the grounds of racial and ethnic allegiance, Gina serves as a parallel figure of multisubjectivity against which Juani can negotiate her own multi-vocal queer Afrolatina identity. As a US citizen within a woman-centered community of radical Puerto Rican nationalist independentistas, Gina represents one ideal of Afrolatinidad: she is part of a community that acknowledges the political implications of racial, national, and ethnic specificities within Latinidad (Román and Flores 10). Gina's insistence on subordinating sexuality to nationality cements Juani's commitment to queer identification and institutes fissures in their relationship. For Juani, "It didn't matter that all our friends, and eventually my family, said our names together Juani and Gina, as if it were one word—*juani-gina*—because the bottom line was simple: Gina wasn't out" (121). The figure of "juanigina" serves as an emblem of thwarted queer Afrolatina possibility, foregrounding the queernesses the two women share—the shared nuances of their gender, their Afrolatinidad, their working-class status, and their same-sex desire—but ultimately signaling the failure of these mutual identifications to sustain them due to heteronormative hierarchies of difference.

This failed identification through the queer nuantial is replicated in Juani's and Gina's larger queer Latina community. In a discussion of Latin American global politics, Hilda, one of Gina's Puerto Rican friends, refers to Juana as a "Gusana" and a "Bad Cuban" (*Memory Mambo* 127). Literally translated as "worm," gusana is a signifier for hybrid Cuban immigrant identity, signaling, as Myra Mendible states, "the 'in-betweens' [who] cohabit two or more identities at once; we are insiders/outsiders . . . both Cuban and American and yet neither simultaneously" ("Growing Up Cuban in Miami" 1). By linking this ethnic and racial heterogeneity with the image of the "Bad Cuban," Hilda deploys more derogatory usage of gusana, which links emigrants from Cuba after Fidel Castro's takeover with sociopolitical treason. As a "gusana," Juani thus is an outcast in several communities of outcasts; she is alienated from non-US Cubans (who for reasons of political loyalty, socioeconomic constraints, and family ties, remain in Cuba) as well as from the community of queer Latina women who condemn her emigrant status on nationalist political grounds. Further, as an out lesbian, Juani is also barred from identification with the novel's "in-between" community of Cuban emigrants on the grounds of her sexual difference.[23]

These multiple alienations precipitate Juani's search for a queer Afrolatina identification through history. Recognizing the isolating heterogeneity of her own subject position, Juani begins the process of establishing what Mendible refers to as "a grounded identity and social space" that bridges the gaps among national, ethnic, and other aspects of Cuban American identity (2). As Mendible observes, this process is closely linked to the manipulation and renegotiation of historical narrative. For Cuban emigrants, "the condition of exile separates a people from their homeland and their history. Like colonized subjects, Cuban exiles and their bicultural sons and daughters carry fragments of a shattered history like baggage" (15). For Juani, establishing a "grounded identity" means assembling from this baggage a cultural history complex enough to accommodate her interstitial subjectivity.

## Heteroglossic Temporality and Multi-Silent Death

The need to articulate multiple subjectivities and identifications shapes black/queer women's narrative temporalities, both in coming-of-age stories and in other narrative forms. Temporal collages such as those of Gayl Jones's *Corregidora* (1975), Toni Cade Bambara's *The Salt Eaters* (1980), Edwidge Danticat's *The Dew Breaker* (2005), Chimamanda Ngozi Adichie's *Half of a Yellow Sun* (2006), and Heidi Durrow's *The Girl Who Fell from the Sky* (2010) reflect the mutuality and collaboration of past and present in contemporary Afrodiasporic women's literary texts in particular. In these texts, as in *Memory Mambo*, the past, present, and future are structured as shifting timescapes that both protagonists and readers must negotiate to engage black women's multisubjective identities.

Ed Pavlić uses the notion of "syndesis," borrowed from Robert Plant Armstrong, to chart the complex functions and multidirectionality of time in modern Afrodiasporic texts and worldviews. Syndesis, Pavlić notes, signals the "dynamic, multidirectional relationships between 'ancestors' and 'descendants'" in Yoruba cultural practice and aesthetics, which serve as structuring features of many Afrodiasporic modernist texts. In syndetic formulations of time, "'new' cultural performances explore various combinations of previous cycles and improvise changes in existing patterns. . . . The result [of this syndesis] is a multilayered ritual present that relates, through the consciousness of performers and audiences, to preexisting voices" (21, 22). In diasporic coming-of-age narratives structured around syndetic aesthetics, youth cannot rush toward "the *future* rather than . . . the past" in its quest for self; in these texts, the future is coterminous with the past, and both exist "right alongside" the present, as Juani states, in much the same way as multiple, potentially dissonant stories are "captured in" protagonists' narrative voices.

Obejas's poetics of difference reflects this syndetic "multilayered present" through Juani's multisubjective voice, establishing history as, itself, a queer, creative artifact. The multi-vocal narrative "lens" with which Obejas presents history allows Juani to infuse her account of history through multiple aspects of her subject position, shifting her narrative relationship with time and tense as she confronts specific facets of her difference. Rather than "relating to" pre-existing voices, Juani relates the voices themselves to the reader in an effort to better understand her own multisubjective identity. Recounting the story of her family's immigration from Cuba, Juani remarks on memories of events for which she was not present:

> Why do I remember driving around senselessly, for days, in and out of the beaches outside La Habana . . . combing through tall grasses and dirt, as fascinated by the tiny, translucent frogs on the tree branches as by the malevolent shadows scurrying underneath? My father planned out escape this way, but I never went along on these excursions . . . if these aren't my memories, then whose are they? Certainly not my father's—he always casts himself as the stoic hero . . . if these were my father's stories, they would be wholly congratulatory and totally void of meaningful detail. (11)

Juani's narrative is so deeply rooted within the re-membered scene that she is able to anthropomorphize the shadows between which her father crawls as "malevolent," assuming her father's epistemic and affective engagement with the story she tells. Juani's narration here is "multilayered" in several ways—it signals a present-tense recollection of an event occurring in the past and fuses her own perspective with her father's, creating a version of family history that contains the experiences of both self and other, past and present, and is directly attributable to neither. Juani narrates from what Achille Mbembe terms a "time of entanglement"—an interconnection of "presents, pasts, and futures that attain their depths of other presents, pasts, and futures, each age bearing, altering, and maintaining the previous ones" (*On the Postcolony* 16). Here, her multilayered perspective allows her not only to speak multiple entangled temporalities at once, but also to speak from multiple perspectives in order to tell a fuller story of diasporic migration and family history.

Juani's narrative temporality finds further rupture as she comes of age in Chicago and confronts various forms of ethnic, national, racial, and sexual alienation, particularly within community of her queer Latina peers. When Hilda hails Juani as a "Gusana," Juani seeks identificatory solace in Gina. She probes Gina for evidence that the latter "was hurt and torn by what had happened," but she finds instead that "the gulf between [them] was wider than the ninety miles from Havana to Miami" (135). The spatial terms on which Juani imagines her alienation from Gina signal the failure of their relationship to offer her the "grounded" social identification she needs to pursue her own becoming as a queer Afrolatina subject in the United States (Mendible 2). The argument that follows this rupture becomes a complicated, erotic, and violent fight that produces several parallel ruptures in Juani's narrative voice:

> All the screaming had dissolved into a high-pitched hum interrupted only by the thud of a fist on muscle, the labored work of our angry lungs, and the crack of an elbow or leg hitting bone.

> *All of the blood pours savagely from my limbs, all of my limbs are severed, veins sliced open, blood blinding—and here you are, teeth bared, blowing air—I go this way then that, push you away, hit you, bring you to me in a vice-like embrace, feel, again, your muscles stretch underneath my bones, my bones crushing your bones, dark blood congealing blue/black/magenta—my blood like a fountain from my nipples, like a geyser, like rain—and I kiss you, my tongue running inside your bloody mouth, gums, teeth, down your throat, then we both gasp and choke and spit—and I love you, monstrously and uselessly.* (135)

Juani's efforts to come to a meeting of the minds with Gina result in an explosive physical confrontation that destabilizes boundaries between self and other, and past and present, through voice. The two women's bodies merge into sound in Juani's narrative, their voices becoming an indifferentiable "hum" of violence and voice. The narrative temporality bends Juani's first-person past-tense account of the fight into a stream-of-consciousness interior monologue located in the immediate present. As the narrative's sentence structure scatters to accommodate the many differences at play, the narrative point-of-view also shifts to carry the characters' stories into a shifting present tense.[24] Here, the narration expands to include the only second-person address in the novel. Juani's "you" is a relatively open signifier, hailing not only Gina, but also the larger presences of xenophobia, homophobia, patriarchy, racism, sexism, and other violently oppressive forces that complicate the potentially pleasurable, affirming queer Afrolatina communities to which Juani yearns to belong, rendering the relationship violent and toxic instead.

This violent moment of interstitial alienation forces Juani to reconsider the linearity of time, and the possibility of a "real" history—deliberations that are reflected in the novel's larger temporal structure. Prior to the dissolution of "juanigina," the novel's temporality is rooted predominantly in the present tense and shifts consistently into the simple past tense when recounting passages of received or recollected memory. In narrating her fight with Gina, however, Juani's narrative moves from the present, back to the past, and then into the future. She introduces the scene by noting that "this *is* the part when I *left* my body," and concludes with the future-tense declaration "I will always love Gina." Juani performs a syndetic collapse of time, carrying the reader's attentions with her into the past-tense action of the scene and imagining a sutured identity in a speculative narrative future. As the violence mounts, the multiple layers of the narrative's syndesis accrete as well, and the fantasy of a stable narrative of the past "literally "crack[s]" under the weight of un-reconciled queer Afrolatina difference.

Coming to terms with the failure of her queer Afrolatina community prompts Juani to reconsider her relationship with history and to imagine historiography as source material for her identity development. Musing on her alienation, she remarks: "I was jealous that [Gina] and her friends knew so much about my country, and I knew so little, really, not just about Cuba, but about Puerto Rico and everywhere else. . . . I hated their independence movement, not for political reasons, but because it seemed to give them direction. And hope. Suddenly I hated that I was just sitting there like a big black hole" (133). Juani's characterization of herself as a "big black hole" inverts the yonic imagery of the wet-wrung waist Brand deploys in Elizette's erotic encounters with queer history. Here, Juani's yonic imagery signals both her feelings of ethnic difference within this queer Afrolatina community and the consuming absence of a history that reflects her interstitial subjectivity.

Hilda's attack on Juani's intra-group difference—her expressive departure from the intra-group ideological and political norms Hilda sets—prompts Juani to crave a self-construction that is "not just about Cuba" but about the multiple locations and identities that link her nationality, race, ethnicity, and sexuality through the nuantial. As Kate McCollough points out, the condition of exile links separations of place with separations of time, as "located at the intersection of temporal and spatial vectors, and mediated by memory, exile presupposes a relationship to a lost physical place or land that comes to embody the temporal zone of the past" ("Marked by Genetics and Exile" 580). The knowledge of "Cuba . . . [and] everywhere else" is itself a syndetic phenomenon for Juani, marking not only a desire to know about contemporary Afrolatinx politics, but also Afrolatinx histories. In response to this desire, she sets out on a quest to cull and construct these nuantial histories of Afrolatinidad, which, she imagines, will offer her the "direction" she needs to enact her own becoming as a queer Cuban American woman.

Juani's older cousin, Titi, emerges as a symbol of this historicized identity.[25] Whereas Brand's characters look to the everpresent ancestral figure of Adela to shape their queer history through narrative, Obejas's Juani's persistent belief in "real" history prompts her to search for historical grounding in a living family member. She hopes Titi will offer objective information and practicable guidance in constructing her queer Afrolatina identity. Titi lives in what McCollough calls "the lost place/past of Cuba," accessible only through scrap vestiges of material pasts and fragments of received narrative. Juani's encounters with Titi thus occur entirely in the realm of communal memory. Juani reflects on what it means to "know[s] about Titi only through stories," most of which narrate

Titi's many unsuccessful attempts to flee the island (McCollough 581; Obejas 76). The family constructs Titi simultaneously as a badwoman ne'er-do-well and as an emblem of a Cuban desire for freedom, as well as of the tragedy of class difference and powerlessness. In family lore, Titi is "the archetypal would-be exile [who has] heroism alive in her because of her great heart, and because of her insanity" (Obejas 76). Still, Juani reads Titi's story in much the same way as Brand's characters attempt to "calculate the heart" of people in order to identify their subjective nuances. Through photos of Titi, Juani "decode[s] her every gesture and look," intuiting in her a sense of alienation and desperation that extend beyond nationalist longing and are instead "connected to how she loves, or more precisely, how she's not allowed to love" (75). Juani apprehends Titi's sexual difference by reading "between the lines" of the family stories that circulate about Titi, and knows "from the shadings, omissions, and insinuations, that she's been loved . . . powerfully and jealously" by women (75, 76).

Juani constructs Titi as a foil for the alienating voices of her nationalistic Afrolatina community in the United States, which refuses to prioritize queer sexuality among its defining differences. Musing on Titi's imagined loneliness, Juani states: "even though I'm here, in what's supposed to be the land of the free, I share this desire with my cousin Titi. Every lover I've ever had has been closeted" (76). In her efforts to reconcile her national, ethnic, and sexual identities, Juani uses Titi's figure to help her construct an alternative Cubanidad predicated on queerness. She describes Titi's face as "a map of a sealed island, surrounded not by water but by an invisible, electrified barbed wire" and later refers to herself as "my own island, with my own practical borders" (75, 79). By positioning Titi's face as "a map" to the islands of Juani's own queer Afrolatina identity, Juani cements her belief that Titi's story may provide the "direction" she needs in order to pursue her own identity formation.[26] In contrast to Juani's mother's fantasy of respectable, proper, non-African ancestry, Titi's defining features are her "crazy hair," "bloody red lips," and a face etched with "lines" of "desperation and bravery," counter-images for the family myth of a lineage defined by white colonial power. Titi thus represents not only "the existence of the lesbian in the lost past of Cuba and the promise of its continuance in the future of the Cuban American who is Juani," as McCollough suggests; she also signifies the possibility of a new kind of spatialized identification in which the alienating differences of Cubanness, Americanness, queerness, and Afrolatina womanhood are intrinsically and historically joined (588–589).

Juani's biomythic historiographic effort ultimately fails as a result of her inability to imagine this identification outside of the contexts of objective history and truth. Whereas Elizette and Verlia of *In Another Place* are self-aware in their narrative constructions of black/queer history, Juani is able to imagine history only in the context of "reality" and her own identity as a matter of "truth." Unable to understand her queer Afrolatina subjectivity outside of the binaries of "truth" and fiction, Juani is unable to initiate the creative historiographies she hopes to construct. Thus, though she understands her voice as a funnel for multiple subjectivities, her efforts to make narrative contact with Titi fail. Following her epiphanic split from her community, she plans to write Titi to "let her know [she is] coming, ask what she needs" (Obejas 154). Obejas introduces the possibility of a further splitting of Juani's voice to accommodate Titi's historicized queer Afrolatina voice and incorporate her nonnormative "needs"[27] and nuantial desires into Juani's narrative. Yet when she attempts to compose a letter to Titi, she complains: "nothing was coming to me. What, after all, do you say to someone you've never met? . . . someone who you suspect is a lesbian, like you? I didn't want to make assumptions, but I also wanted to make a connection" (176). Juani's inability to privilege intuited connections of what Brand calls "spirit" over objective interpersonal histories of shared experience, and her attachment to binaries of suspicion and imagination, prevent her from making the historical connection she hopes will guide her into her future.

The consequences of Juani's failed efforts at queer Afrolatina historiography are reflected in the narrative and temporal reversals at *Memory Mambo*'s culmination. The novel's final scene depicts Juani attempting to write to Titi once again, but producing only what her dialogue refers to as "rough drafts," which her narration reveals as a series of dots on a napkin. Juani quickly submerges the napkin in a puddle of water, watching "the dots, the lines, all the connections, vanish" (Obejas 234, 235).[28] Obejas symbolizes the effects of this failure through the deliberately anti-triumphal image of a fly that circles Juani's head as she sits with her sister, watching her unwritten "drafts" dissolve and admitting defeatedly, "I don't know what I am." When the fly "throws itself at [Juani's] face," Juani swats at it, casting it into the puddle in which she has submerged her imagined letters. This final gesture signals both agency and self-defeat, each of which is reflected in the novel's ambivalent closing lines: "I flick my finger at the fly, freeing it from the puddle of water. It crawls a bit, then takes off, making an aimless loop in the air, then smashes itself against the window pane. It's quiet now" (237).

Unable to forge a creative engagement with history, Juani's attempt to locate her queerness in the past of Cuba is "aimless," and results immediately in silence, immobility, and an anti-triumphal death. This death opposes itself directly to the white queer anti-futurist "death drive," in which the foreclosing of the future appears as a radical move against social normativities, and an anti-hegemonic rejection of "hope itself as an affirmation" (Edelman *No Future* 4). Juani's figurative death—figured in the silence of both her own voice and that of her social world—reflects the real, material loss that occurs when black/queer life narratives are drained of hope. In the absence of a history that reflects a "dream of eventual self-realization"—that is, without the "imaginary past" white queer anti-futurism critiques—it is not a symbolic Child or heterosexist discourse that fails, but, rather, it is *Juani herself* that is rendered inert (Edelman 10). Barred from sustaining links to a history that looks, lives, and sounds like her, Juani has neither the social privilege nor the narrative agency to "*insist* that the future stop here" (31; emphasis added). Her future "stops" not as a result of radical queer agency, but as a function of isolation, historical erasure, and the silencing of Afrodiasporic queer pasts and presents. Juani's queer death thus functions not as an end to "futurity's unquestioned value," but as a death of her own narrative (4). It is not an idealized, metaphorical, socially constructed "other" that is sacrificed by her failure to connect past, present, and future; Juani's afuturity is an *experience* of death—an end to the possibility of a queer Afrolatina self. This death also refuses to acquiesce to possibility in social deadness as some Afropessimist logics suggest. For Juani, death is not an inhabitable location beyond lethal structures of antiblackness—a life, as Jared Sexton puts it, "lived not in the world that the world lives in, but . . . lived underground, in outer space." For Juani, death is a form of silencing that dislocates her from temporality and collectivity, leaving her in an "aimless" quiet from which there is no future and no escape (Sexton "The Social Life of Social Death" 29; Obejas 237).

This death of black/queer possibility haunts the final lines of Obejas's narrative. Whereas the "rough drafts" of Juani's letter signal the failed potential of a narrative movement through the past into the future, Juani's narrative leaves her in a space of syndetic paralysis, in which barriers to history preclude futurity as well. Rather than sounding the shared history she has worked to create—a chorus of historicized voices nuantial enough to include her own—even the narrative itself is "quiet." Instead, a self-destructive silence lingers, "smashing" promises of mobility and futurity, and leaving Juani ultimately constrained to a still, voiceless present tense.

## #*SayHerName*: Social Media Poetics as Recitatives for Survival

The invention of black/queer histories marks a radical, transformative act that has effects not only on literary and historical narrative, but also on the viability and livability of black/queer lives. Media attention to queer youth deaths by suicide in the first decade of the twentieth century in the United States illustrates the importance of such histories for black queer youth whose deaths are grossly underrepresented in mainstream cultural discourse. The 2010 suicides of lesbian-identified Howard University student Aiyisha Hassan, openly gay Johnson & Wales College student Raymond Chase, and queer youth activist

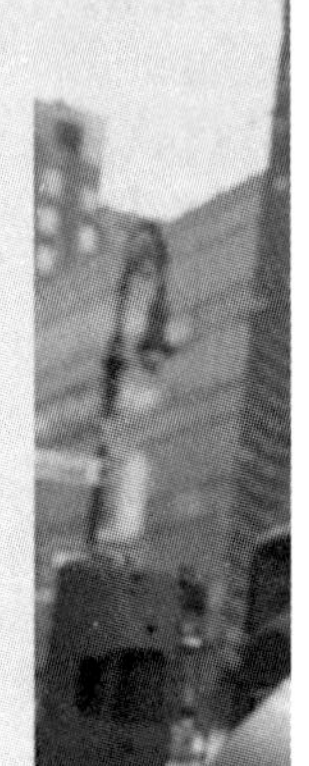



Figure 1.1a. "#SayHerName Tweets" (from AAPF #SayHerName Social Media Guide). Image © 2015 African American Policy Forum.

Joseph Jefferson received startlingly little media coverage. The underreported murder of queer fifteen-year-old Sakia Gunn (in 2003), the gross and innumerable killings of queer and trans people from Michael Sandy (in 2006) to Islan Nettles (in 2013) to Nina Pop (in 2020), and an all-too-brief 2011 study on the "significantly increased risk of suicide" among black queer youth published in the *American Journal of Public Health* illustrate what black/queer people have known for decades: death is not simply a social metaphor, but a constant threat shrouded in multiple levels of silence.[29]

There have been few critical studies of black queer women's history, or of Afrodiasporic queer history more broadly.[30] This is a striking absence, given white queer studies' recent (and long-standing) concerns with history and historiography.[31] As Alison Oram and Annmarie Turnbull point out in their introduction to *The Lesbian History Sourcebook*, queer theorists "are inevitably drawn towards evidence about behaviour in the past which has some parallels with that which signals same-sex desire today" (1). As Juani's, Yasmine's, Verlia's, and Elizette's stories suggest, this is equally the case—if not more so—for black queer women of the African diaspora.

Examining the #SayHerName social media movement through a black queer feminist interpretive lens attentive to the poetics of new media reveals the important moves #SayHerName makes toward addressing this erasure of gender from contemporary popular discourses on blackness and power and offers an example of how the logics of biomythic historiography can function across mediums and in contemporary black queer feminist activist contexts. By constructing black/queer histories as creative, imaginative, biomythic processes of affirmation, #SayHerName introduces textual narratives of black/queer futurity as a tool of activist praxis and points to the possibilities of biomythic historiographies in the digital space.

Popularized in 2015, partly by the African American Policy Forum (cofounded by Kimberlé Crenshaw with Luke Charles Harris), #SayHerName is a political media movement that moves across genres to document and highlight the names of black women whose lives have been lost to police violence and to center black women—including black queer and trans women—absented in much popular Black Lives Matter rhetoric (*#SayHerName: Resisting Police Brutality against Black Women: A Social Media Guide*). The absence of queer people, trans people, and women in dominant popular conceptions of national Black Lives Matter discourse has been, of course, a gross misreading of the foundational objectives of Black Lives Matter and of its three founders—Patrisse Cullors, Opal Tometi, and Alicia Garza—two of whom identify as black queer women. As Garza states in her "Herstory of the #BlackLivesMatter Movement":

> When you design an event / campaign / et cetera based on the work of queer Black women, don't invite them to participate in shaping it, but ask them to provide materials and ideas for next steps for said event, that is racism in practice. It's also hetero-patriarchal. Straight men, unintentionally or intentionally, have taken the work of queer Black women and erased our contributions. Perhaps if we were the charismatic Black men many are rallying around these days, it would have been a different story, but being Black queer women in this society (and apparently within these movements) tends to equal invisibility and non-relevancy.
>
> (Garza, "A Herstory of the #BlackLivesMatter Movement by Alicia Garza")[32]

This erasure is, importantly, both historical *and* rhetorical. The refusal to acknowledge black women and queer people as central to BlackLivesMatter not only erases Garza, Cullors, and Tometti from the historical record of one of the most important antiracist movements in recent American history, it also relies on a distorted understanding of the aims of the movement by misreading

"Blackness" (the "Black" in "BlackLivesMatter") as a signifier that cannot name gender, sexuality, and race at once. This in turn, of course, relies on a misreading of the movement's founding documents—or a failure to read them at all. Yet, for its emphasis of black queer feminist politics to the movement, Garza's "Herstory" warrants quoting at length:

> When we say Black Lives Matter, we are talking about the ways in which Black people are deprived of our basic human rights and dignity. . . . It is an acknowledgment that Black women continue to bear the burden of a relentless assault on our children and our families and that assault is an act of state violence. Black queer and trans folks bearing a unique burden in a hetero-patriarchal society that disposes of us like garbage and simultaneously fetishizes us and profits off of us is state violence; the fact that 500,000 Black people in the US are undocumented immigrants and relegated to the shadows is state violence; the fact that Black girls are used as negotiating chips during times of conflict and war is state violence; Black folks living with disabilities and different abilities bear the burden of state-sponsored Darwinian experiments that attempt to squeeze us into boxes of normality defined by White supremacy is state violence. And the fact that the lives of Black people—not ALL people—exist within these conditions is consequence of state violence.
>
> *When Black people get free, everybody gets free.*

Garza echoes the 1977 Combahee River Collective's statement: "if black women were free, it would mean that everyone else would have to be free since our freedom would necessitate the destruction of all the systems of oppression," emphasizing that the founding vision of Black Lives Matter is a black queer feminist one in which issues of race, gender, sexuality, class, disability, and nationality are inseparable (Combahee River Collective 15).

#SayHerName addresses both the linguistic and historical dimensions of this erasure by foregrounding gender in its wording and using that language to create, identify, and circulate an archive of the names of women whose stories have been erased from dominant narratives on race and state violence. This is evident, for example, in the "Can You See Them?" infographic published in AAPF's #SayHerName Social Media Guide, a meme-able word puzzle graphic depicting the names of dozens of black women killed by police, along with the caption "Black Women Are Killed by Police Too. . . . Can You See Them?" (*#SayHerName*). Moreover, #SayHerName pays explicit attention to black queer and trans womanhood in its archives of black life and black death.[33] In this project of historical rewriting, the poetics of the #SayHerName movement echo and extend the literary practices of biomythic historiography that Lorde, Brand, and Obejas engage. In #SayHerName, "Her" becomes a polysemous, nuantial signifier that signals not only the many named individual lives claimed by the state, but also the specific dynamics of gender, gender identity, and sexuality written out of dominant narratives of black mortal vulnerability. By moving

**BLACK WOMEN ARE KILLED BY POLICE TOO.**

GABRIELLANEVAREZMICHELLECUSSEAUXTANISHA
ANDERSONPEARLIEGOLDENNATASHAMCKENNAAU
RAROSSERSHELLYFREYTARIKAWILSONAIYANASTA
NLEYJONESELEANORBUMPURSSANDRABLANDREKI
ABOYDSHANTELDAVISALBERTASPRUILLMARGARET
MITCHELLFRANKIEPERKINSKAYLAMOOREMIRIAMC
AREYKYAMLIVINGSTONALEXIACHRISTIANMEAGAN
HOCKADAYMYAHALLTYISHAMILLERSHEREESEFRA
NCISYVETTESMITHKENDRAJAMESBETTIEJONESMA
RQUESHAMCMILLANINDIAKAGERREDELJONESMON
IQUEJENEEDECKARDJANISHAFONVILLEYVETTEHE
NDERSONKORRYNGAINESJESSICAWILLIAMSDERES
HAARMSTRONGKISHAARRONELARONDASWEATTIN
DIABEATYKISHAMICHAELSAHLARIDGEWAYJANET
WILSONDEBORAHDANNERMICHELLESHIRLEYCHAR
LEENALYLESDECYNTHIACLEMENTSATATIANAJEFF
ERSONREGISKORCHINSKIPAQUETBREONNATAYLOR

**CAN YOU SEE THEM?**

# #SAYHERNAME
AFRICAN AMERICAN POLICY FORUM

Figure 1.1b. "Can You See Them?" (from AAPF #SayHerName Social Media Guide). Image © 2015 African American Policy Forum.

across various textual and media forms—from its original twitter hashtag to, for example, visual memes, GIFs, video media, visual art, message shirts, and other apparel listing the names of black women, queer people, and trans people killed by the state—#SayHerName and related movements create queer archives of black women's lives. They write them into a historical narrative that provides not only a crucial corrective for incomplete dominant histories, but also a creative political tool to be used by black women and trans people ourselves as they imagine and work toward visions of history in which our lives—and deaths—hold meaning.

In this sense, we might read the poetics of #SayHerName—and the poetics Lorde, Brand, and Obejas develop—as forms of black queer feminist recitative.

The *New Grove Dictionary of Opera* defines the recitative as "a type of vocal writing, normally for a single voice, with the intent of mimicking dramatic speech in song." The recitative form is most often associated with white Western operatic texts that emerge alongside the "liberalization of poetic forms" in the mid–seventeenth century and continue to be taken up in contemporary classical music ("Recitative"). The recitative uses formal variation—specifically a melding of musical and narrative forms—"providing . . . textual or musical repetition to lend coherence" to the narrative integrity of the text. Varying across temporal and geographic contexts, the recitative generally functions by "striking bold and unexpected harmonic progressions, affective melodic intervals and other musical means to elevate textual expression," particularly in delivering past-tense information or back-story crucial to the progression of the narrative at hand ("Recitative").[34]

While useful for its articulation of how art forms use multiplicities of voice, genre, and narrative to rearticulate history, this definition of the recitative fails, of course, to acknowledge the centrality of oral multiplicities to African diaspora narrative forms or the ways in which music and narrative have worked together in diasporic storytelling strategies since long before colonial contact. Considered together, the biomythic historiographies examined here close that gap, revealing how black queer women have used difference across forms and genres to tell the stories that imagine—and thus enable—our survival.

In her 1978 poem, "A Litany for Survival," Lorde offers a meditation on the importance of cross-temporal linguistic connections for black queer women. For women, she reminds us,

> who love in doorways coming and going
> in the hours between dawns
> looking inward and outward
> at once before and after
> seeking a now that can breed futures . . .
> it is better to speak
> remembering
> we were never meant to survive (*Collected Poems*, 255)[35]

Lorde offers a meditation on the importance of cross-temporal linguistic connections for black queer women. As Lorde reminds us, for those who live "at once before and after/ seeking a now that can breed futures . . ." creative voice is necessary for survival (*Collected Poems*, 255). For queer women of the African diaspora, investment in history is inextricably linked to an investment in futurity—and to belief in a survival that is, itself, radical. This need to cull from the past "a now that can breed futures" is, for queer Afrodiasporic women writers, a primary creative strategy and a precipitating push to the page. It is the condition that demands the construction of Lorde's generic innovation of the biomythography. It is this need, too, that infuses multiple voices into Brand's queer social novel and shapes the narrative and temporality of Obejas's bildungsroman. It challenges white queer anti-futurism's call to "refuse the insistence of hope itself as affirmation, which is always affirmation of an order whose refusal will register as unthinkable, irresponsible, inhumane," and critiques Afropessimism's insistence on locating black survival within the "outer space[s]" of death (Edelman 4; Sexton 29). Instead, they expose and undermine "unthinkable, irresponsible, inhumane" silencing of black/queer women's subjectivities and lives, and imagine narrative modes of black/queer feminist survival through imagination and self-expression, and collective voice (Edelman 4).

As Brand's and Obejas's poetics of difference illustrate, this sustaining voicing is heterogeneous, heteroglossic, and reflective of multiple voices and multiple subjectivities at once. These biomythic historiographies retool voice to provide what Essex Hemphill calls "evidence of . . . being," but also provide evidence of *having been*, which, read in terms of a poetics of difference, can serve as evidence of future being, and fodder for faith in the possibility of survival (*Brother to Brother* xxiv).

By constructing black/queer histories as creative, imaginative processes of affirmation, writers such as Lorde, Brand, and Obejas work against foreshortenings of black/queer history. They introduce narratives of black/queer futurity where there seem to be none and empower readers to construct their own affirming narratives of black/queer historicity, presence, and continuance. Through their poetics of difference, these writers provide not only "litanies" for black queer women's survival, but also sustaining *recitatives*—formally subversive texts that mobilize heterogeneities of voice and genre in recounting history and imagining toward futurities. They announce a black/queer presence that creates its own past to invent the possibility of its future. In so doing, they make space for "new spellings" of the names of lives lost unendingly to bodily death and narrative erasure, new ways of "Saying Our Names" that will allow us to imagine, create, and insist upon our existence—then and there, here and now, and in the innumerable timescapes beyond us.

# "walkin on the edges of the galaxy"

## Queer Choreopoetic Thought in the African Diaspora

**flesh memory** (flesh mem'e re) 1. a text, a language, a mythology, a truth, a reality, an invented as well as literal translation of everything that we've ever experienced or known, whether we know it directly or through some type of genetic memory, osmosis or environment. 2. The body's truths and realities. 3. The multiplicity of languages and realities that the flesh holds. 4. The language activated in the body's memory.
—Akilah Oliver, *the she said dialogues: flesh memory*[1]

if you are . . . female & black in the u.s.a/ . . . you have one solitary voice/ though you number 3 million/ no nuance exists for you/ you have been sequestered in the monolith/ the common denominator as persona . . .
—Ntozake Shange, "takin' a solo/a poetic possibility/ a poetic imperative"

In this chapter I explore the ways that black women artists express the queerness of blackwoman embodiment through the performative capacities of body/language. Articulating the nuantial contours of blackwoman experience through the body, black women performers incorporate into their poetics an idea of "queerness" as an identification of sexual difference that cannot be disentangled from differences of race, gender, nation, class, and the numerous other silenced subject positions that black women's bodies can signify. They deploy queerness as a collectivizing and healing language in which, as Cathy Cohen suggests, linked experiences of racial, gender, sexual, and class oppression can form "the basis for progressive transformative coalition" and anticolonial community through shared languages of difference ("Punks, Bulldaggers and Welfare Queens" 438).

Ntozake Shange's *for colored girls who have considered suicide/ when the rainbow is enuf* is a touchstone text for black queer women artists and for writers, readers, and critics concerned with blackwoman voicing. Though not typically read as a "queer" text, *for colored girls* queers norms of genre and form to articulate the nuantial, nonnormative complexities of black women's sexual, bodily, and interior lives, speaking against hegemonic silencing through radical reimaginings of voice. Reading Shange for the queer nuance of her poetics highlights the importance of interstitial hermeneutics for black performance studies. I bring Shange's vision of poetic "nuance" in black feminist voicing into conversation with Spillers's notion of the blackwoman erotic "nuantial" to consider the queer possibilities of the choreopoem form. Read through a black queer feminist lens, Shange's poetics enact and expand what Thomas F. DeFrantz and Anita Gonzales identify as a key aim of black contemporary performance theory: "queering the capacities of theoretical intervention [to do] the productive work of disidentification that produces the synchronous singularities of black performance" (*Black Performance Theory* 10). Shange's vision of "choreopoetic" performance in *for colored girls* makes poetic space for generations of contemporary black queer feminists artists working, as Omise'eke Natasha Tinsley puts it, "*in the tradition*" of queer gender-subversive performance—"in a black tradition of finding healing in expressing multiple ways of performing gender, desire, soul, music" in a range of genres (*Ezili's Mirrors* 37). For black queer artists, these performances are crucial acts of political praxis, enacting what D. Soyini Madison calls "a poetics of understanding and an embodied epistemology [of] activism . . . its dimensions of imagination and creativity, and its rhetoric and politics" (*Acts of Activism* 2). Shange's choreopoetic vision functions as a queer link between voice, body, and praxis, offering contemporary black queer feminist artists a model of nuantial genre subversion that extends from the page, to the stage, to sites of digital and cultural activist work.

First staged in Berkeley, California, in 1974 at the Bacchanal, a women's bar, *for colored girls* portrays the overlapping poetic narratives of seven "ladies" as they describe their experiences of growth, sex, violence, and love. In its structure and thematic focus, the choreopoem is an exemplar of the poetics of difference. Even in its genesis as a poetry collection (published under the same title the following year by Shameless Hussy Press), *for colored girls* explores the dynamism of black women's voices as tools against patriarchy, racism, and several concurrent oppressions. Yet, as the name of Shange's generic innovation suggests, *for colored girls* is not simply a chorale of seven disconnected, disembodied voices. Instead, Shange's poetry is culled and reshaped into written drama on the page and then choreographed into a work of body, motion, and performance for the stage.

Shange's refusal to acquiesce to a genre that would deny the interrelatedness of poetry and dance reflects larger concerns with voice and embodiment in much of contemporary Afrodiasporic women's writing. As an indispensable tool for asserting and validating the human intellect, voice is a tool whose value, particularly for African diasporic writers, cannot be overstated. These writers are tasked not only with expressing their characters' thoughts but also, absurdly, with demonstrating the validity, relevance, and existence of a complex black subjectivity and inner life, or to prove that, as Shange puts it in her 2011 essay collection, *lost in language & sound*, "[b]lack folks do have brains" (22). This task multiplies in the hands of black women writers, whose bodies are *imagined* in terms of chattel and sexual property from colonization and enslavement onward, and who are vulnerable to silencing within contemporary Western systems of publishing and dramatic production as well.[2] In a cultural milieu that is, as Shange states, "a legendary male-poet's environment," how does a black woman writer account linguistically for the dramas and traumas of the body without sublimating pain and desire entirely into voice? (*for colored girls* x).[3]

Responding to this dilemma, Shange develops the "choreopoem" form, a genre that brings together lyric, verse, narrative, and bodily movement in both print and stage contexts. In Shange's work, the choreopoem form emerges as one of many ways to bridge the chasm between the demands of racial representation and the expressive, subjective "nuance" representation elides. The choreopoem instantiates a poetic melding of body and voice that allows Shange to probe what she calls elsewhere "the meaning of a contradiction in anybody's body" (*See No Evil* 20). By rendering body and voice inextricable components of creative expression, the choreopoem form allows Shange to write nuance back onto black women's bodies through the communicative properties of the body, including gesture, dance, movement, and color.

In the past three decades, the choreopoem has held striking meaning for queer and lesbian artists in the African Diaspora. Queer Haitian American poet and playwright Lenelle Moïse, for example, borrows the generic designation for her 2002 choreopoem, "Cornered in the Dark," which explores black women's sexuality and sexual violence. Likewise, queer-affirming performance group Body Ecology takes up the choreopoem genre in their mixed genre dance performance, "Choreopoetic Aesthetics," while Keith Boykin plays on Shange in the title of his 2012 anthology of gay men's prose memoirs, *For Colored Boys Who Have Considered Suicide When the Rainbow is Still Not Enough*, following the gross lack of media attention to queer-of-color suicides in the queer suicide rash of 2010. Likewise, lesbian filmmaker Aishah Shahidah Simmons and queer scholar and writer L. H. Stallings have both written a choreopoem and a "choreostory," respectively, exploring black women's sexual desire, pleasure, and autonomy in recent years.[4]

These artists have looked to choreopoetic thought as a means of articulating black queer experiences, identities, and lives. They take up Shange's "poetic imperative," musing on the choreopoem form to explore and explode contemporary conversations on race, gender, class, and ethnicity, and to mark the places in these discourses where queer sexuality lies, unspoken and untouched. Their works invite several questions about black sexuality and formal subversion:

What are the queer potentials of embodied voicing? What are the choreopoem's erotic antecedents in Shange's oeuvre, and how does the form echo in the works of other writers? What does the blending of body and voice do for Afrodiasporic artists invested in speaking the many nuances of black sensory, sensual, and erotic life? In other words, what is queer about the choreopoem form?

For contemporary queer women performance and literary artists of the diaspora, choreopoetic thinking offers pathways for speaking oneself out of social structures that constrain the voice through willful misreadings of the body. Kara Keeling points out that the inscription of racist, sexist, anglocentrist, and homophobic idioms onto black queer women's bodies limits the range of subjectivities and experiences that black queer women are allowed to express in dominant cultural imaginaries ("Joining the Lesbians" 217). Class difference, differences of gender expression, and the subjective "nuance" Shange points to are erased in popular readings of black queer women's bodies. This erasure of the expressive reaches of black queer women's being reiterates the significance of what Hortense Spillers terms "the *nuantial*" for black women's literary histories and forms.

Shange's innovation of the choreopoem offers such a form, forwarding a mode of expression designed explicitly to represent the complexities of intersectional identity through constant meldings of linguistic and bodily expression. For Shange, voice and body are intimately linked in creative praxis. She describes the development of her own poetic voice as a negotiation of self and body in which "with the acceptance of the ethnicity of my thighs & backside, came a clearer understanding of my voice as a woman & as a poet" (*See No Evil* 14). This mutuality of voice and body is evident even in the creative process through which *for colored girls* was developed. In her essay "A History: *for colored girls who have considered suicide/ when the rainbow is enuf*," Shange explains that the choreopoem form is as much informed by dance as by poetry, and positions both as more influential on her poetics than dramatic form. Among her greatest influences in developing the piece were dancers Raymond Sawyer and Ed Mok, with whom she studied in San Francisco while drafting the poetry collection that would become *for colored girls*. The evolution of the genre continued in collaboration as dancer Paula Moss created partly improvisational choreography for readings of the poems in the summer of 1974, "inspiring," as Shange states, "my words to fall from me with her body (*See No Evil* 115). This collaborative process linked her identification as a black woman to both bodily and poetic expressions of diaspora. As she states: "Just as Women's Studies had rooted me to an articulated female heritage & imperative, so dance . . . insisted that everything African, everything halfway colloquial, a grimace, a strut, an arched back over a yawn, waz mine" (ibid. 114). For Shange, poetic fusion of body and voice is a matter of blackwoman identity, and all of these elements—the body, the voice, and the identificatory matrices of black women's subjectivity—are crucial in the development of the diasporic poetics of blackwoman embodiment that characterizes the choreopoem form.

Shange's fusion of corporeality and vocality responds to a history in which the commodification and desubjectivation of black women occurs on the grounds of the body and the voice at once. Michelle Wright, Hortense Spillers, Janelle Hobson, and others have argued that the history of black women's subjectivity as a conceptual and economic object in Western culture is replete with fissures and disjunctures between the body and the mind. Many of these complex associations occur as a result of the stigmas of sexual deviance that are imposed through rhetorical processes beginning in enslavement and continue to define black women in contemporary Western imaginaries.[5] This cultural history has direct effects on the structural choices of black women writers, who, as theater artist and critic Glenda Dickerson notes, are necessarily caught in "an ethos of contradictions" between the long-standing sexual stigmas of blackness, the gender and sexual mores of the cult of true womanhood, and, most importantly, the desire to shape their writing into "subversive weapon[s]" of cultural re-visioning legible enough to have their impact (Dickerson "The Cult of True Womanhood" 179).[6]

Shange creates such a "weapon" through the choreopoem form. She develops what I term "body/language"—a strategic means of inscribing the blackwoman body with new languages that both rewrite that body's meanings *and* expand the creative and conceptual terrains on which that body can speak. Body/language allows black women artists to articulate and emphasize the many meanings of their bodies (including the many identities those bodies signify); it also enables them to create new formal modalities for inserting black feminist intersectionality into discourses on identity and embodiment. Body/language allows black women writers to revise oppressive narratives of difference inscribed on their bodies, and to use these rewritten forms to create new possibilities for diasporic identification. Body/language complicates Afrodiasporic womanhood in several different ways: it rewrites blackwoman bodies, using textual markings and scripted movements to reconfigure black women's sexuality and multiple difference; it rewrites the space of the text through manipulations of voice, language, and typography; and it rewrites blackwoman communities by providing new, shared languages of difference.

For black queer writers in particular, airing the silenced far reaches of several unsanctioned subjectivities requires creative feats of both body and voice. For these writers, body/language acts as a form of what black American lesbian experimental poet Akilah Oliver terms "flesh memory," an approach to lyric that links "the body's truths and realities" with "the multiplicity of language and realities that the flesh holds." For Oliver, and for other black queer women writers and performers, body/language rearticulates, as Oliver puts it, "the representational idioms of 'blackness,' 'femaleness,' [and] 'homogeneity'" from a specifically black queer feminist perspective and operates on black expression by re-embodying the "terms of the internal discourse: what is permissible to speak" in conversations on sexuality, desire, and queer erotic experience (Oliver 5, 6).

The erasure of subjective nuance from dominant conceptions of black identity occurs largely through ideological structures and practices that disaggregate black bodies from the complex capabilities of the human voice. The overwhelming and enduring presence of stereotypes of black women in American and global narrative culture attests to dominant cultures' structural resistance to imagining black women speaking in multiple different ways, about multiple different things, individually or collectively.[7] In the US context, caricatures such as the Mammy, the Jezebel, and the Angry Black Woman or Sapphire stereotypes instantiate what Melissa Harris-Perry terms an "intentional misrecognition of black women," which pervades American social and civic life (*Sister Citizen* 22).

This misrecognition of black women occurs largely through willful and repeated misreadings of black women's bodies. The stereotyping of black women's bodily expression (seen, for example, in the "eye-rolling, neck-popping" angry black woman stereotype) supports cultural and civic power imbalances in which, as Harris-Perry notes, "black women's concerns can be ignored and their voices silenced in the name of maintaining calm and rational conversation" (36). Yet, as many scholars have noted, the will to resist and critique these "misrecognitions" often enacts a politics of respectability that ultimately castigates, polices, and invalidates several facets of black women's lives and cultures. For black queer women, this willful misreading of the body produces multiple burdens of representation, in which the body is required to un-write several different stereotypes—racist, sexist, homophobic, xenophobic, classist—at once, leading to the kind of distorting visibility that Keeling discusses. In this dynamic, the black queer woman body must respond to so many kinds of misreading that it cannot readily speak its humanity—its impulses and its strangenesses, its fantasies, needs, and desires.

Centering nexuses of body and voice allows black queer writers to create routes of passage out of this bind of stereotyping and representation, reaffirming the kinds of pleasure, fulfillment, and healing that imperatives of monolithic representation preclude. E. Patrick Johnson points out that, "for black gay people, dancing and singing at once have transcendent spiritual potential not afforded them" in other spaces, including the black church, where external interpretations of their sexuality and erotic bodily life bar them from fully experiencing the spiritual healing available to non-queer people. For Johnson, "the simultaneous acts of dancing and singing bridge the sacred and the secular," allowing black queer people to create experiences of spiritual and personal fulfillment unavailable to them in spaces where their bodies and identities are stigmatized, misrecognized, or misunderstood ("Feeling the Spirit in the Dark" 410).

Choreopoetic thinking creates similar opportunities for healing and transformation in literature. They serve as poetic instantiations of what Cherríe Moraga terms "theory in the flesh," in which "the physical realities of our lives—our skin color, the land or concrete we grew up on, our sexual longings—all fuse to create a politic born out of necessity" ("Entering the Lives of Others").[8] Undoing the boundaries between body and voice allows black queer women writers both to represent the processes by which their voices are un-written and to develop new languages that can write against the erasure of their complex subjectivities, desires, and lives.

Artists such as Oliver, Moïse, Body Ecology, Zanele Muholi, and burlesque performer Chicava HoneyChild Tate explore the interstices of body and voice in ways that articulate the nuantial dimensions of black queer women's lives, extending the logic of Shange's choreopoetics to "sing a black girl's song," as Shange puts it, in languages of their own (*for colored girls* 18). In so doing, they demonstrate how literary expression must not only *tell a black queer woman's story*, but also *represent the bodies* through which that story moves and on which it makes its meanings.

## "Conversations Intricate and Tactile": Ntozake Shange's "Two"

While Shange's strategy of blending voice and body is perhaps most recognizable in the 1976 choreopoem version of "for colored girls," her choreopoetic thinking is evident both before and beyond the life of the Broadway production. Exploring the experimental poetics of Shange's earlier works reveals the formal workings of body/language, and its particular usefulness for black queer women artists.

The poems collected in the chapbook version of *for colored girls*, published in 1975 by Shameless Hussy Press, chart the development of Shange's choreopoetic thinking, both in *for colored girls* and beyond. Alta Gerrey, Shameless Hussy publisher, noted, even before the poems' publication, that Shange preferred to perform the poems to music, always with "someone dancing" in the background ("Alta and the History of Shameless Hussy Press" 28). This early emphasis on the body is evident in the front matter of the chapbook's first edition printing, in which an image of a black woman's body accompanies the text, indicating the place of blackwoman embodiment in Shange's poetry even before the emergence of the "choreopoem" as a form.[9]

The poems, from which several sections of the choreopoem version of the

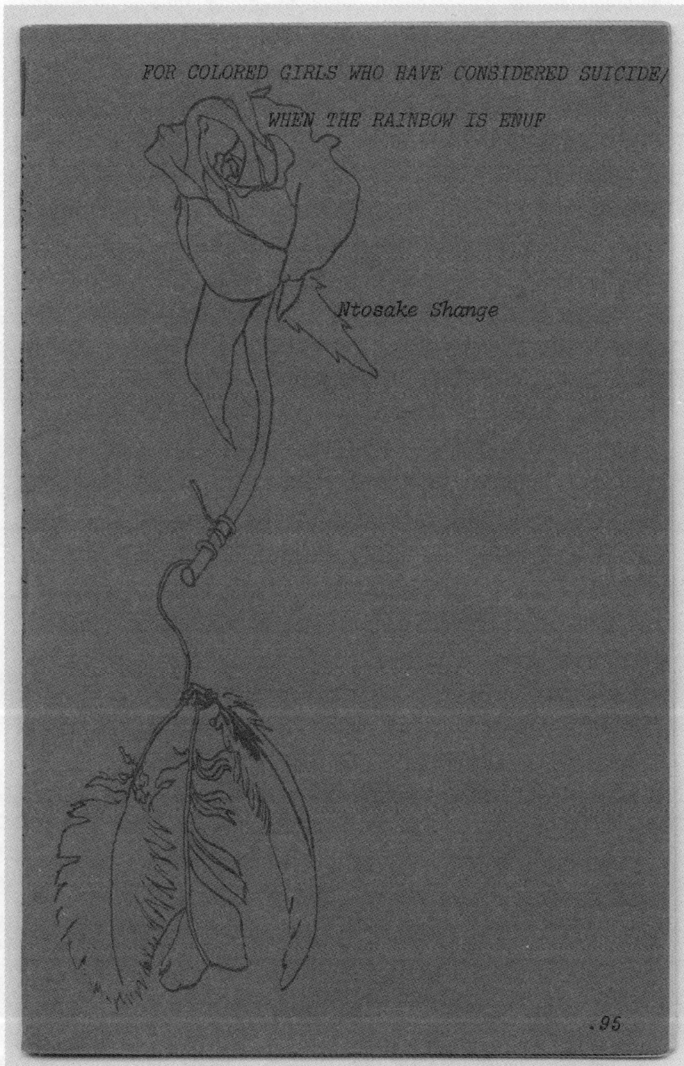


Figure 2.1a. Cover of the poetry collection version of Ntozake Shange's *for colored girls who have considered suicide/ when the rainbow is enuf*. CA: Shameless Hussy Press 1975 (1st ed., 1st printing). Copyrighted material is reproduced by exclusive arrangement with the Ntozake Shange Revocable Trust. Paul T. Williams, Managing Trustee Donald S. Sutton, Literary Trustee.

Figure 2.1b. Front matter of the poetry collection version of Ntozake Shange's *for colored girls who have considered suicide/ when the rainbow is enuf.* CA: Shameless Hussy Press 1976 (1st ed., 1st printing). Drawing by Wopo Holup. Copyrighted material is reproduced by exclusive arrangement with the Ntozake Shange Revocable Trust. Paul T. Williams, Managing Trustee Donald S. Sutton, Literary Trustee.

text are culled, demonstrate the importance of embodied speech and expressive corporealities in Shange's landscape of black feminist erotics. In "between a dancer & a poet," a free verse poem that appears in the Shameless Hussy Press collection, Shange lays the conceptual groundwork for choreopoem form. The poem follows a dancer as she falls in love with a poet, exploring the ways in which the two figures' divergent modes of creative expression (dance and poetry) transform each figure and coalesce into a new form. As in the choreopoem, this new form of black "union" is replicated through the form of the poem, which employs irregular white spaces and stanza breaks to illustrate the divergences and mergings of the two figures and the creative forms they symbolize. The poem begins as the dancer

> swayed from the barre taut in control
> her legs hurt mercilessly she even laughed
> while he took notes . . .
> the poet signed his name to lines eclipsing reality
> he cdnt catch his breath the language waz
> overpowerin . . .
> he put his pencil in his pocket & sat
> in the middle of a whimsical circle
> the dancer plieed she contracted she sweat
> & grew confident in her struggle
> to surpass form transcend calves ankles hips merely
> accoutrements like a music stand . . .
> the waz an impudent lover & the dancer
> was righteous chosen to conquer space . . .
> while the poet fondled his own cheek
> she slid round him her body swirled like a cobra-wind
> & she located the poet's soul in space

The dancer seduces the poet with her body, "sway[ing] from the barre [] taut [] in control," until the poet, "overpower[ed]" by the "language "of dance, is pushed breathlessly from words and must relinquish his writing tools to find new implements of expression in his body. The dancer likewise grows "confident in her struggle [] to surpass" the physical form of her body, the disparate parts of which quickly become "accouterments [] like a music stand" as she and the poet collaborate to re-write her body into music and lyric. (Because the marker "/" often appears in each of Shange's texts as a formal device which does not, most often, indicate a line break, I use the marker "[]" to indicate line breaks and/or whitespace between characters as needed.) As the figures' bodies and voices transform through their merging, the poem "surpass[es]" form as well—it eschews any regular line break pattern and uses equally irregular white spaces in place of both standard punctuation and the slash marks (or virgules) that become Shange's signature signifiers of poetic pause and shift. The speaker thus joins the poet and the dancer in "transcend[ing]" form and "conquer[ing]" space through unions of formal and generic difference. Through these figures Shange establishes the liberatory possibilities of bodies and voices transmuted through generic intermixture. The body becomes "music," and the word is drawn to touch and "fondle [its] own" physicality in order to "locate" itself "in space." It is here that Shange begins to develop the body/language of corporeal movements and markers through which she complicates blackwoman identity and desire.

The collection's second poem, a narrative piece titled "Two," stands out as a particularly rich example of how Shange's choreopoetic body/language is useful in expressing black women's queer erotics. Dedicated to fellow poet and playwright Thulani Davis, "Two" tells the story of Graciela and Smoke, nonspeaking focal figures whose relationship illustrates the corporeal and sensory dimensions of black women's language and communication. Early in the poem, the third-person speaker informs us that the women are so close to one another that "even when they spoke different languages/ the voice was the same" (*for colored girls* Shameless Hussy Press 2). Likewise, the unidentified speaker describes the intimacy between the two in specifically corporeal terms, explaining that "they never missed anyone else/ like they missed each other/ a deep hole crawled through all . . . marrow/ so they stayed round/ together/ most time the . . . thoughts they shared waz private" (ibid.). Smoke and Graciela's relationship is defined by a same-sex intimacy that is erotic and corporeal, and that is facilitated by languages of both the body and the voice.

Shange echoes this embodied language of blackwoman intimacy in formal properties of the poem. "Two" departs from Shange's signature free-verse poetic style, taking on a prosepoetic stanza structure that uses minimal white space and literally fills the pages with the body of the text. This structure is underscored by the poem's handling of dialogue. Although the text introduces Smoke and Graciela through metaphors of language and voice, the third-person speaker never yields to their polyglossia; the figures' speech is rendered only through indirect discourse embedded within the poem's paragraph structure. The reader must thus work to excavate the women's voices and try in vain to disentangle those voices from the formal body of the text.

Nestled deep in the anatomy of Shange's poetic structure, the voices of Smoke and Graciela—and their erotic connection—are most readily heard through languages of the body. The speaker gives us to understand that the two spend their time doing "what brought them secrets to cherish & purposes for rising at sunrise/ dancing & writin," and that each woman shares stories about her many lovers with the other in "conversations intricate and tactile/ as whoever's legs had been between hers" (*for colored girls* Shameless Hussy Press 2). In this relationship, the simultaneity of language and movement in the joint practices of dancing and writing—the core juncture of the choreopoem form—also forms potential for a radical black women's sensuality. Here, Shange's slashes perform

                                two
                            (for thulani)

graciela and smoke waz like outta the same womb/ cept it
waznt so/ graciela waz born some where in a different time
from smoke/ but even when they spoke different languages/
the voice waz the same/ & the bangles the/same/ gods patted
them to sleep at night/ & they never missed anyone else/
like they missed each other/ a deep hole crawled through all
marrow/ so they stayed round/ together/ most time the
thoughts they shared waz private/ aired only tween the two/
& solid fronts of ignorance or familiarity met any intruders
some mother or man or lover wantin to know/ why graciela
always knew when smoke needed quiet/ a hand/ some water or
actual lewdness/ & smoke didnt allow anyone who waz distrac-
ting or gauche within a hair's breath of graciela/ waz prone
to desperation when someone didnt understand/ & smoke under-
stood/

one time at this ridiculous fete/ jumbled with glitter boys/
butch whacks/ wd-be dancers writers painters & butch whacks/
real dancers painters jewelers & writers in multiple tongues/
smoke and graciela encountered a mimist recently returned
from europe/ where he'd endured boundless adulation & pov-
erty/ pyssed in women's mouths on request/ & worked once/
in oslo/ the mimist haunted women/ cuz he had chosen celibacy/
& cuz he loved them more than himself/ & cldnt offer the
imperfect/ when more waz needed/ graciela waz a dancer & res-
ponded immediately to the flow of the mimist's hands as he
spoke/ & smoke liked the way his lower lip dipped under an
auburn mole/ then continued to the last hairs of his moustache
graciela glanced at smoke & saw the same/ a desire to know
this mimist more intimately/ & though he waz the flower to be
plucked by each/ they laughed/ wantin to know what wd happen
now the two/ smoke & graciela/ seriously plotted intentions/
for one other/ than themselves/

for aeons/ it seemed/ graciela & smoke attracted the same
lovers/ at the same time/ or a while after someone met gra-
ciela/ he met smoke/ & began to harbor desires for his lover's
closest companion/ usually confessing to graciela/ this coincidental lust for smoke/ & graciela wd buoyantly suggest/
this lover/ go right over to smoke & get it if you can/ but
i dont think so/ smoke & i have an arrangement/ & they really

Figure 2.1c. Shange, "Two." *for colored girls* . . . Shameless Hussy Press chapbook, 1st ed., 1976. Copyrighted material is reproduced by exclusive arrangement with the Ntozake Shange Revocable Trust. Paul T. Williams, Managing Trustee Donald S. Sutton, Literary Trustee.

did/ it waz called 'no trespassing'/ & the lovers were
shared in conversations intricate and tactile/ as whoever's legs had been between hers/ & the lovers of graciela & smoke never knew both/ only one & that waz that/
the two prided themselves on loyalty rare among women/ &
snickered when men insisted on some prerogative of choice/
choosin both smoke & graciela waz cosmically impossible/
& its said one or another lover never got over bein
refused/ & here the two were quite emphatic/ 'no man
on the face of the earth/ has enough to hold both of us/
it'd have to be a colored man from saturn or uranus/
not one from here'/ & then they wd go off to do what
brought them secrets to cherish & purposes for rising
at sunrise/ dancin & writin/ & possible lovers/ waz
their lives & graciela & smoke waz good/ if not over-
whelmin & that too/ waz all they cared abt/

but this mimist/ waz the key to something both were
looking for/ graciela heard him talking& he was not
talkin/ smoke felt his heat & his hands were chill-damp/
how waz a choice to be made/ neither knew how & both
became the essence of themselves to avoid bein involved
in the final tappin of shoulders/ the forces wd have to
work/ & they did/ graciela waz energy of unseen waterfalls
nurturin immense jungle vegetation/ & smoke flowed outta
herself like horizons in tahiti/ hot rose & melon tinted
vastness/ & the mimist thoroughly enjoyed himself/ never
before in his very worldly life/ had he encountered two
women of such/ compelling dimensions/ & he also performed/
becoming singularly muted language/ using each second/
every space of his body/ to project/ himself/ & the three
of them/ smoke/ graciela/ & the mimist created so much
energy/ they all thought they were walkin on the edges
of the galaxy/

the mimist waz endowed with/ above all other things/ a
sense of unity/ & between smoke & graciela/ he felt precise & categorical ties/ like those he'd known on mars/
before there waz no water/ & colored people moved in the
same tone/ like graciela & smoke/ they had one voice &
delighted in sharing secrets & food &/ like on mars/
where colored men placed themselves among two women/ &
begat & beloved & held each closely/ the mimist set
celibacy aside/ for smoke waz drawin him into her &
graciela waz plungin thru him/ & he chose to do so/ which
is more important/ the two graciela & smoke/ didnt know
why the choice waznt theirs/ the mimist/ bein a colored
man from mars/ not from earth/ never admitted to makin
one/ true unions are imperative/ are commanded/ transient
lovers are chosen/ & occasions have no meaning/ it is the
motions of unnamed stars/ burnin thru acres of sky/ that
is not for sale/ & not arbitrary/ that the mimist respected
& he took them both/ graciela & smoke/ assumed it waz god's
will/ the mimist knew/ the integrity of his person/

Figure 2.1c. Continued.

what Jennifer DeVere Brody identifies as one of the queer functions of punctuation: "the simultaneous suturing and separating of text(s)" (*Punctuation* 109).
Yet, Shange's queer punctuation performs the same act on the subjects' bodies. It
is through the women's embodied languages—and in their "intricate and tactile"
conversations about sexuality—that they divvy up the many sexual partners who
approach them, seeking to sleep with both Smoke and Graciela at once. This

endeavor always ultimately fails, the speaker informs us, because "choosin both smoke and graciela waz cosmically impossible" (*for colored girls* 2).

Despite the explicitly sensual dynamics of the women's intimacy, the possibility of a shared erotic experience between Graciela, Smoke, and a third lover remains foreclosed until they encounter a figure who shares their understanding of the inseparability of body and voice. At the midpoint of the poem, the two attend a "ridiculous fete/jumbled with glitter boys" and "butch whacks" (ibid.). At the party, they encounter a "colored mimist . . . from mars" who redirects the poem's narrative and opens new possibilities for black women's sexual expression through embodied voice. Immediately, the three connect through the erotics of embodied voice: "graciela heard him talking & he was not talking/ smoke felt his heat & his hands were chill-damp" (ibid. 3). The pair sleeps with the mimist, an act that has transformative implications for all three, leading to amalgamations of body and voice and broad-scale reconfigurations of both material and textual terrains. In erotic engagement with the mimist, all three bodies become "singularly muted language/ . . . & the three of them/ smoke/ graciela/ & the mimist created so much energy/ they all thought they were walkin on the edges of the galaxy" (Shange "Two" 3). This encounter establishes the queer reach of Shange's choreopoetic thinking. Here, communication through voice and body at once offers transcendent possibilities for articulating nuanced modes of black sexual expression; by becoming "singularly muted language," Shange's figures introduce the possibility of a queer space in which two deeply intimate blackwoman friends and "a colored mimist from mars" can create inroads into new galaxies of subjectivity and sexual connection (*for colored girls* 3).

## "Visual Fusion" and "Textual Impairment": Zanele Muholi's "what do you see when you look at us?"

By creating the genre of the choreopoem as a new form for articulating multiple modes of voice and body, Shange invites similar modes of generic subversion beyond dance and theatrical performance realms. While the queer legacies of choreopoetic thought are most readily visible in the works of diasporic writers and stage performers, the formal melding of body and voice opens important pathways for black queer visual art as well. The work of South African lesbian photographer and visual activist Zanele Muholi illustrates the resonances of choreopoetic thinking for queer visual artists in the diaspora.

Muholi's 2011 mixed-genre text, "What do you see when you look at us," compiled with queer South African poet Pam Dlungwana and Namibian-born poet Olivia Coetzee, demonstrates the usefulness of choreopoetic thinking for

Figure 2.2a. Muholi, "Apinda Mpako and Ayanda Magudulela, Parktown, Johannes-burg, 2007." From the "Being" series, in *what do you see in us when you look at us* (a visual fusion). © Zanele Muholi. Courtesy of Stevenson, Cape Town/Johannesburg and Yancey Richardson, New York.

articulating the links between body, voice, and black queer women's subjectiv-ity on the visual plane. Part visual chapbook and part photo essay, the text is comprised of portraits of black South African lesbian women and poems ex-ploring black queer women's experience. The poems and images are collected under headings that flag specific aspects of queer life such as "On Poverty," "On Blackness and Body Politics," and "On Race and Representation." Muholi terms the text a "visual fusion," following Shange not only in developing a new genre for exploring Afrodiasporic women's sexuality, but also in *naming* that genre as both an amalgamation of and an extension beyond other recognizable forms. Muholi's generic invention of the "visual fusion" echoes the logic of the choreopoem by highlighting the epistemological properties of the image of the black queer woman body, but also by insisting that even the poems themselves be read as "visual" texts.

"What do you see?" begins with a section titled "On Black Lesbian Youth," opening with a photo from Muholi's "Being" series. The image shows two black women laying in a bed, entwined in each other's arms as they look frankly at the camera, one smiling, the other's face partly illegible, cast in the shadow of her arm, which cradles her own head. The greater part of the women's bodies, too, is unintelligible through basic technologies of vision; light and shadow compel the reader to imagine the touch of the women's flesh as it continues in the background of the front-lit scene. This image, however, is followed by the free verse poem "Caught," written by Dlungwana, describing an experience of erotic black / queer intimacy through a metaphor of captivity.

Because of its stanza structure and its use of whitespace, "Caught" bears reproducing in full:

cupped in love
inherited
from lovers past

fist full of fury
new lust birthed,
a sweet decay of
inhibition and doubt

gently creaming into
warmth eminating from
a heart now residing
between thighs
greedily holding I captive,
Captured.
(Pam Dlungwana in Muholi "what do you see" 2 *sic*)[10]

The speaker of "Caught" remains unidentified until the last of the poem's three stanzas, in which she describes "warmth eminating from/ a heart now residing/ between thighs/ greedily holding I captive/ Captured." The "I" serves a function similar to the "language intricate and tactile" that Shange's Smoke and Graciela speak; the speaker invites the reader to engage the sensory and sensual aspects of black queer women's love unmediated by distancing pronouns—or the obscuring shadows of the visual; only once scenes like the one pictured in "Being" have been conjured does the poem's speaker announce itself.

And, as in Shange's "Two," the form of "Caught" echoes its body/language. Dlungwana's line breaks and the collaborators' choice to arrange the poem at the center of the page evokes both a curved human form and the letter "I" that lays unspoken at the poem's center. This visual fusion positions the poem itself both as a textual signifier of an individual black queer woman subject *and* as a body open and available for reading. By articulating the physical embrace the poem describes in terms of an erotic captivity, Dlungwana uses this ambiguous "I" to write narratives of black women's sexual subjectivity that are erased, as Spillers puts it, in moment[s] of colonial, imperialist, and perhaps even psychic "capture" (Spillers 15). The fusion of image and text here reimagines capture as a moment of mutual erotic exchange between black women, a subversive instantiation of the kind of "sheer sensual pleasure" around which both Shange and Spillers define black women's subjective nuance (Shange *for colored girls* 47). The poem invites viewer/readers to find subjective grounding—that is, to search for the "I"—within a subversive queer erotics consistent with Moraga's ideas about the radical potential of sexual power dynamics in the lives of queer women of color, for example, and with Audre Lorde's notion of radical erotic expression as a means of intervention against social dominance.[11]

Here, Muholi's "visual fusion" complicates the visual meanings of black embodiment by centering the black lesbian South African self—the "I"—an ineluctable subversion that confronts the reader even across shifts in genre and the turning of the page. In this sense, the genre of the visual fusion intervenes in what Nicole Fleetwood terms "the process of deciphering" black visuality, which, as she points out, "itself is a performative act of registering blackness as visual manifestation" (Fleetwood 6). Muholi's visual fusion activates the queer, anticolonial, and diasporic potentials of visual hermeneutic decipherings of blackness, showing not only how "[b]lackness and black life become intelligible and valued, as well as consumable and disposable, through racial discourse," but also how black queer sexualities can undergo—and critique—similar processes of consumption and valuation on the diasporic visual field (ibid.). Following this subversive poetics through to the poem's orthography, we might read Dlungwana's disruptive spelling of "eminate" as part of this rewriting, a formal disturbance that reveals the "I" where it is not supposed to be, doing what it is not supposed to do.

The fusion of bodily image and text continues throughout Muholi's visual fusion, requiring the reader to navigate *both* as part of a single set of utterances about diasporic lesbian identity. The portraits that follow "Caught," titled "Nothing Lust For-ever I" and "Nothing Lust For-ever II" map the poem's poetic rendering of embodied black women's sexuality back onto the plane of the photographic image.

The photographs, which appear under the heading "On Black Lesbians and Safer Sex," share the composition of Dlungwana's poem, rendering visually scenes of black queer women's erotic pleasure, but also inserting into that image the nuanced imperatives of sexual health and responsibility, and an ethic of care shared between black queer women's bodies. The composition and tonal contrast of the black-and-white image focalizes not the act of sex performed

Figure 2.2b. Muholi, "LiZa I, 2009." Published as "Nothing Lust For-ever" I (2009) in *what do you see when you look at us* (a visual fusion). © Zanele Muholi. Courtesy of Stevenson, Cape Town/Johannesburg and Yancey Richardson, New York.

by two black queer women's bodies, but the image of the white latex glove, which represents both an erotic care and mutual responsibility, and the violent threats that HIV and AIDS pose to black South African lesbian women's lives. In centering the glove, the image interrupts the exclusion of black lesbians and black queer women from public health discourses on HIV/AIDS and safer sex in South Africa, discourses in which, as Zethu Matebeni points out, "[w]hile much has been written about gay men's sexuality and its interplay in HIV and AIDS debates, there continues to be silence about female same-sex relationships and how HIV and AIDS affect women in these relationships," highlighting a discursive erasure that forms a core concern of Muholi's digital and artistic activist vision ("Sexing Women" 102).[12]

The photograph and the poem together work as doubly rhyming images: the photograph echoes the poem's use of white space, positioning black queer women's bodies in a visual continuity first with the form of the poem, which itself invokes the shape associated with feminine bodies, and then with the poem's speaking voice—the missing capital letter "I" which both the photo and the form of the poem evoke. Reading the visual fusion for choreopoetic typographies, we can also read the diagonal arrangement of the bodies in "Nothing Lust Forever I" as evocative of the forward slash, which in Shange's poetics indicates a semiotics of both distinction and inclusion—a division of breaths and a joining of thoughts made material on the page.

Like Shange's choreopoetic works, Muholi's "visual fusion" thus trains readers in a new literacy, requiring them to come to new understandings of black lesbian subjectivity that take into account the affective and emotional nuances expressed in Coetzee's and Dlungwana's poems. Its visual registers tap what Kobena Mercer, in his recent study of African Diaspora visual culture, terms "the interruptive agency of blackness in unsettling long-standing habits and traditions" of dominant critical hermeneutics, "open[ing] our understanding of art to a broader range of interpretive pathways" for imagining blackness (*Travel & See* 3). Yet, for Muholi, as for Shange, the project of correcting external understandings of black womanhood arrives beside the point; that is, not what or whom these texts are *for*. Indeed, Muholi herself states that her visual fusion is "for all black women who are intimate and in love, women and transmen, regardless of their age, ethnicity, race, and borders. Ultimately, this work is for all humans who are textually impaired but able to feel." Echoing Shange's title and the closing lines of *for colored girls*, Muholi offers a dedication that is both subjectively expansive and pointedly precise. Where Shange's choreopoem closes with a tight circle of brown women physically joined in an intimacy of black woman "color" and nuance—the choreopoem's climactic "layin on of hands"—Muholi opens her text by naming the absence of nuantial expression against which Shange's colored girls speak, dance, and move (Shange *for colored girls* 60). Muholi identifies the grammars of colonialism, racism, sexism, homophobia, transphobia, and xenophobia as afflictions of language and corporeal misreading that, she says, render viewers "textually impaired" and bar black queer women from both textual and visual recognition. By blending word and body, then, Muholi extends Shange's choreopoetic tradition, inviting the viewer to read, hear, and *see* against the afflictions of text that unwrite black queer women's voices, and to understand, as she writes in full-bodied capital letters at the close of the text: "We are here NOW!" (Muholi 11).

## The Queer Uses of Quiet: Choreopoetics in Black Women's Erotic Performance

Muholi's notion of "textual impairment" as a condition of sociopolitical illiteracy that can be repaired only by learning how black queer bodies speak points to the importance of choreopoetic thinking and body/languages not only on the visual field, but also in back queer women's performance texts. Reading black queer women's performance strategies and poetics for body/language reveals the ways in which vocabularies of the body appear both in concert with and in tension with spoken language to critique and reimagine black women's experiences with embodiment and the erotic. If we take seriously Audre Lorde's claim that the erotic is a source of power precisely for its capacity to establish a bodily and therefore deeply experiential standard of pleasure around which the viability and livability of social and political life can be measured—and toward which collaborative anti-oppressive action can work—then black queer women's performances of erotic and sexual life make visible and audible the contours of this work, inviting and challenging audiences to share space with both the traumas and pleasures of black queer women's bodily being, and to bear witness to the collective labors of healing and pleasure that black queer women's living requires.

The choreopoem form reveals the possibilities of black feminist performances of the erotic beyond amplification. Reading black women's performance strategies for a body/language propelled by both voicing and quiet invites us to examine what is possible when black women's bodies speak their desires wordlessly on stage and how these tensions between verbal and bodily voicing demonstrate what we might think of as the queer potentials of quiet—the ways in which quiet can function as a poetic strategy for rethinking how difference, subjective nuance, and complex self-expression can take place.

While Shange's choreopoem is widely (and rightly) understood as an iconic text of black feminist voicing, it is meaningful to note that *for colored girls* itself operates through an erotic aesthetic of quiet, a mode of inaudible bodily communication that must be accessed before verbal voicing can happen effectively. The choreopoem is perhaps best known for its famous spoken lines "somebody almost walked off with alla my stuff" and "being alive and a woman and colored is a metaphysical dilemma I have not conquered yet" and the iconic "I found god in myself and loved her fiercely" (23, 26). Yet beyond and before these spoken lines, the choreopoem demonstrates the radical possibility of quiet for recasting black women's bodily connections and desires, possibilities that have been taken up and expanded on by black queer women artists in the decades since the choreopoem's first performances. Consider the opening stage directions of the choreopoem:

> The stage is in darkness. Harsh music is heard as dim blue lights come up. One after another, seven women run onto the stage from each of the exits. They all freeze in postures of distress. The follow spot picks up the lady in brown. She comes to life and looks around at the other ladies. All of the others are still. She walks over to the lady in red and calls to her. The lady in red makes no response. (3)[13]

*for colored girls* begins not with the radical black feminist voicing that the choreopoem is most known for, but in stillness and silence. "Harsh" music eventually underscores the muteness of the characters and their inability to reach one-another through voice alone. It is only once the "harsh" music becomes danceable—a conduit for wordless bodily movement—that the characters are able finally to connect with one another. The stage directions indicate that Martha and the Vandellas' "Dancing in the Streets" is heard, and the characters are unfrozen, finally able to reach each other silently through hand-clapping games, freeze-tag, and dance, and creating space to "come to life" *together* through body, touch, and physical pleasure.

This opening moment of *for colored girls* demonstrates the logic of the choreopoem form, and it reveals why the choreopoem has been of such use for black queer women artists. In insisting on the body as a tool for radical self-expression and connection between women, the choreopoem suggests that voice, alone, is insufficient as a means of communication between black women's bodies "frozen" by the layers of psychic, linguistic, representational, and corporeal violence that characterize black queer women's experiences of embodiment and the erotic. It is only through the expressive technologies of the body—technologies that understand movement *as* language—that black women can fully touch each other and forge spaces defined by our disallowed pleasure, desire, healing, and joy.

This queer healing through expressive embodiment is the animating concern of Haitian American lesbian poet Lenelle Moïse's 2002 choreopoem *Cornered in the Dark*. Moïse uses the choreopoem form to explore experiences of rape and sexual violence, and to propose sensual contact between women as part

Figure 2.3. From The Black Rep Theatre Performance of Ntozake Shange's *for colored girls who have considered suicide/when the rainbow is enuf* (2014). Stewart Goldstein/ The Black Rep.

of a reclamation of erotic agency and power. Like Shange, Moïse uses the choreopoem form to juxtapose bodily and verbal modes of expression and highlight the insufficiencies of spoken language alone in expressing black women's experiences of embodiment—and of rape in particular.[14] In her interpretation of the choreopoem form, however, Moïse explicitly positions same-sex bodily explorations of both sexual trauma and erotic pleasure as central to the work of black feminist healing. For her, the choreopoem is an opportunity to create a sensory experience that simulates on multiple registers the pain, trauma, and unspeakability of sexual violence, as well as the collective healing capacities and political potentials of queer erotic pleasure.

*Cornered in the Dark* tells four women's stories of rape, molestation, intimate partner violence, and other forms of assault, all of which occur in their homes. As in Shange's choreopoem, Moïse names her characters to invoke both anonymity and interconnection: they are named "Woman 1," "Woman 2," "Woman 3," and "Woman 4." The only further linguistic individuation Moïse assigns each character is the designation of a single element at the close of their brief character description: Fire, Wind, Earth, and Water. Moïse's description of the text's setting is similarly spare; we are told only that the performance takes place in "Dream Space." By invoking the four elements through her characters, Moïse announces immediately one of the text's central concerns: to reimagine the constitutive elements of global, social, and domestic space and to "dream" a world made up of black women's collective expressive embodiments. Moïse includes within a prefatory "Playwright's note" the statement that "A choreopoem is a danced dramatization of free verse" (a definition that Shange does not provide) (2). This seems to be a primarily descriptive summary consistent with the form as Shange uses it. Yet, Moïse's definition highlights the important lexical particularities of "choreopoem" as both a neologism and an invented genre: the absence of reference to aural voice or oral speech—and the emphasis, instead, on dance and "free verse" (a term that connotes poetic text more than spoken performance) suggest that, even as the "choreopoem" is a mode of voicing, its expressive action takes place through and in relation to expressive embodiments. It is in this context of expressivity defined by embodiment (that is, in this context of definitive body/language) that Moïse offers the play's first stage directions: "I leave it up to the director/ choreographer to decide how and when the actors move in their own production of *Cornered in the Dark*. All sounds mentioned in the script are generated by the ensemble. The text, itself, is music" (2).

This is an important departure from Shange's choreopoem, in which specific songs are referenced in the stage directions (such as Martha and the Vandellas' "Dancing in the Streets") and facilitate the characters' individual and collective communication through dance. Moïse, in contrast, frames the "text" as music, and stipulates that that music must be generated by the characters' bodies, thus pushing Shange's choreopoetic thinking to emphasize even further the centrality of the body to black feminist expression. Without the body, for Moïse, not only is there no voice but there is no music, and, in fact, no *sound*.

Framing the choreopoem's entire soundscape through black women's bodily expression—on both visual and aural fields—allows Moïse to remake the stage as a space defined primarily by black women's embodiment and sensory experience. In this space, movement and touch work as a contextualizing frame in which spoken language can make meaning, facilitating the text shifts between discussions of sexual violence and erotic pleasure, both of which are dramatized through collaborative movement and touch between women. Through body/language, Moïse figures the blackwoman body as one that can experience both violence and erotic pleasure sometimes almost seamlessly, and positions erotic touch between black women as an expressive mode of healing that language alone cannot offer.

As in Shange's choreopoem, the incompleteness of voice without body is clear from the opening scenes of *Cornered in the Dark*. Yet where Shange positions this failure of verbal voicing as one that can be repaired through music (as a conduit for dance), in Moïse's choreopoem, it is only the bodies themselves that can overcome silence and forge connection. Moïse writes:

WOMAN 3: Listen!

WOMAN 1: I . . . have discovered . . . something . . . in thought?

Lights shift. The women blindly trickle onto the stage, their collective Dream Space. They are still only sonically aware of each other. They line up behind the stuttering WOMAN 2, reaching out their hands in a vain attempt to touch her voice. As WOMAN 2 struggles to name her feelings, the ensemble, likewise, gropes for her words. WOMEN 1, 3 and 4 physically echo WOMAN 2's ticks and gestures.

WOMAN 2: What I'm—what I'm thinking is—is that you—you just kind of—you don't really—don't—you don't really understand—what—what I'm trying to say to you . . . because . . . I think that if you did—if you—if you understood what it was like to—uh . . . if you understood, then—then I wouldn't have to say a word. I wouldn't have to do this. I wouldn't have to talk to you about it. It'd just be something that you felt and—knew . . . (4–5).[15]

In addressing the limits of "only sonic" awareness by "groping for" and "reaching" to "touch [each other's] voice[s]," Moïse's characters attempt a synesthetic contact, a reach across the rules of materiality and perception in hopes of accessing a kind of communication that can help them understand each other and have their own bodily experiences be understood. Woman 2 calls for recognition through what Oliver terms flesh/memory, a shared understanding of past experience transmitted through the body and thus more effective than spoken language. Here, Woman 2 imagines flesh/memory will save her from having to endure the pain of verbal recollection and will also allow the pain of her assault to do the work of connection, transforming trauma into a means by which the women can "feel" and thus "know" each other in both psychic and corporeal ways.

Yet, verbal voicing plays an important function in Moïse's work as well. Whereas in Shange's choreopoem, voice works *in tandem* with the body to forge black feminist connection, Moïse often positions verbal voice *in tension* with bodily expression to highlight both the traumas and the pleasures of the body and to show the power of queer erotic pleasure for black feminist healing. As Woman 4 tells the story of her sexual assault at the hands of her husband, the stage directions note:

The women stand beside each other, keenly listening to one another as they face the audience. Although the following lines are assigned, each woman repeats each line several times as if to confirm that she can, in deed, hear the words. The effect is symphonic, tidal.

WOMAN 2: This is a true story.

WOMAN 1: Don't you dare say I didn't because I did!

WOMAN 3: I did.

WOMAN 2: I said no.

WOMAN 4: I said a thousand times, no (6).

The women deliver the narrative of Woman 4's assault collaboratively, returning repeatedly to the sonic dimensions of the scene:

WOMAN 2: The sound.
WOMAN 1: Him.
WOMAN 3: His sound. [ . . . ]
*"His sound" is repeated; a horn section, blaring.*
ALL: It was louder than the voice in my head (6, 7).

Here, Moïse presents sexual violence as an act of both bodily and sonic assault:
voice appears as a menacing corollary and accomplice to rape, subsuming the
women's minds and wresting authority over their thoughts just as the physical
violences of rape permeate and incapacitate the body. The "symphony" of the
women's voices facilitates the "blaring" of the assailant's voice, yet also offers
the women a sonic escape to collectivity. Moïse uses the body/language of the
choreopoem form to mobilize what Tina Campt terms "a haptic mode of engaging the sonic frequencies" of visual narratives of black life. Reading photographs
for their sonic contours, Campt argues for a strategy of "'watching' photos that
materializes their transfigurations" to highlight their potential for subversion
and fugitivity. For Campt, these "transfigurations" occur "at the haptic frequency
of vibration, like the vibrato of a hum felt more in the throat than in the ear"
(*Listening to Images* 8). This practice of reading the visual for sonic simultaneity and dissonance in order to access its transformative potential is crucial to
Moïse's poetics, and to the interstitial hermeneutics Moïse asks her audience to
develop. The women's collective voices serve as an embodied materialization of
the haptic, offering departure from the visual scene of the assault and a pathway
to a site of shared blackwoman voicing. The image of the women's bodies stand-
ing side-by-side onstage echoes this sonic departure from the visual scene of the
rape. In its loudness and chaos, the women's "symphonic" chorus allows them
to tell the story of the rape in its "true" sensory registers of traumatic fracture,
violence, and overwhelm; yet it also provides a sonic context of mutuality and
collectivity for narrating the rape, and a way of re-membering sexual violence
within a space of blackwoman voicing.

In Moïse's choreopoem, then, shared voicing allows black women to create a
soundscape for articulating and reframing sexual assault through explorations of
sonic violence; yet, effective movement beyond articulation and toward *healing
from* sexual violence requires body/language. In *Cornered in the Dark*, black
women's sonic articulations of sexual violence are juxtaposed with reclamations
of the erotic through queer bodily contact. As Woman 3 tells her story, in which
she is slut-shamed for her dress and her sexual freedom and thus blamed for her
rape, the women's collective verbal/sonic recognition takes on deeper expression
through erotic touch:

WOMAN 3: "Besides, everyone saw you . . ."
*Hesitant, erotic movement which emphasizes the syllables "dance," "dirt," "touch," "tight" and "want."*
WOMAN 3 CONTINUED: They'll say, "I saw her dancing." [ . . . ]
WOMAN 3: "She was dirty dancing with him."
WOMAN 2: She was dirty—
*Throughout the following, the women explore the sounds of a sensual excitement. Slow and easy at first, then progressively less contained, exquisitely tense. The women move fluidly, ecstatically. They touch each others fingertips.*
WOMAN 1: It . . . feels . . . good.
WOMAN 2: Good.
WOMAN 1: It feels so good.
WOMAN 2: So good.
WOMAN 1: It feels so good—
WOMAN 3: To be touched.
WOMAN 1: I mean really—
WOMAN 3: Touched.
WOMAN 4: Like soft. Like really soft. Like gentle. Like really, really gentle.
WOMAN 3: Warm—
WOMAN 2: And sweet—to be, like—
WOMAN 3: To be, like—
WOMAN 4: To be—
WOMAN 3: Like—
WOMAN 4: Loved—
WOMAN 1: Shit, loved. It feels so fucking good—
WOMAN 4: To be loved . . .
WOMAN 1: Does that feel good?
WOMAN 4: Yes (8–10).

Woman 3's struggle to reconcile her desire for sexual expression with her rape and its aftermath catalyze the blackwoman collective into a new project of communication—one that is specifically erotic, and that is carried through explicitly erotic "touch" between black women. Body/language allows the women to think through and critique sexist visual and sonic restrictions placed on black women's sexuality ("Besides, everyone *saw* you. . . . They'll *say* 'I saw her dancing'"). It also allows them to develop an alternative mode of bodily and verbal engagement through which they can re-visit the scene and access it as a site for both antisexist critique and queer erotic pleasure.

The women introduce a black queer feminist interpretation and expansion of what Jennifer Christine Nash terms "visual pleasure," a site of subversive erotic performance underexplored (in Nash's view) by black feminist criticism. Nash imagines that reading black women's performances of the erotic for "visual pleasure" reveals how black women pornographic actors in particular emphasize the simultaneity of violence and pleasure, thus pushing beyond what Nash sees as a dominant "black women have it bad" logic of black feminism and forwarding a reading strategy that can understand black women's performances of eroticism in terms of pleasure rather than critique (*The Black Body in Ecstasy* 11). Yet Moïse's choreopoetics unsettle this juxtaposition of blackwoman pleasure and black feminist critique. By situating meaning-making at an inescapable nexus of visual and verbal expression, Moïse deploys black women's queer erotics *as* a critique of sexual violence and of the structures of sexual stigma and bodily shame that support rape cultures. That these critiques occur not only on the vocal register but through the tension between spoken and physical expression—in "exploring the sounds of pleasure" through touch—demonstrates the importance of body/language to black queer feminist critique. For Moïse, the body intervenes when aurality/orality is trauma, enabling black women to experience and express dissent, refusal, and bodily sovereignty through—and *as*—erotic pleasure.

This, then, is the erotic face of quiet's "sovereignty" in black cultural expression. Through body/language, Moïse's characters mobilize quiet to create an erotic and sexual sovereignty defined not only by healing but also by pleasure.

I read the erotic movements of Moïse's characters here as "quiet," not to suggest that they occur in an absence of sound (they don't) but rather to emphasize that they happen *in tension and contrast* with sound, overlaying the interiority of intimate touch onto the soundscape of sonic violence such that, through the movements themselves—the wordless languages of the body—the women wrest sovereignty over both body and word. Through their bodily expressions of erotic "excitement"—and the deep contrasts they bear to the narrative accounts of rape that surround them—Moïse's characters are able to recast the vocabulary of sexual violence according to blackwoman interiorities and thus to experience those vocabularies as objects of both critique and pleasure. As Kevin Quashie suggests, quiet is distinct from silence, though this is an unfamiliar mode of listening for black cultural analysis, given the long-standing emphasis on orality in black cultural scholarship. Yet, quiet is not silence; unlike silence, quiet is "[i]nevitable, essential, sovereign; expressive and lush; a little foreign to our thinking on black culture, but there all the while" (*The Sovereignty of Quiet* 10). Invoked as anathema to the sonic violences of rape, Moïse's quiet performance of queer erotics cancels the noise of white, straight, and masculinist proscriptions of—and standards for—living. The women's erotic dance and, specifically, the touching of each other's fingertips echoes the iconic "layin on of hands" that closes Shange's text. Here, Moïse recasts this scene in light of Lorde's model of the erotic, situating black women's bodily collaboration toward healing as a specifically erotic project, one in which black women's shared desire, excitement, and erotic touch facilitates not only survival but a survival predicated on the heights of erotic pleasure as a standard for being.

Moïse's body/language highlights the place of expressive embodiment in this erotic standard-shifting and demonstrates the uses of quiet queer expressions of the erotic. As Quashie notes, quiet is a practice toward an "interior self-measure," that, through engagements with interiority, imagination, and intimacy, provides modes of value beyond those offered black subjects by anyone other than themselves (45). It is this interior self-measure that Shange's colored girls access when they declare, "i found god in myself/ & i loved her/ I loved her fiercely," and that Lorde names when she says: "If I didn't define myself for myself, I would be crunched into other people's fantasies for me and eaten alive" (Shange *for colored girls* 64; Lorde "Learning from the 60s" 137). Moïse frames this self-measure around a black queer feminist erotics, (re)defining black women's bodily experience according to their own erotic fantasy. In so doing, she shows us how body/language conjures blackqueerwoman gods that offer both transcendent re-memberings of sexual violence and new hereafters of erotic bliss.

Considering the place of erotic fantasy in queer performances of body/language also points to the important ways in which body/language reshapes the inhabited, shared publics of the stage according to quiet. This re-creation of performative space is particularly evident in black queer and feminist burlesque performance, in which woman-centered erotic fantasy becomes the standard of "measure" both of internal (and in-group) valuations of blackwoman embodiment *and* of the political possibilities of the social and material worlds in which black women's bodies and subjectivities move. As Quashie suggests, the "expressiveness of quiet is not concerned with publicness, but instead is the expressiveness of the interior" (21). In black queer feminist burlesque, quiet makes space for visions of new publics shaped precisely by black women's erotic inner life. Body/language, in black feminist burlesque, enacts intimate articulations of erotic interiority on a (semi)public stage, re-creating the burlesque theater as a spatial metaphor for publics of black feminist freedom.

In several twenty-first-century urban centers, burlesque performance serves as a crucial site for black queer women's social, communal, and erotic life. Burlesque troops such as Body Ecology, Chocolate City Burlesque in Washington, DC, Brazen Booty Burlesque in Los Angeles, Dark Side Burlesque and Sister BEAR Burlesque in Philadelphia, and New York's Harlem Shake Burlesque and Brown Girls Burlesque, as well as popular black queer burlesque performers such as Maine Anders, Essence Revealed, and Chicago and St. Louis's Jeez Louise, curator of the traveling show Jeezy's Juke Joint and 2019's #1 Burlesque Figure in the World, all engage in queer-affirming, body- and sex-positive, women-of-color-centered burlesque forms.[16] These forms are part of what is known as the "neo-burlesque" movement, which began in the early 1990s. According to Reisa Klein, the designation "neo-burlesque" refers to "a resurrection and a reinterpretation of the burlesque tradition that emerged in the nineteenth and twentieth centuries in European and North American" contexts. These historical burlesque forms, Klein suggests, "engaged in the practice of striptease but used humour, through its application of parody, satire, imitation, and exaggeration, as a technique to critique elements of Victorian culture." For Klein, neo-burlesque extends those critiques both in form and content, encompassing "various embodied performances through exaggerated gestures, costumes, a focus on pleasure and playfulness, coupled with striptease and the other attributes of traditional burlesque [to] challenge normative social conventions of beauty, gender and sexuality" (247).

Notably absent from Klein's description of neo-burlesque is its concerns with race, racialized gender and sexuality, and embodiment. Chicava HoneyChild Tate, Brown Girls Burlesque, and several other black woman burlesque performers and groups understand discourses of race and racialized gender and sexuality as central to their burlesque critique. Many of these performers of burlesque explicitly name burlesque as a way of forging important intersectional critique. For example, The Lady Ms. Vagina Jenkins, part of Harlem Shake Burlesque (described by one writer as the US's "first black neo-burlesque troupe") states: "It's amazing how graceful one becomes dancing at the intersections of race, class, gender, and sexuality." Jeez Louise, cocreator of Jeezy's Juke Joint, a popular black queer burlesque show in Chicago, expands on this point: "The Juke Joint is not just about celebrating unapologetic Blackness, we also are a cast full of queer-ass people!"[17]

In this project of staging a black queer feminist intersectional critique of and through the erotic, many burlesque performers have turned to the choreopoem form. For example, Detroit-born black burlesque dancer JanTina attributes her burlesque work to her history as an "English major with a concentration in poetry." JanTina, who began exotic dancing after college, became fascinated by both the other "strippers' . . . everyday lives [and] their stage personas." To better understand both the dancers' own lives and the personae they embodied, JanTina began to write poems about them, which soon "became a poetic burlesque play, a choreopoem, and a book." The choreopoem, "Silhouettes," was later staged Off-Off-Broadway in New York City.[18] Similarly, during their 2011 "Creativity and Transformation Residency" program, queer-affirming New York–based burlesque and dance group Body Ecology offered a "Ritual Theatre & Choreopoem Aesthetics" workshop as part of their "Public Performing Arts and Activism Workshops" community series, which also featured workshops on reproductive justice, environmental justice, and spiritual activism.[19]

Figure 2.4a & b. Perle Noire at "Jeezy's Juke Joint" Chicago. Photos by MC Newman.

For these black burlesque performers, the choreopoem offers an important language for describing the centrality of intersectional critique and social activism to their embodied erotic performance. Yet even those that don't explicitly take up the choreopoem form often tap into the quiet expressivities of body/language to make space for radical forms of sensual storytelling, embodied narrative, and community building through the communicative capacities of the flesh. By using this embodied narrative both in concert and in tension with musical narrative and sound, these black feminist burlesque performers access the queer uses of quiet, remaking the pubic space of the burlesque stage into an interior and intimate space of shared blackwoman erotic fantasy.

Brown Girls Burlesque creative producer Chicava HoneyChild Tate's performance "Evil Beautiful Sunshine" stands as an example of what I read as queer choreopoetic performance.[20] "Evil Beautiful Sunshine" illustrates this embodied storytelling in burlesque, and the place of wordlessness for expressing black queer feminist nuance, complexity, and community. Tate makes radical use of wordlessness to express subversive blackwoman desire and subjective complexity through the body. This creative act of bodily self-expression makes space for black queer feminist connection and community. A 2008 recording of the

Figure 2.5a. Chicava HoneyChild Tate performs "Evil Beautiful Sunshine"
(Movement 1: Eartha Kitt, "I Want to Be Evil"). Courtesy of Chicava Roslyn L. Tate.

performance at New York City's Zipper Room Cabaret (which Tate describes as
"a very black and queer space") illustrates how Tate uses the quiet expressions
of costuming, dance, and what Mireille Miller-Young terms "facial stunting"
work—a technique in which black women actors' pointed facial expressions
parody and critique the scenes they dramatize—to provide context for the language of the lyrics to which she dances, and to rearticulate those lyrics as erotic
critique (63).

Tate begins her performance dancing to Eartha Kitt's 1953 song, "I Want to be
Evil," in which Kitt laments: "I've posed for pictures with Iv'ry Soap/ I've petted
stray dogs, and shied clear of dope/ My smile is brilliant, my glance is tender/
But I'm noted most for my unspoiled gender."[21] Tate's white dress and playful
performance of bodily longing echo on the visual plane Kitt's lament about
"unspoiled" black femininity and sexual propriety, and mirrors the speaker's
deep desire for the freedom of sexual dissidence, the erotic power that comes
with being bad. As a still from the 2008 Zipper Room performance shows,
Tate's facial expressions articulate this longing, enacting "facial stunting"—a
particularly useful and resonant expressive strategy in silent film pornographic
genres (ibid.). Tate's facial stunting enacts both parodic and critical modes in its
exploration of the constraining purity Kitt's lyrics describe; her face tilted toward

Figure 2.5b & c. Chicava HoneyChild Tate performs "Evil Beautiful Sunshine" (Movement 2: Marilyn Manson, "The Beautiful People"). Courtesy of Chicava Roslyn L. Tate.

the spotlight in a longing gaze, she is at once enacting and overemphasizing the fantasy of youthful feminine purity that Kitt laments.

Tate's burlesque also highlights the construction and instability of this fantasy of "unspoiled" black womanhood, and the slim skin it shares with more complex modes of blackwoman eroticism. Seconds into her performance, the lights dim, signaling only subtly a new tone—more a dynamic shift of mood than a change of scene. In a repeating circular twirl that signals both playfulness and literal physical revolution, Tate sheds the "Iv'ry" costume and begins to dance to the harder metal beat of Marilyn Manson's "The Beautiful People," clad in scraps of leather and clasping an oversize fringe whip. The absence of lyrics here amplifies Tate's choreopoetic body/language in this part of the dance as she becomes the "evil" woman Kitt's speaker yearns to be, performing erotic power, dominance, and joy wordlessly as a room full of women shout their appreciation.

As the dance continues, Tate's bodily expression becomes increasingly vigorous and emphatic. Her cartwheels and splits occasion a form of call-and-response that performs a community-building function not unlike that which Cheryl Clarke and others find in Shange's choreopoetic form, and particularly in the climactic "layin on of hands" with which the choreopoem closes (98). Yet, here, Tate's performance queers and completes the fraught call-and-response of Shange's opening scene; in Tate's performance, it is the explicitly erotic, desiring, wordless body that makes the successful call for verbal touch and connection. This yearning for queer connection reaches its realization as Tate's performance shifts to its final movement. Lying supine, Tate undresses and covers her body slowly with a sheer yellow cloth as the hit 1967 song "Aquarius/Let the Sunshine In" by The Fifth Dimension—the full title of which is, aptly, "Let the Sunshine In (The Flesh Failures)"—is heard. As she dances playfully around the stage once again—this time nude, her movements broader and the sun-yellow cloth flying freely through the space of the stage—the audience spontaneously joins in the song and sings loudly along. As the still image from the Zipper Room performance suggests, this participation is not only a vocal but also a bodily engagement; the audience members' raised and clapping hands traverse the boundary between spectator and stage. Simultaneously, in the recording, we hear women's voices singing and laughing as the audience takes part in the play, pleasure, and recognition that body/language enables, offering their voices to Tate's wordless performance of black erotic bodily joy.

Tate's performance demonstrates the great potential of body/language for black queer women's self-expression and connection, and the transformative potential of the haptic (Campt 8). Moving quietly in a scape of several sounds, she accesses multiple nuanced modes of blackwoman subjectivity and inner life: she is playful and longing, dominant and desirous, powerful and contemplative as she invites her audience to experience *and express* the queer simultaneity of multiple

Figure 2.5d. Chicava HoneyChild Tate performs "Evil Beautiful Sunshine" (Movement 3: Aquarius, "Let the Sunshine In [The Flesh Failures]"). Courtesy of Chicava Roslyn L. Tate.

modes of black girl being. Here, we see, as The Lady Ms. Vagina Jenkins puts it, as mentioned earlier, "how graceful one becomes dancing at the intersections of race, class, gender, and sexuality" (McDaniel, "PHOTO Essay").[22] Yet around this "grace," Tate's body/language intertwines other interior modes such as anger, desire, longing, and rage, using the expressivity of the body to articulate what Quashie terms "the full range of [the character's] inner life" (6). By inviting the audience to supply language for the complex subjectivity expressed in her erotic performance, Tate's burlesque reconstitutes the expressivity of quiet according to a queer iteration of what Clarke terms a "black feminist communalism," in which collectivity and shared expressions of community affirm and empower the black woman erotic self (Clarke, *After Mecca* 94). In Tate's performance, quiet is concerned with both interiority *and* publicness; it works to express the "desires, ambitions, hungers, vulnerabilities, [and] fears" of blackwoman erotic subjectivity, and to use that expressive embodiment to reshape the space of the burlesque theater into a public for shared blackwoman pleasure.

In his essay "The Trouble with Publicness: Toward a Theory of Black Quiet," Quashie considers, provocatively: "Could the concept of quiet help to articulate a different kind of expressiveness, or even stand as a metaphor for the interior? In everyday discourse, quiet is synonymous with silence and is the absence of sound or movement, but for the idea of quiet to be useful . . . it will need to be understood as a quality or sensibility of being, as a manner of expression. Such expressiveness is not concerned with publicness, but instead is the expressiveness of the interior" (333). Black queer women's choreopoetic thinking responds to this provocation through the many tones and movements of the body, using the body as a way to productively communicate "the full range" of black women's erotic and subjective interiority in ways that spoken language (alone) cannot. This, for Tate, is the function of bodily expression of the erotic. When asked if she ever mouths or sings song lyrics during her performances, Tate states: "That's not a part of my work . . . To mouth the words is to need to do something outside to signify. Are you doing this outside signifier as an expression of something that's happening on the inside, or because of a lack of something happening on the inside?"[23] For Tate, words and lyrics are important external context for the stories burlesque seeks to tell, but it is the body speaks the language of the interior.

Through the creative technologies of body/language, Lenelle Moïse, Zanele Muholi, and Chicava HoneyChild Tate rethink the bounds between publicness and interiority, trauma and pleasure, embodiment and speech. These artists write black women's bodies as tools for the expression of their dazzlingly queer, complex lives, desires, and inner worlds. Through quiet gestures of pleasure, longing and critique, they create spaces where the interior galaxies of black womanhood find recognition, connection, and the expressive power of queer erotic life.

# CHAPTER THREE

# Feeling Colors and Seeing Speech

## *Body/Language and Black Women's Diasporas of Difference*

"[T]he next time someone asks me if I've seen the paper
I'll say / I've seen more news than is fit to print . . .
My households understand the rhythm of our lives
n speak colloquial universal language . . .
EXTRA EXTRA READ ALL ABOUT IT
ZIMBABWE CELEBRATES FIFTY YEARS OF INDEPENDENCE
EXTRA EXTRA READ ALL ABOUT IT
THOUSANDS OF WRITERS FLOCK TO INTERNATIONAL CONFERENCE
    ON FREE SPEECH IN ARGENTINA
EXTRA EXTRA READ ALL ABOUT IT
WHITE SOUTH AFRICANS DENIED ENTRY TO THE UNITED STATES AS
    WAR CRIMINALS
EXTRA EXTRA READ ALL ABOUT IT
CELEBRATION OF CAMPAIGN AGAINST NATIONAL ILLITERACY
    EPIDEMIC HELD IN BED-STUY"
—Ntozake Shange, *boogie woogie landscapes*, 126[1]

These are the declarations of a set of dreamed-up fantasy personae that appear to Layla, the black woman protagonist of American writer Ntozake Shange's 1978 staged long poem, *boogie woogie landscapes*. Layla imagines voicing these transnational black news headlines after eating the pages of several different newspapers from the *Philadelphia Inquirer* to the *Zimbabwe Herald* to the *New York Times*. She scarfs the "gritty" pages in hopes that "news of the outside world would soothe her," only to find that, like the bland, meatless papers themselves, their telling of "the outside world was black & white & thin like where she lived." "She never thought," the speaker states, "people places or ideas were anything but black & white/ no one printed books in colors" (*three pieces* 116).

This provocative scene from one of Shange's least-known works illuminates the relationships between body, language, and transnational identification in black women's writing. For Shange, and for a number of other genre-bending contemporary women writers of the diaspora, language is at its most expressive when it becomes a part of the body, and it is only through "rhythm[ic]" amalgamations of word and flesh that full mappings of the world can be forged. Shange's body/language here is part of a larger move in twentieth- and twenty-first-century black women's writing to push the limits of language, voice, and genre in order to highlight the nuantial complexities of blackwoman identity on a global stage.

## Diasporas of Difference: Reimagining Diaspora on Black Feminist Terms

Chapters 1 and 2 explored the poetics of difference as a means of complicating interpretations of black / queer experience in African Diaspora literary cultures. I shift now to consider the functions of the poetics of difference as a black queer feminist interpretive strategy and creative methodology that forwards anti-normative critiques for queer and non-queer black feminist communities on a transnational scale. In the chapters that follow, the poetics of difference serve not only to make claims about black queer women's experience, but also to insist on a nuantial hermeneutic of the interstice—that is, on queer ways of reading that are constantly attentive to the nuantial, interstitial, and intersecting dimensions of blackwoman subjectivity and political life. Building on Shange's logics of textual embodiment as a mode of diasporic connection, this chapter explores the relationships between body and voice as creative tools for reimagining diaspora on black feminist terms. I focus specifically on the ways in which contemporary black women US-born playwright Shange, Trinbagonian Canadian poet M. NourbeSe Philip, and queer Afro-Cuban hip-hop group Krudxs Cubensi (also known as Las Krudas) deploy an embodied poetics of difference to redefine black and to map queer and intersectional frameworks of diaspora. Taking up the poetry collection and choreopoem versions of *for colored girls* alongside the 1982 telefilm adaptation of the text and Shange's 1981 play-in-poems, *A Daughter's Geography*, this chapter first examines how black women writers write heterogeneities of voice onto the bodies of their characters. I then consider how body/languages perform similar work in black feminist poetic form and performance, particularly in Philip's poem, "Discourse on the Logic of Language" and Lxs Krudxs's song and music video, "La Gorda," which centers on a fat black woman.

These writers create what I term "body/language": a set of linguistic modes in which black women's bodies articulate their multiple nonnormative subject positions and use a complex model of difference to reinscribe identity and community on black queer feminist terms. In chapter 2, body / language is understood as a formal means of expressing the queerness of nuantial subjectivity. In this chapter, I consider the implications of body/language for signifying

Afrodiasporic identifications through a queer black poetic *reading strategy* and *methodology*; in their use of body/language, Shange, Philip, and Lxs Krudxs reframe the body as inextricable from the heterogeneous voice and position both as tools for reconceiving black communication, identification, and community across global space.

This focus on queer readings of embodiment is crucial to feminist models of diaspora; in this chapter I also consider the implications of body/language for signifying Afrodiasporic identifications. By articulating black women's communities through a corporeality that signals difference, these writers create what I call "diasporas of difference": networks of boundary-crossing identification and communication organized according to the multiplicities of blackwoman difference across stages, pages, genres, and texts.

By using black women's interstitial difference as a conceptual starting point for understanding both the interconnectedness of diasporic locations and the complexities of black identity in specific diaspora locales, diasporas of difference allow for simultaneous, anti-hierarchical recognition of black multiplicities. They comprise a tradition in black feminist literary and artistic practice in which, as Samantha Pinto points out, "Diaspora becomes not only a set of physical movements, then, but also a set of aesthetic and interpretive strategies" (*Difficult Diasporas* 6). Yet in their aesthetic and interpretive formulation of black globalities, diasporas of difference take as their specific starting point the interlocking power dynamics of race, gender, nation, sex, and sexuality—as well as the subjective coils of pain, pleasure, fantasy, and desire that constitute black women's interstitial difference.

The project of articulating a diasporic identity is inevitably fraught. Yet, rejecting any attempt to express the multiple identifications between, among, and within black subjectivities in diaspora risks not only misunderstanding diasporic blackness in general, but also recapitulating the erasure of black women as diasporic subjects. Imagining linguistic articulation of diaspora as an unreachable vision also obscures the crucial political work of many black feminist writers. These writers' poetics work not to "translate" black women's experience from one grammar of identity to another, but rather to expose the multiplicities of diaspora through *new* languages that are better able to articulate interstitial subjectivities. By writing these languages as inseparable from black women's embodiment (through body/language), they use poetic form to "reconsider the primacy of location and the geography of bodies that often defines" diaspora and feminist studies, while also deploying black feminist models of embodiment to create new languages for articulating diaspora (ibid. 9).[2]

Afrodiasporic feminist writers' diasporas of difference communicate those differences of identity that might otherwise escape language, and push the bounds of "diaspora" and "difference"' simultaneously. They reconfigure hierarchical models of difference to do the formal work of what Brent Edwards calls *décalage* (exposing the overlapping differences of black diasporic experience through language).[3] If, as Edwards puts it, "a discourse of diaspora articulates difference, then one must consider the status of that difference—not just linguistic difference but, more broadly, the trace or residue, perhaps, of what resists or escapes translation" (*The Practice of Diaspora* 13). Rather than yield to diaspora's "resist[ance]" to translation, diasporas of difference develop new modes of articulating diasporic space and identity, models constructed specifically to express the "missing" interstices of difference that language cannot otherwise hold (Spillers "Interstices" 156).

Important critical conceptions of diaspora by Edwards, Paul Gilroy, and others acknowledge difference as a major theoretical component of diasporic experience; yet the range of possibilities this difference presents for illuminating the interconnectedness of race, gender, class, sexuality, and other differences, as well as the implications of such a difference-based diaspora for Afrodiasporic poetics, have yet to be fully explored. Diasporas of difference move away from hierarchical of theorizations of diaspora that rely on "internal" and "external" differences as the defining contours of the diaspora concept. Instead, I propose a horizontal weave of "simultaneous . . . and interlocking" differences to map diaspora (Combahee River Collective 272). In diasporas of difference, "blackness" is always already inflected with gender, age, sexuality, class, and more. Here, the "external" differences of nation and geographical location remain intact as sites of identification across space, but they also serve as signifiers of subjective boundary crossing and cross-difference identification.[4]

In presenting the nuantial space of the interstice as a grounds for viewing multiple difference, diasporas of difference draw on recent feminist and queer theories of diaspora, as well as theories centered specifically on the "new African diaspora" (produced by economic and political displacements beginning in the mid–twentieth century). These theories have begun to destabilize vertical hierarchical models of diasporic subjectivity, and to examine the simultaneity of diasporic identifications. Filipina feminist critic Neferti Xina M. Tadiar's notion of "personal diaspora" as a means of describing several forms of affective belonging and Louise Shabat Bethlehem's description of international and cross-geographic identifications as diasporic "double-crossings" are useful in examining the place of plural, concurrent geographic identifications in diaspora. Yet, in their efforts to address diasporic plurality, these models rely, on one hand, on a limited quantification of a "doubled" difference, which ultimately cannot account for the innumerability of diasporic differences, or, on the other hand, on the overly abstract mode of the "personal," which risks obscuring the specificities of the multiple identifications it aims to hail (Tadiar 253; Bethlehem 264). In this binary of quantification and abstraction, such models fail to provide means of addressing the crucial specificity of African derivation, enslavement, colonization, and neocolonialism that shape African diasporic movement.

Diasporas of difference address these concerns by maintaining "blackness" as a legible identificatory marker of diaspora but expanding it to include a nexus of differences that range from the personal to the geographic and beyond. Each of these discourses speaks to what is arguably the major challenge facing twenty-first-century diaspora theorizing: the need to reconcile what Edwards, Gilroy, and others frame as the "external" differences of blackness that they find at the core of diaspora with the "internal" differences of gender, class, nation, ethnicity, and sexuality that define specific bodies' experiences of blackness in global space.

Black feminist writers' body/languages write past this problem by taking the nuance of intersectional embodiment—the fleshy site of the interstice—as a language of definition and a point of departure into geographies of global black space. They use the body to construct languages that articulate and expand what Katherine McKittrick has termed the "demonic grounds" on which black women author geographic and spatial subjectivity. For McKittrick, black women writers' literary engagements with space allow for the production of "black feminist geographies": "black women's political, feminist, imaginary, and creative concerns that respatialize the geographic legacy of racism-sexism" (53). Shange, Philip, and Krudxs Cubensi demonstrate the queer dimensions of such a black feminist geography when it is mobilized as creative praxis and show how queer readings of embodiment are central to feminist visions of diaspora. Rooting their re-worldings specifically in a poetics of the nuantial—that is, in a black feminist rejection of intersectional power and silencing specifically at the site of the nonnormative blackwoman body—these artists demonstrate models of diaspora that escape masculinist and patriarchal conceptions of global blackness by insistently attending to several queerness of blackwoman bodily experience (Spillers *Black, White, and in Color* 15). By undertaking their creative respatializing projects specifically through the multiple, simultaneous expressivities of blackwoman bodies, these writers and artists develop black feminist geographies that not only renegotiate the nexuses of racism and sexism, but that also expose connections between racism, sexism, and interconnected structures of nation, sexuality, and (non)normative embodiment. By articulating their black feminist geographies through body/language, these writers move beyond the hierarchical paradigms of "external" and "internal" difference that others have proposed, which subordinate gender, sexuality, and desire to ostensibly more central priorities of race and blackness. Black feminist writers' diasporas of difference acknowledge these defining heterogeneities of global blackness by depicting boundary-crossing identifications that are shaped by both membership in specific identity groups (for example, race, gender, class, ethnicity), and by an intimate identification with a wider, antihierarchical horizontal axis of difference. They thus work against the carefully constructed, received, and protected fantasies of a coherent blackness whose primary variables on the global stage occur on the grounds of nationality and geography. They extend the work of queer diasporas, "transDiasporas," and "personal diasporas," presupposing intersectional experience as the central locus of its diasporic identificatory ties and bridging not only geographic locations, but also social locations and modes of embodiment, expression, and desire.[5]

These writers construct their characters' and speakers' bodies not merely as vehicles for enacting a larger articulation of a stable "external" transnational blackness, but rather as organs or limbs of a larger body whose distinct parts converge, disperse, and, most importantly, *converse* through difference as they move toward new meanings of diaspora—meanings to which black women's political, subjective, and bodily multiplicities are central.

## Locating Blackness as the "Color" of Difference

Many critics have explored *for colored girls* as a voicing of blackwoman collectivity, with analyses that vary from the celebratory, to the dismissive, to the punitive. Writing on iterations of *for colored girls* from the 1974 West Coast production of the choreopoem through Tyler Perry's controversial 2010 film adaptation, critics have noted the presence of a heterogeneous voice of difference and collectivity in the text. Critic Jean Young, for example, reads the poetic structure of the choreopoem as an effort "to evoke the collective power of voice" in a communal black feminist self-affirmation through black diasporic call-and-response strategies (300). Shange corroborates this notion, considering the text an "individual" work resultant of a "collective effort" of writers, dancers, and musicians working in the Bay Area at the time of the work's development (Anderlini 89). Conversely, Robert Staples's editorial, "The Myth of Black Macho: A Response to Angry Black Feminists," which appeared in *The Black Scholar* in 1979, exemplifies an expansive body of male-authored criticism of the choreopoem, arguing that Shange's protagonists are joined primarily not by shared experiences of black womanhood, but by "a collective appetite for black male blood" (26).

Despite their divergent (and, in many cases, masculinist) perspectives on the text, these assessments of the poetics of *for colored girls* all succeed in identifying its crucial linking of black gender and vocal heterogeneity. Yet both popular feminist and patriarchal critiques fail to acknowledge the text's central set of creative objectives, which reflect a crucial aggregate of concerns for contemporary black women writers more broadly. *for colored girls* uses its collective vocalities not simply to celebrate black womanhood or to critique black masculinity, but rather to emphasize the expressive technologies of the body through multiplicities of voice and to use the expressive body to complicate blackwoman community across global space.

Read through an interstitial hermeneutics, the heteroglossic collective in *for colored girls* serves not only as a metaphor for the nuances of black women's difference, but as a set of embodied markers of a diaspora rearticulated in black feminist terms. As Cheryl Clarke points out, the text is both "a feminist communal project and a representation of nascent (black) feminist community" across cultures (*After Mecca* 98). For Clarke, Shange's "revision of Afro-American call and response, Afro-American folk rituals, and the pastiche of signifiers from other diaspora cultures [allow black women to] function synecdochally for women of color and indeed all women—in community" (98). This understanding of the simultaneously cross-cultural and feminist core of the text's heteroglossic collective illuminates Shange's interventions into conceptions of African diaspora. However, reading *for colored girls* through a lens of voice and expression rather than "representation" and visual iconography (as Clarke does) reveals a further nuance of Shange's transnationalism. By melding choreographic motions of the body with poetic movements of the voice, Shange's text creates a model of black diasporic women's identity that is written on the body, echoed through the voice, and tuned to critique dominant assumptions about both. Working on both the form of her heterogeneous genre and on the bodies of her heteroglossic cast, Shange's expressive corporealities allow her to produce a blackwoman diasporic identity forged through "nuance," "singularity," and interstitial difference (*Nappy Edges* 6, 3).

Shange's use of body/language makes several interventions into contemporary models of diaspora identification. If, as playwright Glenda Dickerson suggests, "the language of oppression is the same the world over"—or if, at least, the world's various languages of oppression share common fundamental grammatical structures and orthographies—body/language serves as a means of counter-discourse, a move toward freeing black women's subjectivities from the many grammars that link interstitial experiences of oppression in the diaspora ("The Cult of True Womanhood" 180). It straddles what Saussure terms a "langue" and a "langage," constituting a mode of communication and expression that, like diaspora, is as integrally rooted to communicative regulations of the "social body" as to the technologies of the "individual" human form (9). Moving beyond the "basic grammar of blackness" that "official" conceptions of black internationalism strive to write, body/language introduces corporeal signifiers of difference concurrent with, and analogous to, race but symbolic of difference more broadly (Edwards *The Practice of Diaspora* 9). Through this language, black feminist writers break down and reconfigure both human and poetic forms, expanding the technical mechanisms through which black women characters can speak, *and* creating new systems of signification around which diasporic women's communities of belonging can be imagined.[6]

Shange's body/language functions on two planes of embodiment: (1) it works on the generic and aesthetic bodies of her texts—that is, through the heteroglossic voices of the characters; the fusion of choreography, poetry, and drama within individual poems and within the choreopoem genre; the multiple typographies and formal modes she deploys in the print text; and the interconnections of black women's subjectivities that link various iterations of the text itself across genres and mediums; and (2) it works on the corporeal/fleshy bodies of Shange's characters, including the designations of "color" ascribed to each character; the movements, gestures, and bodily expressions mobilized in performances of the piece; and the movements of the characters across and through the space of the stage as articulated in the stage directions of the text.

Shange's theorization of "color" in the choreopoem version of *for colored girls* illuminates the transnational and diasporic potentials of body/language as a collectivizing idiom of difference written on the blackwoman body. For most critics, Shange's "color" acts as a metonym for gendered ideas about ethnicity and/or race. Clarke, for example, reads Shange's notion of "color" as an effort to extend her gender critique "beyond the specificity of black women," and as a reflection of "her multicultural feminist roots," in which the characters "function synecdochically for women of color and indeed all women—in community—recovering their voices and doing their work" to articulate a multiethnic "(black) feminist community" (98). Shange critic Neal Lester maintains this logic but reverses its gender focus, imagining the "colored girls" as representatives of "women of color specifically and people of color generally" ("At the Heart of Shange's Feminism" 718).

As these readings suggest, Shange's characters reflect a range of cultures over the course of both the choreopoem. Yet, read through an interstitial hermeneutics attentive to the languages of both voice *and* body, *for colored girls* shows the complexities of blackwoman difference *beyond* (though integrally linked to) the concerns of womanhood and race. While the color can be read as a racial or ethnic difference, Shange's insistence on assigning each character a distinct color suggests that her "ladies" cannot be read simply as identical members of a single identity group (black women). Nor does the difference of color signal a specific identity category (such as race or ethnicity); the fact that each of the ladies *wears* her color (rather than embodying it) suggests that the difference being presented is mutable, performative, and polysemous.

Shange's "color" expands the faulty racial/ethnic significations of skin color as an indicator of coherent blackness, emphasizing instead the illimitability of blackwoman difference and the linkages race and gender bear to subjective but equally bodily experiences of blackwoman pain, pleasure, feeling, and desire. In both the collection and the choreopoem, Shange introduces "colored girls" nominally linked by gender and visible differences of racial "color"—that is, black embodiment. Yet the action and language of each text reveal that what ultimately connects these figures is the nexus of this racialized embodiment and the subjective and interior experiences of interstitial blackwoman difference itself. In other words, Shange's "color" signifies a shifting legible bodily marker of the multiplicity of black women's difference.

This is most clearly articulated by the choreopoem's Lady in Orange, as she states "I cdnt stand bein sorry & colored at the same time/ it's so redundant in the modern world," and by the Lady in Yellow, who proclaims famously that "bein alive & bein a woman & bein colored is a metaphysical dilemma/ I haven't conquered yet" (46, 48). Color, for Shange, figures as a condition of multiple "sorrow[s]" that cannot be disambiguated simply along the lines of race or gender, and to which subjective and interior experiences of difference are as important as—and, in fact, inseparable from—blackness and womanhood.

As exemplars of complex difference, Shange's "colored girls" embody Spillers's vision of "the *nuantial*" in black women's identity. For Spillers,

> winning the right to the *nuantial* . . . goes with the territory of subjecthood, which must be *earned* for some; it is also intimately proximate to "sexuality." In order to name black women in the sexual, the investigator is obliged to back all the way up to that suspenseful chapter in the unfolding of subjecthood, which begins for Africanity in the West *not* with a body (which one sees well enough) but what the body was made to *mean* via the powerful grammars of capture. ("Peter's Pans" 15)

The "right" to express complex black subjectivity is thus "earned" and made legible through bodies specifically marked to make meaning in the context of "powerful" historical languages and narratives. The differences Shange's speakers and protagonists perform are subversively subjectifying "nuan[ces]" of identity that insert themselves into historical and social narratives of black women's identity, not simply through voice and not simply through bodies, but through corporeal expressions and reconfigured forms that speak collective, heterogeneous experiences of black womanhood. Shange uses color to paint heteroglossias of difference on the stage, making visible the inexhaustible nuance of blackwoman subjectivity.

Through Shange's choreopoetic body/language, "color" becomes not only a signifier of concurrent "sorr[ows]," but also a way to express fuller black women's identities and map communities that produce blackwoman joy. After the characters have forged their initial connection through body/language, the Lady in Blue reflects on her feelings of hopelessness, stating, rhetorically: "we deal wit emotion too much/ so why don't we go on ahead & be white then/ & make everythin dry & abstract wit no rhythm & no reelin for sheer sensual pleasure" (*for colored girls* 47). Whiteness, here, is figured as an inversion of "color" and all its meanings; it signals the absence of racial/ethnic/skin color *and* the absence of feeling, rhythm, and "pleasure." Shange's "color" signals not only interstitial sorrow, but also the capacity of taking *pleasure* in the nuantial site of the interstice, and the possibility of community defined by shared pleasure taken in the nuantial self. Color makes possible an inter-subjective and inter-identitarian community rooted in the "sheer sensual pleasure" of difference.

This community of difference has marked implications for Shange's conception of textual and performative space as metaphors for Afrodiasporic space. Through their difference-based body/language, Shange's characters work to create what the central figure of the untitled third poem in the Shameless Hussy Press poetry collection version of *for colored girls* calls "some other place to be held" (8). Through Shange's collective of "color," the stage becomes such a "place," accommodating the characters' concurrent alterities and providing them the means for both individual self-affirmation and shared embraces with others marked by interstitial difference.

In using color to signal difference, Shange's body/language applies a cosmopolitan ethic to the humanist communitarian principles of black feminist thought. Kwame Anthony Appiah argues cosmopolitanism holds the potential to vision a collective "global tribe" in which humans acknowledge connections across lines of difference, and also demonstrate a "universal concern and respect for legitimate difference." While Appiah frames his model of cosmopolitanism as a response to changes in cross-cultural and international relationships prompted by the acceleration of globalization, he also notes that the individual is as important as the national in the cosmopolitan worldview. As he states, "people are different, the cosmopolitan knows, and there is much to learn from our difference" (xv). The metaphorical resonances of color are central to transnational communal model of difference. As Appiah states:

> Color language is a good example of the way in which basic features work for most normal people. . . . Someone who was raised inside a house where everything was painted black or white, wore only those colors, was surrounded by people dressed likewise, and was exposed only to black and white food, and so forth could understand only those color terms . . . Whether you have a word for the color purple, on the other hand, won't just depend on whether you've ever seen the something purple; it will depend, too, on the resources of your language. (*Cosmopolitanism* 96)

The perception of color differences is a universal process of human functioning; yet, organizing and making meaning of color depends on the variables of language, culture, and communication. Shange takes up this use of color as a communicator of difference; by refusing to itemize the many differences her colors symbolize, she points to difference as a linguistic "resource" for understanding human experience and making interpersonal connections. What is important to Shange is that difference ultimately works constructively within what Patricia Hill Collins calls a "humanist vision of community" (Black Feminist Thought 201). Shange issues "a communitarian call and an insistence upon a multilingual affront to any centrality—be it language, music, choreography or geography—except 'blackness'" (Clarke, *After Mecca* 104). Yet in writing "blackness" as a "color" always already inflected by gender and a multiply-signifying "sorrow," she destabilizes even race as a "central" trope of blackwoman community. In this sense, Shange's black feminist formulation of "color" anticipates and critiques the rise of color-blindness as a racialist cultural paradigm in the late twentieth century. Anthony Reed points out that as "a hermeneutic and mechanism for shaping allowable discourse, color blindness incorporates, co-opts, or suppresses difference, narrowing and policing the range of the thinkable and imaginable while presenting itself as the imperfect culmination of past struggles" (*Freedom Time* 1). By positioning "color" as the defining language of both her characters' individual subjectivities (as "Lady in Brown," "Lady in Red," and so forth) and of their collective identity (as the group of "colored girls" for whom the text is named and dedicated), Shange constructs an important interpretive barrier to the dismissal of (racial) difference that Reed discusses, while simultaneously *expanding* the fields on which blackness can (and must) be thought by defining it specifically through a poetics of ongoing black feminist critique.

Shange's logic of multiple differences of identity collected in a single visible trope is repeated in the Lady in Green's famous declaration "somebody almost walked off wid alla my stuff" (52). Here, "stuff" figures as a consolidation of complex, heterogeneous identity, without which she is unable to "hang out in [her] own self." This model of "stuff" also participates in Shange's body/language, as the Lady in Green describes her lost "stuff" as "my arm wit the hot iron scar/ & my leg wit the flea bite/ I want my calloused feet & quick language back in my mouth" (58). Like "color," "stuff" signals both difference *and* the power to speak that difference through the body.

Through technologies of song and movement, color and touch, Shange's body/language deploys a poetics of difference that re-anatomizes genre and re-articulates the meanings of black women's embodiment. As her "colored girls" dance, sing, feel, and speak themselves free from "sequester . . . in the monolith" of black representation, they paint the stage as polychromatic a space of subjective possibility (*Nappy Edges* 6). Shange's "rainbow" of blackwoman difference forms a corporeal counterpart of the heteroglossic play of voices that joins the "colored girls" in the choreopoem's opening scene, and gestures toward the communitivizing functions of interstitial difference. Through their body/language, the characters reveal "color" not only as a set of signifiers of difference, but also as a communalizing experience, a collective bodily state as intimate as a hand-clapping game or a shared dance to a familiar "black-girl's song." In this act of liberation, Shange's characters (and, by extension her variously "colored" readers) are free to forge connections across boundaries of difference and to reimagine the planes on which identification across difference is possible.

## Mapping Diasporas of Difference

As an African American writer, Shange is a complicated but important figure through which to begin an exploration of black feminist poetic diasporas. Because she is a US writer exploring diasporic experience from a vantage point of cultural US-centric power and privilege within the neocolonial economies of twentieth-century global culture, Shange's perspective on diaspora is necessarily shaped and boundaried, at least to some degree, by some of the very power structures she works to critique. At the same time, Shange's black American feminist vision of diaspora extends and critiques the many other black American models of globality through which we often understand blackness and black literary expression at the close of the century. For example, Shange's interventions into Black Arts–era models of blackness force us to consider blackness not only as a gendered phenomenon, as Clarke suggests, but also as one whose gendering takes on meaning and import within a specifically intersectional framework to which nation and ethnicity are central. Likewise, her poetics insert intersectional models of gendering into US-based Pan Africanist and Afrocentrist visions of black global space, ultimately suggesting that twentieth-century blackness cannot be fully articulated except through an intersectional lens that prioritizes both gender and nation as constant facts of blackness.[7] Shange's diasporas of difference demonstrate how, for black women, historically specific structures of American racism have never been the only defining factor of black difference. For black feminist writers, black literature—and blackness itself—have always been intersectional and always multiply located; its languages of (re)production, articulation, and circulation have always constantly created themselves anew.[8]

For many black feminist writers, the viability of a new model of diaspora depends largely on its ability to reconceive transnational collectivity so that it not only acknowledges *but is shaped by* the ever presence of difference. Black feminist diasporas of difference thus work to reconceive the spatial dimensions of difference and reimagine the identificatory capabilities of space through form and language.[9] Black feminist writers' diasporas of difference call into question critical claims that the full complexity of diasporic difference necessarily "resists or escapes translation" (Edwards *The Practice of Diaspora* 13). Shange's poetics challenge the assumption that diaspora's defining differences are inexpressible. Her strategy of "coloring" black women's bodies with the nuances of interstitial difference transforms spaces of diaspora such that they allow for communication and, indeed, "translation" of diasporic identifications and experiences specifically through difference. Shange's body/language offers a creative response to what Houston Baker terms the "tight place" into which black identity is historically inscribed through social narrative (Baker, *Turning South Again* 15). Shange illustrates that these constraints on black subjectivities are imposed not by the fact of Afrodiaspora or its complex configurations but by the ways in which dominant languages and ideologies limit the expression of black difference. Her fusions of body, voice, and black subjective complexity offer a radical idiom for expressing the multiplicities and nuances of blackness that enslavement, imperialism, and global oppressions—rather than the nature of diaspora itself—render untranslatable.

For Shange, the technologies of choreopoetic body/language play a crucial role in in re-inscribing diasporic collectivity. Again, one goal of the choreopoem form is to free Afrodiasporic identity from constraints of colonial language. The conscription of black identity occurs not only through social narrative, but also through constraints of genre. As Shange states, "'the perfect play,' as we know it to be/ a truly European framework for European psychology/ cannot function efficiently for those of us from this hemisphere" (*three pieces* ix). For Shange, Western generic constrictions of a mute choreography funneling narrative exclusively through the body, a static poetry extricable from corporeality and bodily experience, or a drama in which music, lyric, and gesture are merely incidental to plot are all inadequate for telling stories of blackwoman difference. By subverting these constructions, the choreopoem form emerges not as a deconstruction of genre altogether, but as a counter-genre defined explicitly by its multiplicity. It offers an escape route through which black transnational identity can be freed to express a fuller range of body and voice simultaneously. Yet, in naming the genre through terms that explicitly hail multiplicity, Shange positions the choreopoem as a generic a parallel to "Afrodiasporic blackness"—a designator of a heterogeneous identification that exposes and articulates several layers of difference.

Shange's 1981 play-in-poems, *A Daughter's Geography*, demonstrates the collectivizing functions of Shange's diasporas of difference. In this text, as in *for colored girls*, Shange's heterogeneous narrative and poetic strategies introduce models of black diasporic identification in which "unifying" signifiers of race and differentiating markers of nation are reoriented around black women's interstitial identity. In these reimagined diasporas, "blackness" is recalibrated through Shange's model of "color" as signaling not only race but also the differences of gender, sexuality, and class/power, as well as the differences of unquantifiable "singularity" Shange emphasizes (*Nappy Edges* 6). In complicating blackness to include the many differences black women represent, Shange also complicates diaspora's defining differences—those of geography and nation. In diasporas of difference, geographic and national identifications remain crucial loci for the specification of transnational black identity, yet they also take on larger resonance as metaphors for other forms of connection and boundary crossing.[10]

*A Daughter's Geography* exemplifies the logics of black women's diasporas of difference and points to the interplay of genre, diaspora, and body/language in other black feminist explorations of black globality. The piece was first staged in 1981 as *Mouths: A Daughter's Geography: A Performance Piece* at New York City's Kitchen theater. The following year, it was produced as *Triptych and Bocas: A Performance Piece* at Mark Taper Theatre Lab in Los Angeles and then published as a section in Shange's 1983 poetry collection, *A Daughter's Geography*, as "Bocas: A Daughter's Geography."[11] As these titles indicate, what unites the piece in each of its generic iterations is a central concern with mapping woman-centered geographic spaces imagined in terms of speech, performance, and relationships of belonging.

Through its form and structure, *A Daughter's Geography* maps a multinational community consistent with the logics of a diaspora of difference. Of the ten poetic "scenes" that comprise *A Daughter's Geography*, seven directly address social and political crises impacting African diaspora locales toward the end of the twentieth century. These include, for example, urban poverty in the favelas of Brazil, the violence corruption of Jean-Claude Duvalier's regime in Haiti, and the Atlanta child murders of 1979–1981.[12] This international scope is echoed within each of the individual poems, in which Shange uses the specificity of place to invoke ironic ubiquities of oppression throughout the diaspora. While the title of each of these scenes references a specific diaspora locale, the reader quickly learns that Shange's Haiti, for example, is inseparable from "niggahs in philadelphia" and from "all the prostitutes/in . . . el barrio . . . from santo domingo," and that the Brazilian city of Itapuã is chilled by "winds as rough as [New York's] avenue 'c'" (*A Daughter's Geography* 5, 8). Yet, interspersed among what critics have termed the play's explicitly "third-world" anti-oppressive interventions are personal narratives of black women's erotic, intimate, and bodily lives. In this structure, Shange emphasizes black women's love, desire, intimacy, and pleasure as crucial to global "histories of oppression" and larger diasporic identifications. Shange offers what we might read as a black feminist iteration of "Malungaje," which, as Jerome Branch points out, is a Bantu-derived term used in colonial Brazil to designate "my comerade-with-whom-i-shared-the-misfortune-of-the-big-canoe-that-crossed-the-ocean" (*The Poetics and Politics of Diaspora* 2). In *A Daughter's Geography*, the traumas of global black history are inseparable from subjective experiences of pain, and both are crucial in forging identifications and alliances across black space. For Shange, it is only by traveling through the personal that the political dynamics of black globality can be reached.

Perhaps because of its multi-genre trajectory, the Historical Dictionary of African American Theatre refers to *A Daughter's Geography* as "a choreopoem"

(444). This label, however, is incomplete. Like *for colored girls*, *A Daughter's Geography* is a stage work comprised of several poems. Unlike the choreopoem, however, the text of *A Daughter's Geography* does not feature a cast or chorale of speakers; its front matter lists only one "character," named "Speaker," who delivers each poem as a monologue. And where *for colored girls* features movement and choreography as the entwined means of its collective expression of blackwoman difference, *A Daughter's Geography* develops its body/language by narrating the construction of black women's bodies that reconfigure diaspora through poetry and prose.

While problems of race- and class-based oppression are consistent links in Shange's diasporas of difference, structural and linguistic elements in *A Daughter's Geography* reveal the centrality of gender, feminist sensibilities, and a broader concern with interstitial "singularity" to Shange's model of diaspora.[13] She insists on the interrelatedness and (sometimes literal) translatability of the experiences of different peoples of color, to the extent that one contemporary reviewer claimed that "the major theme of the book [in which the play's appears] . . . is that Third-World peoples are united by a long history and current oppression" (Honey "A Sensibility of Struggle and Hope" 111).

Yet, *A Daughter's Geography* enacts its critique of such "third-world" oppressions through an explicitly feminist lens that privileges interstitial difference and nuantial experiences of the body as a language of transnational connection. Interspersed among the play's explicitly "third-world" anti-oppressive interventions are narratives that, in their focus on intimate relationships, domesticities, and interior evolutions may seem, at first, to depart from the global and transnational concerns of Shange's geography. For example, in "You are Sucha Fool," the third scene of the play, the speaker issues a dulcet, playful second-person address to a lover foolish enough to "give me/the poet [] the poem" (*A Daughter's Geography* 1981, 6).[14] While the poem bears traces of Shange's global sensibility (she remarks on the lover's tendencies to "speak spanish like a german & ask puerto rican [] marketmen on lexington if they are foreigners," and revels in the lover's ability to make her feel "like the sub-saharan animal i am"), it is ostensibly and primarily a love poem, exploring similar cross-genre intimacies as those that characterize "Between A Dancer and a Poet" and the choreopoem version of *for colored girls* (5–6). Shange reinforces the speaker's relationships to intimacy, interiority, and love regularly and systematically throughout the play, positioning narratives of Afrodiasporic women's embodiment, sexuality, and "love" literally at the center of her discussion of black diasporic politics.

By situating feminist intimacies and embodiments at the center of global politics, Shange maps a diaspora defined by both a feminist perspective on personal violence, trauma, and healing *and* by the political circumstances of global black genocide, trauma, and liberation, showing how global black politics and transnational feminist politics are, for black women, one and the same. Critics in various discursive traditions have warned of the dangers of theoretically side-stepping these that Gilroy terms the often violent "push factors" of diaspora and over-abstracting diaspora from its original political and social context (*The Black Atlantic* 207).[15] As Malawian historian Paul Zeleza notes, "If the term 'diaspora' is to retain analytical specificity, it has to be conceived in some bounded way, but not too narrowly if it is to remain useful. . . . Diasporas are complex social and cultural communities created out of real and imagined genealogies and geographies" ("Rewriting the African Diaspora" 41, 42).

Shange's diasporas of difference address this challenge by reading the complexity of diaspora as inseparable from what scholars have called the "complexity of intersectionality, mapping both onto the representational spaces of stage and text.[16]

Blackwoman love, desire, intimacy, and nonnormative embodiment are crucial to the global "histories of oppression" Shange's diaspora connects. The opening and closing scenes of *A Daughter's Geography*, titled "Bocas: A Daughter's Geography" and "New World Coro," form a poetic frame that articulates the problems of difference in diasporic identification. Citing several different diasporic locations from "cuba puerto rico charleston & savannah" to "angola . . . salvador & johannesburg," the speaker positions both herself and each diaspora location within a kinship network of thwarted communication in which, as she states,

> i have a daughter/ la habana
> i have a son/ Guyana
> our twins
> santiago & brixton/ cannot speak
> the same language
> yet we fight the same old men. (3, 13)

This refrain continues throughout both the opening and closing poems, linking various characters, stories, and diaspora locales in an identificatory network into which difference constantly inserts itself through language. Shange's "sameness" here takes on a crucial nuance much like that of her model of "singularity," in which the details of subjective difference constitute the furthest possible form of individuality (*Nappy Edges* 3). Here, "sameness" assumes a similarly subversive valence: it is pernicious in the hands of the "old men" who historically wield their sameness (that is, ostensibly, their whiteness, maleness, and power) as a means of oppressing diasporic people; yet, deployed as language shared by diaspora subjects in different locales, "sameness" holds potential for facilitating conversation across difference. The speaker's project in *A Daughter's Geography* is to create this missing language in order to allow diaspora people to forge not only anti-oppressive but *anti-normative* communications across difference.

This "language" not only connects stories of race- and class-based "third world oppression" in specific diaspora locales, but also links those critiques to broader explorations of gender, sexuality, and subjective experiences of trauma, pleasure, fantasy, and desire (Honey "A Sensibility of Struggle and Hope" 111). It joins the play's more explicitly nation-centered scenes (such as "Tween Itaparica & Itapua," and "A Black Night in Haiti, Palais National, Port-au-Prince," and "About Atlanta,") with less epic, more personal, geographically unspecific stories of women's emotional growth, psychic and spiritual survival, and processes of self-expression.

These stories of women's survival are crucial in the development of Shange's diasporic language of difference. The drama's sixth scene, "Some Men," extends the commentary on violent masculinities, domestic abuse, and rape, which Shange undertakes in both versions of *for colored girls*, and links these violences specifically to failures and abuses of language. "Some Men" is a third-person narrative poem about an abusive man who seduces, deceives, and rapes women in an effort to bolster his masculinity. Like the "ladylike" male figure in "Dancers," the subject of "Some Men" is a "pretty man who liked pretty things" (*A Daughter's Geography* 8–9). Yet where the former figure claims agency by subverting gender norms and is thus defined entirely by his gender nonconformity, the effete male figure in "Some Men" is defined by deceptive contrast: he surrounds himself with "dusty manuscripts," "vintage photographs," and "steadied scarlet tulips before French windows," yet he performs a brutish masculinity similar to that of the Lady in Orange's aggressor on the streets of Harlem and the abusive Beau Willie Brown in *for colored girls* (*A Daughter's Geography* 9). When the poem's black woman protagonist proves "[un]afraid" and un-intimidated by his display of masculine prowess in the form of material possession, he attempts to humble her by ordering her to "SUCK MY DICK & MAKE ME SOME COFFEE." Here, he issues a narrative and typographic rupture that emphasizes both black gender difference and the extreme dangers of absolute distinctions imposed upon masculinity and femininity in larger cultural dialogues (9).[17] That this command precedes the man's anal rape of the speaker may suggest a problematic reinforcement of homophobic narratives in which male "prettiness" and gender nonconformity are conflated with a queerness that is, in turn, conflated with sexual predation. Yet, Shange's speaker insists that the male figure's deficiency is not simply a dearth of appropriate masculinity or an inability to accept and manage his desire for feminine beauty; the figure also suffers from a general linguistic condition in which "men [] have no language that doesn't hurt [] a language that doesn't reduce what's whole [] to some part of nothing" (7).

This gendered failure of language is part and parcel of the diasporic linguistic fissure the speaker aims to bridge. "Some Men" maps the silence produced by linguistic incompatibilities of diaspora onto masculine failures to access what Shange elsewhere terms "emotional language" (Tate 156). These linguistic failures result in a situation in which, as the speaker puts it,

> some men would rather see us dead then imagine
> what we think of them/
> If we measure our silence by our pain
> how could all the words
> any word
> catch us up
> what is it
> we cd call equal (Shange *A Daughter's Geography* 9)

Just as the inability of the text's metaphorical diasporic "twins" to "speak the same language" prompts generations of mortal "hunger," women's silence about violent masculinities, confining femininities, and hegemonic normalcies results in death (13, 9). The fact that Shange does not offer any specific spatial or national identifiers in the 199 lines of this poem speaks to the pervasiveness of this condition throughout Shange's geography. Like the untranslated languages of the litany of countries and cultures with which Shange begins the play, languages of hegemonic masculinity produce a dangerous "silence" that renders black women, black men, and all other nonconforming subjects mortally vulnerable.

In *A Daughter's Geography*, as in *for colored girls*, Shange deploys body/language where verbal communications fail, solving problems of diasporic language by endowing it with flesh. The embodiment of expressions of difference that occurs through "color" and dance in *for colored girls* is made literal, textual, and explicit in the fourth scene of *A Daughter's Geography*. In the scene, titled "Oh, I'm Ten Months Pregnant," Shange continues her fusion of diasporic women's personal experience and black transnational politics, deploying pregnancy as a metaphor for gestation periods of both writing and revolution. Just as Shange refuses to reference national or geographic specificities in her gender critique in "Some Men," the sociopolitical valences of the speaker's figurative pregnancy in this poem remain subliminal; she reveals only that she is pregnant with a "baby [that] doesn't know she's not another poem." Instead, the speaker's account emphasizes the corporeal dimensions of this gestation, insisting that her "literary die-hard of a child" is "no mere choice of words." Much of the poem is given to the details of the "urine test & internal exam" that alert her to her pregnancy, the feeling of the doctor's "fingers . . . circling [her] swollen cervix," and the "amniotic bliss" of the "uterine cave," itself a metaphor for a spatial, physiological, and political situation in which the baby "can't move up till she comes out" (7).

The figurative birth of the over-developed baby reinforces Shange's use of body/language as a means of expressing difference and explains the place of embodied multiplicity in her diaspora of difference. The speaker announces that she is a woman who

> makes up things
> nice things ugly things but made up things nonetheless
> unprovable irrational subjective fantastic things
> not subject to objective or clinical investigation
> . . . this baby wants to jump out of my mouth
> at a reading someplace/
> . . . she wants to come out a spoken word.

Establishing herself as a woman who "makes" contradictions and complexities, she positions her word-child as an embodiment of both language and difference (7). The child is a body/language that shapes both the poem's trajectory and the struggle for anti-normative expressivity the poem presents. This anti-normativity, too, is framed in terms of body, as the child "doesn't think she shd come out" through the speaker's vaginal canal, but rather that she "shd come up/not down into the ground." This crisis of body and narrative is resolved only when the speaker, prompted by communication with her own body, is able to name the identity of her literary offspring. She states: "I finally figured out what to say. . . . [] you are an imperative my dear"/ & I felt her startle [] toward my left ovary then I said/ as an imperative [] it is incumbent upon you to present yrself" (8). Here, Shange's notion of literary "singularity" takes on bodily dimensions as the act of identifying and naming the word-child's specific tense and part of speech allows her to be born. The child emerges as an interstitial expression, the fleshy embodiment of the "poetic imperative" Shange calls for in her 1978 essay, "takin' a solo/ a poetic possibility/ a poetic imperative," in which she calls for new creative language to articulate the "nuance" of blackwoman subjective complexity (*Nappy Edges* 3). Her birth as language incarnate allows her to do the work of rearticulating diaspora: In insisting on her own expressivity as "a spoken word," the baby serves as a foil for the poem's "hungry" twins and a bridge for generations of diasporic "kin" disconnected by both inability to translate national idioms and by larger failures of language in general to articulate nonnormativity, singularity, and difference. She becomes a specifically diasporic body/language, the "language . . . tactile colored & wet" the speaker calls for in "New World Coro," which will allow "children of the new world" to replace hegemonic "sameness" with an anti-oppressive translatability and mutual identification. As an "imperative," the word-child embodies both the action that diaspora peoples must take against race-, gender- and class-based oppression and the radical, collectivizing idiom of broader difference they otherwise "cannot speak" (3, 8).

## Staging/Screening Black Feminist Diasporic Space

Shange's use of body/language to forge diasporic communication through difference articulates the importance of physicality, embodiment, and black women's interstitial reconstructions of diaspora. As Susan Stanford Friedman explains, diaspora is "hard on intimacy," primarily because intimacy "needs the body . . . the body of touch, the body of sensation and feeling, the body of speech" ("Bodies on the Move" 190). In the context of Afrodiasporic experience, both "old" and "new" diasporas are propelled by logics that reconfigure black bodies in capitalist terms and disavow black bodies' capacities for both expression and intimate connection. Even in the "voluntary" transnational movements of black people in the twentieth and twenty-first centuries, processes of diaspora tend to render black bodies, as Abena Busia puts it, "the flotsam and jetsam of . . . traumatic moments," reiterating the "same story," of the transatlantic slave trade in a "different century" ("What Is Africa to Me?" 17).

The persistence of this "story" of diaspora and its impact on black bodies requires new modes of storytelling that can reconfigure both diasporic bodies and diasporic space. As Busia states, the constant inscription of trauma onto black bodies in narratives of diasporic movement demands that diasporic subjects look to "the exemplary moments of poetry" as a means of transforming conceptions of diasporic experience (18). Shange's poetics of difference in choreopoem and play-in-poems forms provides this needed generic crossing. By performing "example[s]" of diaspora through mimetic movement of black bodies across space, Shange's poetics provides a means of remapping Afrodiaspora to account for both its subjective and spatial complexity.

The choreopoem version of *for colored girls* exemplifies this remapping of diasporic space. By staging diasporic difference and connection through body/language, Shange subverts the fixity of race, ethnicity, and nationality throughout the text, just as she questions the fixity of gender. The Lady in Blue is perhaps the most explicit in her performance and articulation diasporic ethnic mutability. As the Lady in Yellow describes her first experience of sexual intercourse in one of the choreopoem's best-known scenes, the Lady in Blue interrupts to ask for details about the logistics of the experience and, more specifically, about the rituals of movement and dance that precipitate the Lady in Yellow's first experiences of foreplay. When the Lady in Yellow, less versed in diasporic culture, asks her "what . . . kind of dances are there?" the Lady in Blue begins a monologue on her experiences with "mambo, bomba, merengue," and Afrolatin culture more broadly, identifying herself as a "regal niggah . . . wit hints of spanish." Yet, describing an evening at a "marathon" salsa party, she explains that "if dancin waz proof of origin/ I was jibarita herself that nite. . . . I waz twirlin hippin givin much quick feet/& bein a mute cute colored puerto rican." When provoked, however, she reacts in a display of "niggah temper"; and "talk[s] english loud" (*for colored girls* 11–12).

Through this performance of body and voice, the Lady in Blue interrogates the fixity of race in Afrodiaspora and highlights race's inextricability from gender and class in her diaspora of difference. She identifies first as a "reglar" (that is, US-born American) black subject; yet she soon reveals that her abilities to dance "mambo, bomba, and salsa" allow her access to an Afrolatina identity as well. Though she is unable to understand "a thing" said in the Spanish-speaking dancehall, she is able to become "jibarita herself" through expressions of dance. The term *jibarita* signals the feminine and diminutive form of the Puerto Rican colloquialism "jíbaro," which refers to a rural and often poor or working-class campesino identity and is translated by the Concise Oxford Spanish Dictionary as both *indigenous* and *rustic* ("Jíbaro").[18] By using body/language to evoke a specifically raced and classed diasporic women's identity, Shange not only questions the fixity of impenetrable racial distinctions within diasporic identities, but also highlights the interconnectedness of race, gender, and socioeconomic status in the diaspora and calls attention to the various ways in which those identifications are signaled and discursively deconstructed through dance.

While the Lady in Blue's conceptions of silence as a characteristic of "cute" Puerto Rican femininity and "loud" speech as a trait of African American women's anger[19] reinforce damaging stereotypes surrounding Afrodiasporic womanhood, her ability to access both of these identities through dance and to wield these two ethnic identifications through deliberate calibrations of voice indicates that, for her, voice and diasporic identity are inseparable powers accessed through the body. And while her identification as a "reglar" (that is, African American) "niggah" may indicate a complex fetishization of Afrocaribbean culture, her insistence on framing her relationship to Latina/o dance forms in terms of imagined "origin[s]" expressed through voice and movement calls attention to the performativity of both African American women's and Latina identities. These assumed identities point to Shange's understanding of Afrodiaspora as a nuantial geography of difference. For her, diaspora is not a configuration of verifiable "origin" and stable subjectivity. Rather, it is a fluid, permeable, and dynamic web of expressions donned with the switching of a step, the raising of the voice, the act of joining in a shared performance of race-, gender-, and nation-specific "attitude." In Shange's diasporas of difference, neither blood nor birth can provide "proof of origin;" rather, it is in "twirls" of body and the textures of voice that identity is defined and negotiated.[20]

This body/language of diasporic identification reconfigures the various spaces in which black women writers' characters move and speak. Extending discourses of diaspora that figure its global spaces through metaphors of "home," Shange's diasporas of difference expand the reach of the national, regional, local, and domestic spaces in black women's literature to explore their diasporic possibilities. In her poetics, dance clubs, libraries, and the streets of "avenue 'c'" are as capable as the space between "Haiti" and "santo domingo" of hosting boundary-crossing diasporic connections.[21] Shange deploys her poetics of difference to develop literary expressions of what bell hooks calls "homeplaces," sites in which black women escape objectification and are able to "confront the issue of humanization. . . . [and] strive to be subjects, not objects" (*Belonging* 389). These spaces allow access to a humanity that is resistant specifically because it offers respite from monolithic figurations of blackness and allow black women complex subjectivity.

By remapping diaspora through body/language, Shange's diasporas resist what Susan Stanford Friedman calls "a poetics of dislocation," in which women diasporic subjects find "the source of speech and writing" through emotionally difficult detachments from the primary geographical loci of their diasporic identifications (205). In such a poetics, Friedman observes, women in diaspora access voice by recognizing "'home' . . . as a place where the heart may be, but a place that must be left," because of the oppressive and silencing power dynamics operative there (205). Shange's poetics of difference interrogates the unidirectionality of Friedman's feminist diasporic poetics. In her diasporas of difference, "home" becomes not only a geographical "place" left behind, but also reflects the textual and creative space produced by "spe[aking] and writing" blackwoman selfhood. Moreover, in situating "home" as a creation of the Afrodiasporic woman self, Shange's diasporas trouble what F. Odun Balogun terms an "inward-outward mode" of identification in black women's literature, in which the black woman subject "seek[s] the self" in specific places within or outside of her 'home' (443–444).[22] In Shange's diasporas, the self is neither subordinate to nor primary over place, and the nuances of interstitial difference cannot be separated from identifications of continent, nation, municipality, neighborhood, block, and any other kind of space that may (or may not) be imagined as "home."[23] Instead, in these spaces, the concept of the blackwoman self *becomes its own place*, with its own complex of borders and bridges that must be recognized if useful identificatory ties with geographic sites and subjectivities outside the self are to be formed.

The 1982 Thirteen/WNET Broadcast of *for colored girls* illustrates the role of body/language in forging communicative connections of difference across this reconfigured diasporic space. Directed by Oz Scott (with Shange as assistant to the director) and starring Shange, Alfre Woodard, and Lynn Whitfield, the telefilm pairs the poetry of the choreopoem version of *for colored girls* with a cinematic narrative frame in which the seven women gather first for a slumber party and then for a picnic, each delivering Shange's poetry in flashback scenes. Whereas the staged choreopoem version of the text uses rituals of movement and dance to connect its protagonists' stories, the telefilm uses cinematographic techniques of lighting, color, and costuming to interweave the poetry with its larger narrative thread. And, whereas in the stage version of the choreopoem, body/language foregrounds difference as a means of blackwoman connection through the inexhaustible difference of "color" written on the body, the aesthetics of the telefilm merge embodied heteroglossias with visual and sonic signifiers marking the space of the screen, further emphasizing black women's interstitial difference and its centrality to diasporic space.

The telefilm version of *for colored girls* makes use of cinematic space to illustrate the permeability of diasporic identity through body/language. The telefilm's rendition of the Jibarita dance hall scene begins at a restaurant at which the Lady in Blue, dressed in blue and played by Carol L. Maillard, begins to describe her desire to identify with Spanish language and Puerto Rican culture, occasionally slipping into a salient (if faulty) Spanish accent. As she speaks, the scene slowly fades and reopens on the character, now dressed in red, climbing a narrow flight of stairs in what low lighting and multicolored track lights mark as a crowded dance party. The Lady in Blue continues simultaneously to narrate and perform the scene Shange's text describes. For example, she turns to address the camera as she explains that if potential suitors at the party "cd lead [she] was ready to dance," and then quickly reenters the scene to greet a silent male figure who approaches her, holds her arm, and gestures toward the dance floor. Still narrating, the Lady in Blue rolls her eyes and neck in exaggerated exasperation and turns on her bar stool away from the man while describing for the camera "this attitude [] [she'd] seen rosa do" (11). This performance sets the formal terms of the telefilm and establishes Shange's cinematic poetics of difference. Just as gender, ethnicity, and "color" are interconnected performative elements of black women's identity, bodily movement, narrative, and poetic expression can and must happen simultaneously for Afrodiasporic womanhood to be expressed.

Body/language continues to shape diasporic space as the Lady in Blue narrates her performance of "mute cute colored Puerto Rican" identity through dance—participating, it seems, in raced cultural connotations of Latina feminine "cuteness" with silence and, later, of masculine "temper" and with "loud" African American womanhood. Yet, by narrating this performance in scene (rather than through meta-diegetic voiceover), she enacts an ironic subversion of the problematic silencing she performs. By literally speaking her silence while she dances, she critiques the silencing of black women of various national and cultural identifications against which black feminists like Audre Lorde, Barbara Smith, bell hooks, and others rail. In a complex articulation of body/language, she narrates muteness, revealing this "cute" raced and gendered silence as an artifice of the body by splitting and reconfiguring her voice.

Adding the technologies of cinematography to Shange's choreopoetics, the telefilm version presents a polyglossia that further emphasizes the ability of body/language to facilitate diasporic communication. The scene shows a close-up of the DJ as he announces "lo sentimos mucho, pero Willie Colón no puede estar con nosotros esta noche." Immediately, the Lady in Blue stops dancing, wrinkles her face, rolls her eyes, and turns away again, moving toward her seat at the bar. Only once these gestures are complete does she offer her translation. She repeats the announcement in English, stating "Willie Colón ain't gonna make it today?" and promptly returns to her seat at the bar to narrate the return of her "niggah temper" to the camera while refusing further dance offers. This transition illustrates the reach of body/language as a strategy for translating diasporic experience and emphasizes the crucial role of new linguistic forma-tions for her model of diasporic identity. The logical dissonance of the Lady in Blue's ability to understand the announcement is highlighted in the film version by the interruption of the Spanish-language speech and by her exaggerated physical return to her "reglar" colored identity (11). In her movement from a "regla niggah" to "jibarita" to a "mute cute colored puerto rican" and back, the Lady in Blue illustrates the intersubjective functions of Shange's diasporic space. The space of the dance hall becomes the site of Shange's diaspora of difference. It facilitates identification across linguistic, national, and cultural difference and emphasizes the nuances of concurrent differences of gender and class. By accessing identification through body/language, the Lady in Blue participates in a diaspora defined not by the figurative movement of a monolithic subject from one stable geographic location to another, but by a practice of motion, communication, and complex identification as fluid as a mambo move and as precise as a bomba's downbeat.

This adaptation of Shange's choreopoetic form succeeds in evoking black women's diasporas of difference because of Shange's investment in the choreo-poem as a counter-genre, and her commitment to prioritizing the choreopoem form over the form of narrative cinema. The better-known film adaptation of *for colored girls*, written and directed by Tyler Perry and released in 2010, falls short of such a complex evocation of blackwoman difference precisely because of its adherence to contemporary commercial film structures. In combining Shange's "poetry" with an overarching film narrative, Perry privileges the static cinematic *image* over the dynamic bodily *choreography* of the text. This has implications not only on the visual effect of the piece; the static, montage quality of the film, contrasted with the dynamic motion of stage interpretations or even of the television broadcast, impacts the storyline itself. In Perry's version, the shared dialogues and choruses that occur spontaneously throughout the choreopoem are presented either as monologues or as staged "exercises" for emotional heal-ing, and the film's diasporic connections and resonances are largely silenced.[24]

The most explicit transformation of diasporic space through body/language in the print and stage versions of *for colored girls* occurs in the Lady in Brown's "metaphysical" romance with Haitian revolutionary Toussaint L'Ouverture. Here, as in *A Daughter's Geography*, blackwoman imagination, interiority, and fantasy provide solutions for articulating the diaspora's gaps and rifts. Recount-ing her early reading experiences, the Lady in Brown describes her inability to identify imaginatively with "pippi longstockin/ christopher robin," and other icons of white American children's literature. Frustrated by these "pioneer girls & magic rabbits [] & big city white boys," she defies the library's spatial and organizational structure (and the restricted access to knowledge and text that structure represents) and runs

> inta the ADULT READING ROOM
> & came across
> TOUSSAINT
> My first blk man

She immediately recognizes L'Ouverture as a symbol not only of black social transgression, but also of the possibilities of connection in diaspora. His figure is meaningful to her both because "TOUSSAINT waz a blk man a negro like my mama say [] who refused to be a slave,' and because "he spoke French [] & did not low no white man to tell him nothing." She frames L'Ouverture's revolutionary power in terms of his control of language and identifies with his linguistic power in an explicitly transnational context (26). The presence of "TOUSSAINT" looms large for her as the image of a "negro" who traverses social and political boundaries (like those she has traversed to access his story, knowing that she "waznt sposedta"), and as a black figure who, like her, wields his power through a willful and deliberate renegotiation of language and in a "blk" idiom foreign to standard English (26).

The Lady in Brown's linguistic identification with L'Ouverture across national lines quickly has its effects on her conceptions of her corporeality. When she is disqualified from the library's summer reading contest because of her choice to read books on L'Ouverture, she enacts a metaphoric dissociation of the histori-cal figure from the book in which she has encountered him. She buries "dead Toussaint home in the book," and instead enters a "secret love" relationship with "TOUSSAINT L'OUVERTURE . . . in [her] bedroom [] widda flashlight under [her] covers." This corporealization of L'Ouverture's literary image is ultimately expressed in the Lady in Brown's encounter with a real, living boy named Toussaint Jones, whom she meets during one of her excursions with the imagined "TOUSSAINT." This imaginative incarnation of L'Ouverture as an embodiment of diasporic mobility is reflected in Shange's typography. On her walk with "TOUSSAINT L'OUVERTURE," the Lady in Brown encounters a boy who introduces himself with the statement: "MY NAME IS TOUSSAINT JONES," to which she replies "wow [] I am on my way to see [] TOUSSAINT L'OVERTURE in HAITI" (29).

Even before his fantastical transmogrification into embodiment, L'Ouverture aids the Lady in Brown in accessing diasporic connection through body/language. By endowing his figure with a capacity for death—and separating his "dead" literary image with the possibility of a "livin" being with whom she can imagine a physical interaction—the Lady in Brown is able to maintain her ties with the linguistic power he represents and to explore that power through a corporeally conceived understanding of diaspora.[25] When she resolves to run away from home as a result of the maelstrom of social shifts attending the racial integration of her school and neighborhood, she consults L'Ouverture for direction. In response, she recounts,

> Toussaint said "lets go to haiti"
> I said "awright"
> . . . then Toussaint & I took the hodiamont streetcar
> . . . there waznt nobody cd see Toussaint cept me
> & we walked all down thru north st. louis
> where the French settlers usedta live
> . . . I cd talk to Toussaint down by the river
> like this waz where we waz gonna stow a way
> on a boat for new Orleans
> & catch a creole fishin-rig for port-au-prince
> then we waz jus gona read & talk all the time
> & eat fried bananas (28).

By giving L'Ouverture a body, The Lady in Brown is able to construct an accessible concept of diaspora within the context of her urban US setting. She becomes aware of evidence of transnational histories in her St. Louis neighborhood and notes iconic Afrodiasporic cultural syncretisms of other US cities (such as New Orleans). Moreover, she contextualizes herself within an Afrodiasporic relational system that allows her to imagine "go[ing] to Haiti" in both mind and body while "walkin and skippin" with L'Ouverture's embodied literary figure down the streets of her own neighborhood. By encountering Toussaint through body/language, she transforms the physical space of her neighborhood and accesses a psychic space in which multiple diasporic locations are part of her social reality.

This transformation occurs not only on the spaces of neighborhoods and stages, but on the space of black women's interstitial bodies themselves. Through her "colored girls," Shange demonstrates the extent to which, as Spillers argues, in "[t]he new cultural demographies of the African diaspora, as we slowly, patiently map them. . . . The interarticulatory logic of the *material* and the *symbolic* blends the universal and the particular at the same place—*inside* the one and all" ("Interstices"19). Shange locates the common threads of diasporic difference "inside" the bodies and voices of her characters and situates them within a re-"mapped" diaspora embodied in each "one" of the colored girls, and in the "rainbow" that defines them "all." As the text's climactic moments of choral merging and synchronous dance indicate, Shange's diaspora also signals what bell hooks describes as "the coming together of many 'I's [and] the self as embodying collective reality past and present" (*Talking Back* 31). Shange's diasporic "universal[ity]" depends not only on the contact of interstitial bodies on the shared "place" of the stage, but also on the poetic rhythms, the dramatic beats, and the choreographed timing with which her characters' bodies and voices meet.

This merging of diasporic differences through body/language is nowhere more impactful than in the choreopoem's closing scene. Following the climactic story of a character named "crystal" and her abusive, infanticidal boyfriend "beau willie brown," the colored girls and the women engage in a chorus of utterances parallel to their descriptions of their "outsider" difference in the opening scene. Yet, here, rather than follow repetitions of a common phrase (such as the line "I'm outside" with which they hail themselves in the opening scene) with an articulation of their individual differences (for example, their differing domestic diasporic locales), they collaborate on a single shared narrative about their experiences of difference and their collective lack of access to self:

> *lady in red*
> I waz missin somethin
>
> *lady in purple*
> somethin so important
>
> *lady in orange*
> something promised
>
> *lady in blue*
> a layin on of hands . . .
> I know bout/ layin on bodies/ layin outta man
> Brining him alla my fleshy self & some of my pleasure
> Bein taken full eager wet like I get sometimes
> I waz missin something
> . . . not a man
>
> *lady in purple*
> . . . not my mama/ holdin me tight/ sayin
> I'm always gonna be her girl
> . . . . A layin on of hands . . . (64, 55)

Here, the colored girls form a chorus of voices through which they articulate that which is "missing" in their individual experiences of black womanhood, identifying that missing element as a corporeal gesture. Importantly, the Lady in Blue names this corporeality specifically in terms of "flesh." While, as Sharon Holland suggests, the "body" may describe corporeality as capital and commodity void of subjectivity, "flesh" indicates a subjectivity liberated to corporeal freedom and will (*Raising the Dead* 46). In seeking to reclaim her "fleshy self," then, the Lady in Blue proposes a doubly-emphatic claim over her subjectivity through her body. As the dialogue mounts into a collaborative monologue, Shange's poetics suggest that what is "missing" is not, as the Lady in Blue states, "a man," nor, as the Lady in Purple suggests, a maternal figure speaking blackwoman self-ownership and belonging. The lacking element is not simply a chorus of voices "sayin" words that reify blackwoman connection; it is a collective "layin on" of "colored" hands. What is missing is physical contact with the nuantial—a shared embodiment of "the missing word" of black women's difference (Spillers *Black, White* 156).

This final call for interstitial connection through body/language finds its culmination in the choreopoem's closing stage directions. When the Lady in Red delivers the triumphal penultimate lines—"I found god in myself [] & I loved her/ I loved her fiercely," the stage directions state: "*(a)ll of the ladies repeat to themselves softly the lines 'I found god in myself & I loved her.' It soon becomes a song of joy, started by the lady in blue. The ladies sing first to each other, then gradually to the audience. After the song peaks the ladies enter into a closed tight circle*" (67).

At the text's end, Shange's colored girls use their body/language momentarily to include the audience in their "collective reality," pointing to the expansiveness of Shange's vision of diaspora as a network of difference. Yet by closing the circle "tight" at the end of the choreopoem, the characters return ultimately to the specifically blackwoman identification of interstitial difference they have explored and articulated from the choreopoem's start. Here, again, Shange anticipates canonical black feminist modes of particularized inclusivity useful in defining the expansive scope of black women's political engagement. Like Alice Walker's model of "womanism" and the vision of black feminism laid out by the Combahee River Collective in their foundational "Black Feminist Statement," Shange's vision of blackwoman political and cultural praxis resists separatism;[26] rather, it gestures toward inclusivity specifically in order to highlight the expansiveness of black womanhood and the extent to which blackwoman difference must be acknowledged if blackwoman freedom is to be possible. For Shange, the "colors" of black women's embodiment and subjectivity are useful—and in fact necessary—vectors of connection between black women in diaspora and others committed to their survival. Yet, ultimately the closed circle of colored girl bodies leaves the "pleasure" and healing of black women's interstitial subjectivity at the center of this final tableau. The colored girls' message here resounds: black womanhood is as complex and capacious as difference itself, and if any global healing is to be possible, it must heal black women first. Their closed circle of colored black girl bodies demonstrates the extent to which black womanhood can and must mark its own grounds—grounds on which, as a space, a subjectivity, and a way of imagining globality, black women's interstitial difference is more than "enuf."

## Tonguing the Foreign L/anguish: Queer Erotics and Black Feminist Worldmaking in Diasporic Lyric and Poem Forms

Shange's use of "color" to chart a global space shaped by black women's interstitial difference—that is, by the links between intersectional identity and subjective nuances of blackwoman fantasy, pain, desire, and pleasure—opens space for an important exploration of the place of the erotic in black women's creative constructions of diaspora. As the work of Audre Lorde indicates, the erotic functions in black feminism as not only a source of pleasure, but as a blueprint for political engagement and collaboration and a model and standard for the subjective and experiential possibilities of a liberated life (*Uses of the Erotic* 54). As a practice specifically of nonnormative and anti-normative political vision, black queer feminist analysis is an especially useful lens for investigating the functions of this vision of the erotic on a transnational stage. For contemporary black feminist writers and artists, queer erotics have served as a crucial metaphor for reconceptualizing radical, anti-normative transnational identifications that center black women's bodily experience and place black women's freedom and pleasure at the core of diasporic politics. Poetry and lyric forms are particularly useful in considering the place of queer erotics in black feminist visions of diaspora. As Jahan Ramazani points out, "[b]y virtue of its extraordinary compression, poetry readily evinces the "time-space compression" of globalization" (*A Transnational Poetics* 16). This compression becomes arguably more meaningful in the context of black feminist experimental and multilingual forms, in which various modes of translation—between languages, verse forms, and interpretive modes—require readers to engage in temporal and spatial dislocations of both global black political experience and raced/gendered embodiment simultaneously. For black women poets in the African diaspora, writing transnational identification as bodily experience means both writing time and space—writing histories of transnational movement and connection—and writing *beyond* time and space to articulate the particularities of those histories through the nuances of black women's interstitial difference.

Because of its linguistic economy and its constant engagements with space—both on the printed page and through deliberate spatial engagements with other media forms such as in music videos and multimedia poetry performance—contemporary black women's poetry is uniquely positioned to challenge models of globality and diasporic space. This is especially so for black women's poetry, which, as Samantha Pinto argues, by offering "text in which narrative is decentered, undone, and thwarted . . . does not shy away from the failures, traumas, and unfinished business of diaspora flows and gender's difficult place in those networks" (6). Yet narrative has its place here, as well, particularly in poetic engagements with queer erotics. In various lyric and performance poetry forms, black feminist writers use nonnormative erotics to *re-do* narratives of diaspora, highlighting the racial, gender, and geographic/national limitations of time and space, and offering crucial glimpses into how temporal, spatial, and global location might look in black women's imaginary worlds.

The works of Trinbagonian Canadian poet M. NourbeSe Philip and Afro-Cuban lesbian hip-hop group Krudxs Cubensi (also known as Lx Krudx) offer two such glimpses into the queer poetic possibilities of diaspora. Despite important differences in genre, formal strategy, and modes of circulation, these two bodies of work, when explored together, reveal the breadth of poetic approaches to black feminist worldmaking and the range of visions black feminist poetics opens for models of transnational black gender, sexuality, embodiment, and belonging. Further, they exemplify the formal properties and interpretive functions of body/language in verse forms, making space for queer modes of translation that can articulate both sameness and difference on both linguistic and bodily planes. Read together, Philip's and Krudxs Cubensi's works demonstrate the queer potentials of the "demonic grounds" on which McKittrick has argued black women re-write spatial subjectivity. Through their poetics of difference, they situate erotic and bodily nonnormativity as a nexus around which global/historical locations can be imagined and offer queer forms of blackwoman pleasure as a means of rearticulating diasporic identification, belonging, and freedom.

Philip's *She Tries Her Tongue; Her Silence Softly Breaks* offers an important exploration of black transnational histories framed through body/language and demonstrates the importance of queer and nonnormative erotics in black feminist diasporas. The text, published in 1988 by Casa de las Americas, Cuba, is most often read by critics as an experimental meditation on the problems of language in diaspora—and of the Caribbean in particular. Throughout the collection, Philip's speaker tells, retells, and un-tells histories of transatlantic movement and fracture, constantly charting the ways in which language is reimagined and undone by processes of colonization and enslavement. These histories tap Trinbagonian and other Caribbean histories and languages, drawing connections to broader experiences of Afrodiasporic history through gendered embodiment. Philip joins Caribbean-diasporic women writers such as Lorde, Brand, and Paule Marshall in situating diaspora as a multitemporal and multi-directional experience through which they can, as scholar Angelique V. Nixon puts it, "write and thereby claim multiple homes in transnational spaces through the Caribbean and an African diasporic identity" centering womanhood (28). In this sense, Philip accesses the gendered poetic potentials of what poet and scholar Rosamond S. King terms the "Cariglobal imagination," in which "many aspects of Caribbean culture do not develop in . . . one site or [an]other" (*Island Bodies* 7). In her nonnarrative telling and untelling of diaspora, Philip's poetics of difference proposes a model of transnational movement and identification that not only emphasizes diasporic womanhood, but also places black women's experiences of bodily pain, pleasure, desire, and nonnormative erotics at the center of diasporic history.

The arc of *She Tries Her Tongue* is framed by Ovid's *Metamorphoses*, and particularly by the story of Proserpine and Ceres. In this story, Ceres is abducted and raped by Dis, king of the dead, after which Dis brings her to the underworld, prompting her lover, Proserpine, to go in search of her. Several critics have read Philip's use of Ceres's rape and abduction as a general metaphor for alienation in Afrodiaspora, in which the theft of identities and the rape of cultures result in Diasporic subjects' dislocation from both "mother land" and "mother tongue," both dislocations that are played out in Philip's use of fracture as a structuring form.[27] Other critics, such as Shara McCallum, have considered the gendered dynamics of this disappeared lineage, viewing it as a "parable of mother-daughter relations" and, ultimately, a "too-idyllic and even clichéd account of matriarchal order" (155, 167). In most critical readings, the "tongue" in the title is read exclusively as a metonymy for language, both as la *langue* and la *langage*—that is, as a metaphor for the specific problems of English and creole languages and the problems with verbal communication at large. For these critics, Philip's "tongue" in her poetics of fragmentation functions as a medium for developing new languages and telling dissenting histories, particularly about black women's birth and lineage in the Caribbean and in diaspora more broadly.

Yet, Philip's reflections on (inter)subjective fragmentation, historical alienation, and geographic rupture are not only linguistic, but also bodily. Philip's "tongue" is not simply a metaphor for the fantasy of diasporic history's speakability; it is also a muscle, an element of blackwoman anatomies capable of mediating, articulating, and rearticulating sensory experiences of pleasure and pain. Speaking elsewhere about her own investment in rewriting diasporic histories, Philip says: "I speak . . . of descent. Of enumerated ancestors—intermediate persons—of Africa. Whose public genealogy is one of pain. . . . And genital mutilation. And AIDS. . . . And yet there is another genealogy: of language. Spoken with the whole body" (*A Genealogy of Resistance* 25).

Philip's reworking of diasporic language and lineage is dependent on a simultaneous reimagining of black embodiment, and on the critical capacities of black feminist body/language. Her dissenting genealogies break the rules not only of normative language, but also of normative embodiment. She introduces "tongues" that are "tried" not only in that they are tested for their communicative viability, but also "tried" in that they are pushed beyond conscionable thresholds for sensation—exceeding imaginable limits of pain, but also, subversively, pushing themselves beyond standards of sanctioned pleasure and desire. This exceeding of sensation prompts important fractures and profusions on the body of the text and shape its queer visions of diaspora.

Like many texts that take up a poetics of difference, the first edition of Philip's *She Tries Her Tongue* calls attention to itself not only as a text, but as a material object that must be engaged through nonnormative modes of embodiment, spatiality, and interpretation in order to be properly understood. Each of the collection's nine poems begins with a separate title page, which, in each case, is recognizable as a title only once the reader has referred back to the table of contents. This format requires the reader to engage in a nonnormative reading practice that constantly involves the readerly body, preventing the reader from disidentifying with the stories of bodily rupture and diasporic trauma on which the text centers. Philip's text also demands a reorientation to space and time as part of the reader's interpretive practice: the table of contents is located on the final page of the collection (87), opposite what can be read as either an epigraph, an epilogue, or a continuation of the collection's last and longest poem, for which the collection is named. To understand the shape of the text—how each poem's pieces work together and whether and how they fit into the larger whole—one must be prepared to abandon chronology, temporality, spatiality, and subjectivity, constantly using her own body to begin at and journey back to the speaker's end.

Here, Philip trains the reader in an interstitial hermeneutics that requires the reader to encounter diasporic history and experience as multi-directional, multi-subjective, and multi-chronological, reflecting the interstitial experience of her subjects. Her poetics produce, as Pinto argues, "uncomfortable, sometimes unwelcome recognitions of critical interdependence that force the reader to commit to new routes of diaspora literacy. It is not just the objects of study . . . that accumulate in this formulation of diaspora but interpretation itself that multiplies and becomes the means of sustaining inquiry into gender, race, and location" (180). This new diasporic literacy is "uncomfortable" in part because of the scope and stakes of Philip's subject matter. By resting the knowability of diasporic history on the acquisition of newly gendered and raced languages, Philip situates intersectional experience not only as a requisite for understanding *the text's* language, but also as an indispensable consideration for language itself. As Pinto notes, "[i]f language itself is the key concept of *She Tries Her Tongue*, then its form acts out the drama (and history) of language, structurally and stylistically, as many critics have noted" (189). Yet as a text concerned with the *bodily* dimensions of these raced and gendered histories, *She Tries Her Tongue* uses its poetics to act out the dramas of language and history, specifically through the disruptive, nonnormative, and queer expressions of black women's bodies.

The collection's central poem, "Discourse on the Logic of Language" demonstrates how Philip queers black women's embodiment to offer a model of diasporic history that centers interstitial experience. By emphasizing nonnormative linguistic engagements with diasporic embodiment, she reimagines diasporic subjectivity as a concept shaped by intersectionality—in this case, by the linked racial and gender dynamics of diasporic movement—and by the sensory, bodily, and erotic nuances of black women's subjective experience.

The spatial configuration of "Discourse on the Logic of Language" announces both connection and distinction, singularity and profusion, mirroring Philip's concern with nonnormative embodiment and black women's interstitial subjectivity. The text contains prose, verse, footnotes, and various other kinds of text, all of which crowd both the horizontal and vertical planes of the page, linking fields of page space that would most readily signal separations between distinct stanzas and/or poems in a normative reading practice. In this geography of the page, Philip demonstrates the ways in which, as Anthony Reed puts it, "visual poetics disrupts the accord between sense and sense, multiplying pathways of meaning" (*Freedom Time* 27). In order to navigate this poem, the reader must be prepared to forgo interpretive order and instead confront an un-logic of simultaneity as the poem's speakers "discourse" on the simultaneous bearings of race and gender on diaspora history. The section at the center column of the left (though not first) page of the poem offers its most apparently legible free-verse form. Taking on what appears to be a more-or-less stable first-person speaker, this section offers a historical medical narrative about black and female brain function in language and speech. This section appears at the intersection of three starkly differing modes of text. On the immediate right, the speaker offers "Edicts" limiting slaves' access to language and speech (including, "[w]hen necessary, the removal of the tongue"); on the far right, we see multiple choice exam-style questions and answers about the expressive and erotic functions of the tongue in relation to various body parts (for example, "A tapering, blunt-tipped, muscular, soft and fleshy organ/ describes/ (a) the penis./ (b) the tongue./

## Discourse on the Logic of Language

English
is my mother tongue.
A mother tongue is not
not a foreign lan lan lang
language
l/anguish
anguish
—a foreign anguish.

English is
my father tongue.
A father tongue is
a foreign language,
therefore English is
a foreign language
not a mother tongue.

What is my mother
tongue
my mammy tongue
my mummy tongue
my momsy tongue
my modder tongue
my ma tongue?

I have no mother
tongue
no mother to tongue
no tongue to mother
to mother
tongue
me

I must therefore be
tongue
dumb
dumb-tongued
dub-tongued
damn dumb
tongue

EDICT I

*Every owner of slaves*
*shall, wherever possible,*
*ensure that his slaves*
*belong to as many ethno-*
*linguistic groups as*
*possible. If they can-*
*not speak to each other,*
*they cannot then foment*
*rebellion and revolution.*

WHEN IT WAS BORN, THE MOTHER HELD HER NEWBORN CHILD CLOSE: SHE BEGAN THEN TO
LICK IT ALL OVER. THE CHILD WHIMPERED A LITTLE, BUT AS THE MOTHER'S TONGUE
MOVED FASTER AND STRONGER OVER ITS BODY, IT GREW SILENT—THE MOTHER TURNING
IT THIS WAY AND THAT UNDER HER TONGUE UNTIL SHE HAD TONGUED IT CLEAN OF
THE CREAMY WHITE SUBSTANCE COVERING ITS BODY.

Figure 3.1. M. NourbeSe Philip, "Discourse on the Logic of Language" (Edict II). Excerpts and page images from pages 44, 45, 46, 47. and "Discourse on the Logic of Language" from *She Tries Her Tongue, Her Silence Softly Breaks* © 2015 by M. NourbeSe Philip. Published by Wesleyan University Press. Reprinted with permission.

(c) neither of the above./ (d) both of the above.) Finally, on the horizontal left edge of the page the text offers, in all capital letters, a third-person narrative of a mother using her own tongue to "gently force" her child to speak.[28]

Of the ample criticism on Philip's work, and on *She Tries Her Tongue* in particular, this poem has received relatively little scholarly attention—and this specific section even less, perhaps due in part to the "uncomfortable" engagements with language the text requires, which here are uncomfortable not only for the intellectual destabilizations they require, but also because of the specifically unusual, nonnormative, sensory, and sensual engagements to which those intellectual destabilizations lead.

Critics who do address "Discourse on the Logic of Language" largely understand it as McCallum does, as either a lamentation of the struggle to reconcile English and Creole languages *or* a meditation on motherhood as a metaphor for diasporic belonging. Yet approaching the poem through a black queer feminist lens reveals that Philip is interested in neither languages nor mothers *exclusively as metaphors*. Rather, she constructs a vision of a blackwoman language of diaspora built in and through the body. In this language, the body occurs both as a discursive representation of black women's subjectivity *and* as a conglomeration of organs, muscles, and flesh that can expresses pain, pleasure, and longing as a means of creating identity and belonging.

The poem begins: "English is my mother tongue. A mother tongue is not a foreign lan lan lang/ language/ languish/ anguish/ a foreign anguish" (44). Here, the speaker's tongue is "tried" to the point of *tying* as she attempts to declare herself as a descendant of—and in—the English language. In these lines, the themes of motherlessness and voicelessness that recur throughout *She Tries Her Tongue* converge, culminating in the failure of the tongue both as metaphor and muscle as the speaker concludes: "I have no mother tongue/ no mother to tongue/ no tongue to mother/ to mother/ tongue/ me." (44). The absence of both a "mother to tongue" and a "tongue to mother/to mother/tongue/ me" suspends the strictly representational figurations of the tongue, requiring the reader to read and reread (and thus confront and reencounter) both the important distinctions and the provocative connections between the metaphorical significations of the noun form of tongue-as-language (in which the "tongue" serves strictly as a signifier for language and speech) and the verb form of tongue-as-action (in which "*to* tongue" invokes a range of sensory, sensual, and erotic actions and experiences, including licking, kissing, tasting, and innumerable forms of lingual stimulation).

Here, Philip articulates the queer erotic resonances of what Orlando Patterson and others have thought of as "natal alienation"—the series of social, familial, and historical rifts caused by enslavement of diaspora bodies (*Slavery and Social Death* 5). In order to articulate her rifts from both language and diasporic lineage—that is, to express the absence of both the body of the "mother" and "mother tongue"—Philip's speaker must rewrite the "fleshy organ" of the tongue itself. In the first of these center stanzas, Philip highlights the definitive failure of the tongue-as-language: its inability to reconcile the concept of English with the originary narrative of the "mother tongue" absented in diaspora. For the speaker, this reconciliation is an impossible process that precludes both lineage and language, and instead produces not only alienation but "anguish" and bodily pain. In her efforts to understand this pain and its causes, the speaker turns toward a queer erotics that can help articulate and suture the belonging ruptured in transnational diasporic movement. She imagines the intersection of her voicelessness and her rootlessness as an absence of "a mother to tongue," "a tongue to mother," and "a mother to tongue me," positioning an impossible same-sex erotic expression at the center of both speech and belonging. Soon, the "tongue" that serves as the poem's central image shifts from a metaphor for diasporic belonging to a fleshy bodily organ replete with sensory and erotic functions. The speaker states: "tongue mother tongue me/ mothertongue me/ mother me/ touch me/ with the tongue of your lan lang/ language/ languish/ anguish/English." Here, the yearning for a mother tongue becomes a form of queer desire—a desire for both linguistic and erotic contact with an inaccessible experience of home.

For Philip's speaker, these two desires—the desire for home and the desire for the mother's erotic tongue and touch—are inseparable and at times indistinguishable. By placing uncomfortable, unsanctioned, corporeal desires at the center of the search for black diasporic lineage, Philip offers a corrective to the commodification of colonial histories, in which, as she puts it elsewhere, "the space between the legs [is] the raison d'etre of [the black woman's] importation to the New World" (1997, 91). In "Discourse on the Logic of Language," the radical rewriting of diasporic lineage and language requires an articulation of diaspora's violences against black women's bodies *and* an equally radical reimagining of those bodies' purposes and possibilities according to sensual healing and pleasure. Philip's turn to the erotic capabilities of the corporeal tongue is thus not (or not only) about incest; rather, it highlights queerness of blackwoman healing through shared pleasure, and the expressly rebellious, anticolonial act of producing lineages, languages, and models of transnational belonging governed not by whiteness and masculinity, but by black women's sensory and erotic contact with self and other.

Philip's poetics and stanza structure emphasize the importance of bodily sensation to this model of diasporic belonging. Read through a standard linear horizontal reading practice, these central verses are immediately followed by a multiple-choice examination question in which the speaker offers: "A tapering, blunt-tipped, muscular, soft and fleshy organ" to which the possible answers are:

"(a) the penis/ (b) the tongue/ (c) neither of the above/ (d) both of the above." This is the first of four such questions that comprise the poem's final page. Yet this description also serves as important context for the narrative that appears in all capital letters on the far vertical edge of the previous (left-facing) page. In this second horizontal narrative, the speaker describes: "Then the mother put her fingers into her child's mouth, gently forcing it open; she touches her tongue to the child's tongue, and holding the tiny mouth open she blows into it—hard, she was blowing words—her words, her mother's words, those of her mother's mother, and all their mothers before into her daughter's mouth" (46). Here, both language and diasporic lineage are transmitted through tongue-to-tongue touch between mother and daughter. As Pinto argues, this "mother-to-newborn-child contact via the tongue" is a means of reimagining the gender resonances of diasporic language and history (193). Yet, this gesture also emphasizes the specific place of nonnormative, woman-centered sensory and bodily experience in such an imagining. That this passage occurs as a spatial and thematic parallel to the multiple-choice question on the opposite page that connects the tongue and the penis as "blunt-tipped, muscular, soft and fleshy organ[s]" suggests that the speaker's vision of the tongue extends not only beyond the metaphorical, but that it is connected specifically with genital embodiment and the violences and pleasures thereof. In "touch[ing] her tongue to the child's tongue," the mother invokes the latter, using the sensory and tactile capacities of the tongue to inscribe herself and her daughter in a poetics of pleasure in which self-created language can facilitate not only belonging, but also healing. Here, the queer contact between mother and daughter tongues yields sensation beyond "l/anguish," offering both the feel and the *sense* of language as creations that can sustain blackwoman lineages across diasporic space.

This queer practice of erotic lineage-making demonstrates the extent to which Philip's work is as much about healing as it is about fracture, even when healing decidedly does not, as Shockley puts it "make us w/hole" ("Going Overboard" 816). The visual and sonic poetics of "Discourse on the Logic of Language" echo this simultaneity of healing and rupture as an important feature of black feminist diaspora. In its nonlinear structure and multiple uses of pagespace, the form of the poem replicates rifts from chronology and the disfigurement of black women's bodies. Yet, these same structures also highlight a queer fantasy of possibility—a narrative in which black women's shared pleasure is a condition of possibility for transnational belonging, once diaspora is re-tooled, re-tongued, and reread the right way.

These poetic renderings of queer embodiment as a metaphor for new modes of feminist worlding are useful, in part, because of how they renegotiate black women's embodiment as itself queer and highlight the multiple forms of both difference and deviance evoked by black women's bodies across time and space.

As Philip's work suggests, diaspora is queer because black womanhood is queer—that is, because it is mediated by a blackwoman "mother tongue" that constantly makes space beyond norms of gender, desire, and legibility to create its continuance and survival. This mother tongue is both figurative and fleshy, its very form a spectacular testament to both multiplicity and possibility in diaspora.

In considering the reach and resonance of these spectacular modes of black / queer feminist embodiment for poetic reimaginings of diaspora, then, it is also useful to explore poetic engagements with blackwoman bodies that are, themselves, spectacular—in the sense that they subvert and exceed norms of embodiment both on and beyond the visual plane—and examine how a poetics of difference mobilizes such spectacular blackwoman embodiments to reconceive diaspora as a space of black queer feminist possibility. Poetic explorations of fatness in Afrodiasporic feminist hip-hop offer particularly rich opportunities for such exploration. As a form deeply invested in considering race, gender, class, sexuality, and embodiment—and as a form of poetry often tied to the visual technologies of music video—diasporic feminist hip-hop is an important ground on which to explore spectacular embodiments and the spaces they open up for interstitial models of diaspora.

## "Más Espacio en El Mundo": Interstitial Silence and Fat Black Queer Re-Worlding

The works of queer Afro-Cuban hip-hop group Krudxs Cubensi offer particularly rich examples of such worldmaking. Also known by their founding name Las Krudas (which they use in some interviews and promotional materials), the group's 2009 single "La Gorda" reframes the spectacle of the fat black / queer body to articulate a queer model of gender and diasporic belonging that challenges both individual viewers/readers and several scholarly and activist discourses to reconsider difference, power, and globality according by centering black queer women's experience. Particularly since their 2014 album, *Poderosx*, the group has been explicit about troubling the patriarchal violences inherent in gendered colonial language, and unsettling binary gender in their lives and work. The group uses both feminine-gendered and gender-neutral language to discuss their work, identifying, for example, as "*Cubanas, Negras . . . lesbianas y* [Cuban women, black women, lesbians and] *genderqueer, non-binary conforming.*"[29] Both nonbinary gender and a political stance "contra el binarismo de género" (against the gender binary), are central to the vision of the group and its collective identity (Eimil "Krudas Cubensi: Vivir en Resistencia"). I use the term *woman* here to refer primarily to the figure invoked in "La Gorda," who is explicitly marked as "mujer" (woman) in the song's lyrics. "La Gorda" develops a body/language that mobilizes linguistic heterogeneities of Afrodiaspora (including dialect, code-switching, and creative acts of translation) alongside the formal heterogeneities of hip-hop (including verse, hook, rhyme, and, especially, connections and dissonances between lyrics and music video imagery) to propose models of blackwoman embodiment in which fatness, queerness, and blackness introduce new models of worldmaking.

"La Gorda" is an anthem of fat woman embodiment that positions the fat blackwoman body as both a center of the world, and as a world of difference, desire, and pleasure unto itself. The song celebrates "la gorda," (the fat girl/woman), announcing her arrival in the unnamed space of the song and insisting upon her fatness as a metaphor for national and global capaciousness. Throughout the song, the world of "La Gorda" is unapologetically fat, unapologetically queer, unapologetically Cuban, and unapologetically black. Las Krudas's poetics of difference echoes and further queers those forwarded by Shange and Philip, each of which emphasizes Afrodiaspora as a site of multiple blacknesses and multiple routes of descent. As Flora María Gonzáles Mandri points out, while the term "Afro-Cubanism" often describes cultural movements emerging partly in response to US economic imperialism, African histories, black embodiments, and discourses of and against antiblackness are crucial to Cuban history, identity, and nation-building (3–4).[30] Lxs Krudxs centers a queer feminist discourse of Afro-Cubanidad, explicitly claiming a black feminist ethos and critiquing antiblackness in their creative practice. This critique is evident throughout the group's work, particularly in the closing call-and-response to "La Gorda," in which Odaymar Kruda leads a final chant: "Black!?" "Beautiful!" "Heavy?!" "More beautiful!" resituating "black is beautiful" logics that permeate black nationalist discourses of the 1970s—a more complex, more nuanced diasporic feminist critical context. For Lxs Krudxs, Cubanidad is inseparable from Afrodiasporic identity, queer desire, and fat black embodiment. It is a nuantial location in which blackness, queerness, and fatness bring crucial intersectional complexity to Afrodiasporic nation-building projects.

In "La Gorda," Lxs Krudxs demonstrates the possibilities of black queer feminist diasporas of difference, and the importance these diasporas hold for feminist critiques of embodiment. The song's celebration of fat black queer re-worlding marks an important creative intervention into several discourses on embodiment whose interconnections remain woefully undertheorized in contemporary scholarship, as well as in public health discourse, and fat activism. Viewed through a black queer feminist lens, the song reveals several nuantial connections between blackness, womanhood, queerness, fatness, and diaspora overlooked by multiple discursive fields, even as they are written big and bold all over black feminists' creative texts.

Attention to these connections and discursive contexts is crucial for understanding the impact that creative worlding projects like "La Gorda" make. Fat

Figure 3.2a. "La Gorda," Las Krudas Cubensi (2009). Courtesy of Krudxs Cubensi.

studies, like queer studies, since the 1970s has looked to black antiracist discourses in its interrogations of difference, though few studies have examined the interplay of fatness and queerness on black bodies, or in black diasporic cultural expression.[31] Blackness has served as a structuring resource for both fields. In framing the fat studies project, Kathleen LeBesco argues, "It is useful to examine recent physical identity-based movements of race and gender (e.g., Black Nationalism and second-wave feminism) in order to understand more about the genesis of fat politics. It is also necessary to consider the strategy contributions of queer theory and activism to fat politics" (*Revolting Bodies?* 10). That LeBesco does not address the place of blackness *within* fat politics indicates the need for increased critical attention to the intersections of black, queer, and fat experience. Elena Levy-Navarro's gloss of the links between fat studies and queer studies echoes this point. Race and blackness appear nowhere in her gloss of the historical stigmatizations "used to debase the nonnormative."[32] Yet, despite this erasure of blackness from fat queer critiques, blackness and global black cultural expressions cannot be disentangled from discourses on intersecting difference. We might think, for example, of Grenadian American lesbian feminist writer Audre Lorde who, well before either of these discourses solidified, used the phrase "fat, black, nearly blind and ambidextrous [from] a West Indian Household" to describe the differences that attend her sexual identity. Even outside of black experience, global blackness shapes white Western understandings of both sexual and corporeal aberrance, creating a situation in which, as Amy Erdman Farrell points out, "the connections between fatness, Africanness and a grotesque, 'queer' [gender] have been passed down" in Western culture for centuries, and operate in American cultural production today (*Fat Shame* 174).

Figure 3.2b. Children's Health of Atlanta, "Strong4Life" Campaign.

While critics have paid increasing attention to some of the connections be-tween blackness, queerness, and fatness in recent years, these links have often relied on the familiar trope of invoking black bodies as metaphors for queer and/or fat struggles read primarily as both white and American. In addition, the transnational reach of these conversations remains largely unexplored. One salient example is prominent fat activist Marilyn Wann's 2012 "I Stand" proj-ect, which was a response to Children's Health of Atlanta, GA's *Strong4Life* campaign. The Strong4Life campaign targeted black families with posters and TV commercials featuring fat black children (often girls) over captions such as "It's hard to be a little girl when you're not," "My fat may be funny to you, but it's killing me," and "Fat prevention begins at home. And the buffet line." In response to the campaign's fatphobic message, Wann created a large-scale

Figure 3.3a. "I Stand" Campaign, 2012. Courtesy of Jennifer Jonassen. Photo by Sierra Lisa.

response, putting together 389 posters featuring images of fat activists alongside body-positive and anti-fat-shaming captions like "I Stand against harming fat children. Hate does not equal health." Of these 389 posters, however, fewer than ten featured black fat activists. The images are largely of white cisgender queer and or feminist fat activists culled from Wann's own network and linked circles. While important for its critique of fat-shaming, the project risks reinscribing the myth of systemic fatphobia as a raceless issue—an issue that the People of Color Caucus of fat activist group NOLOSE highlighted in their 2012 response to the "I Stand" project. In the "I Stand" project, the original *Strong4Life* campaign's stigmatization of fatness as a symptom of black social failure, bad black

Figure 3.3b. "I Stand" Campaign, 2012. Courtesy of Amanda Levitt.

parenting, and black pathological embodiment remains unaddressed. Instead, fat black children's bodies become vehicles for a critique of fat-shaming that is ultimately dislocated from race and class.[33]

These media campaigns' silent mobilization of black women's and girls' bodies echoes silences around fatness and blackwoman embodiment in scholarly, popular, and activist discourses. We might consider the lack of public and critical discourse about this ad campaign in contrast to, for example, the antiabortion billboard that appeared in NYC a year earlier, in 2011. Sponsored by the antichoice group That's Abortion, the billboard depicted a young black girl under the caption "The Most Dangerous place for an African American is in the womb," a rhetorical violence which earned the billboard significant critique from both feminist and antiracist thinkers, precisely for its indictment of black

Figure 3.4. "Anti-Abortion Billboard Sparks Controversy" 2012. Mario Tama/Getty Images News via Getty Images.

women's reproductive autonomy and sexuality and its implicit disregard of economic access as a factor in women's reproductive decisions. In contrast, the *Strong4Life* campaign (which received very little public attention) demonstrates the ways in which race and intersectionality are evacuated from public critiques of fatphobia, while fat-shaming and fatphobia are largely absent from black feminist discourses of bodily freedom, even as both of these discourses (critiques of fatphobia and arguments for black feminist freedom) rely heavily on images of black girls' bodies. This recourse to understanding the fat black girl's body as both social *symptom* and social *cause*—that is, a symptom of the failures of blackness and a cause around which white feminist discourses can rally—is perhaps an interesting twist on a familiar move by which homophobic logics nurture moral panics around queerness and sexual difference using the image of an imagined, idealized, and idyllic child. Here, the fat black girl's voice is usurped by, on one hand, the hospital's rhetoric of structural antiblackness and classist medicalized fatphobia and, on the other hand, by the voices of white queer and feminist fat activists in whose anti-bullying campaign race, class, and globality are absent.

These are the under-examined contexts of intersecting racism, sexism, US-centrism, and fatphobia into which works like Krudxs Cubensi's "La Gorda" intervene. "La Gorda" responds to this simultaneous silencing and spectacularization of fat black women's bodies by queering the conventions of form, reimagining the fat blackwoman body as a metaphor for a livable place defined precisely by disallowed pleasure, desire, and difference. Identified in the music video as an "Anthem" of fat black feminist Cubanidad, the song and video offer fat black women's embodiment as a locus of beauty, pleasure, and desire, and a material and spatial center around which conceptions of nation and globality orbit. This emphasis on the fat blackwoman body's political potential for altering and intervening in accepted geographies and spatial configurations is clear in the song's hook: "llegó la gorda, la gorda llegó / llegó la gorda, la gorda soy yo [the fat woman has arrived/ here is the fat woman/ the fat woman has arrived/ I am the fat woman]." This phrase "llegó la gorda," which is repeated often in the song's verses as well, is somewhat difficult to translate, partly because of its investments in announcing the fat blackwoman body as an active force, the arrival of which is a meaningful event that requires the decisive mood and tone of the preterit tense. Thus, while "llegó la gorda" would colloquially be translated as "the fat woman is here," the preterit tense "llegó," literally translated as "arrived," more precisely articulates not simply the *presence* of the fat woman in a given space, but also the definitive and emphatic event of her arrival as an important intervention into the space of both the song and the listener's imaginary, as well as into political and social geographies that seek to exclude her.[34]

The song's lyrics are offered in Spanish, with partial English translations shown at the bottom of the screen in the music video. In interviews, Lxs Krudxs acknowledges writing the song partly in response to popular Cuban group La Charanga Habanera's song "La Gorda," from their 2002 album, *Soy Cubano Soy Popular* [I'm Cuban I'm Popular]. In the song, the lead singer laments his lover's weight gain, commanding her to eat less. Lxs Krudxs takes up that song's title and engages some of its most salient lyrics, recoding them in a critique of body hegemony to which issues of sexual autonomy, colorism, racism, and queer desire are central and using that critique as a centerpiece for reimagining the globality and Afrocubanidad. They respond to masculinist, racist, and sexist body policing logics like La Charanga's, saying "Baja de peso tú porque yo? Yo no. [Lose weight yourself because me? Not me."]"; they issue a challenge to fat activist discourses that silence blackness, nation, and class in discussions of pleasure and body liberation; finally, they situate fat black queer feminist embodiment and desire as focal points for rethinking nation and transnational communication in the diaspora. By maintaining focus on the fat black queer woman's body as a specter of freedom, they insist on an interstitial critique that links politics of race, gender, sexuality, and fat embodiment; further, by positioning that body as a metaphor for a worldmaking practice, they highlight links between artistic visions of nation building and globality, extending a tradition of

Afro-Cuban women's and feminist art which, as Flora María González Mandri puts it, "simultaneously engages the concept of nation and African diaspora in their works" (*Guarding Cultural Memory* 6).

The efforts of "La Gorda" to rearticulate black women's embodiment extend a long-standing Afrodiasporic feminist project of overwriting silence with multiple modes of voicing, and of locating the body and its pleasures as central to both linguistic expression and diasporic feminist critique. Las Krudas engages this tradition explicitly, locating themselves within Lorde's intellectual legacy as they declare "mi silencio no me proteja [my silence does not protect me]" near the midpoint of the song. Yet, here they omit the more popular part of the famous Lorde quote: "My silences had not protected me. *Your silence will not protect you*" (*Sister Outsider* 41). By focusing instead on Lorde's often overlooked preceding sentence, Krudxs Cubensi insists upon on the primacy of the first-person pronoun, shifting attention squarely onto the speaking black-woman body as it articulates and rearticulates diasporic feminism both *in* and *on* the body's own terms.

For Las Krudas, this body/language not only reimagines fatness and bodily difference, but also locates the power of fatness within an imagined space delimited by black / queer pleasure. Early in the song, rapper Odaymar Kruda shows their belly as they rhyme:

> Yo experimento un profundo placer
> En un mundo lleno de muchas formas de mujer
> A la alegría de la vida tenemos derecho
> Las de mas de 40 de cintura y 52 de pecho
> Mira, la gorda llegó a tu casa
> 180 avanza me tengo confinaza
> Y a partir de ahora disfruta de la danza
> De esta gorda con su panza . . .[35]

"Yo experimento un profundo placer/ en un mundo de muchas formas de mujer" translates literally as "I experience a profound pleasure in a world full of many womanly bodies/ forms of womanhood." Yet, here, "muchas formas de mujer" performs a profusion of meanings—signaling either "many forms of woman," as in models of womanhood, or womanly forms, as in "many women's bodies." The "world" the song imagines is thus one in which black womanhood is free to take on multiple forms of embodiment *and* to experience queer sexual pleasure, potentially with many same-sex partners. The next line centers, extends, and queers this proliferation of significations, as they rhyme "Disfruta de la danza de esta gorda con su panza [Enjoy this fat girl's dance with her belly]," invoking images of belly fucking and tummy tribadism, queer sexual practices made possible only by erotic engagements with fat flesh. The speaker clarifies

Figure 3.5a. "La Gorda," Las Krudas Cubensi (2009). Courtesy of Krudxs Cubensi.

the specifically same-sex possibilities of these erotic pleasures of fatness later in the song, as they exclaim "Fatty, fatty, fatty! Papi! Oiste? Esto tambien es pa ti mami! [Fatty, fatty, papi, you hear? This is for you too, mami]," speaking both literally and rhetorically, yelling both at and over the silencing of spectacular fat embodiment and the usurpation of fat women's voices, replacing them with declarations of black fat queer desire. That these radical fat black / queer encounters occur because "la gorda llegó a su casa [the fat woman came to your house]" emphasizes the spatial reach of this deviant queerness, and its potential to reconstruct and reclaim hostile spaces and spatial configurations precisely by exceeding their physical and figurative parameters.

The video's play with queer excesses extends to its linguistic engagements as well, emphasizing the extent to which the coloniality of language—like racist and sexist modes of body policing—must be unsettled in order to make geographic space for the fat blackwoman body. The song's emphatic expressions of erotic desire and pleasure work in productive tension with the discomforts that arise for English-language listeners and viewers attempting to access meaning in the lyrics and link them with the video's visual landscape. Through partial translation and tension between printed text, spoken language, and image, La Gorda critiques colonialities of language, requiring viewers to interrogate their own relationships to language, power, and embodiment in order to access the song's meanings. The song recodes languages of fat blackwoman and black / queer embodiment to rid them of stigma (the hook, for example, translates as 'They call me fat, round, ball. They call me fat. Yeah, I *am* fat!). Yet when engaged along with the video, these recodings are joined by partial, incomplete, and nonliteral translations that invoke multiple meanings, highlighting the untranslatability of black womanhoods that Spillers discusses and situating the black woman body as the ultimate arbiter of meaning. In the second verse, for example, what the English subtitles translate as "Absolute Monarchy" actually occurs in the lyrics as "monarca absoluta," which, translated literally, would mean "absolute monarch," not "absolute monarchy." In this partial mistranslation, this single line signals both the speaker's total and unassailable sovereignty over her individual body as an absolute monarch of her own form *and* alludes to a broader fantasy of a geopolitical terrain—a black / queer feminist monarchy—in which fat black queer women's embodiment is an ultimate marker of power. The sparseness of the English translation requires English-speaking audiences (much of Las Krudas's fan base) to perform the intellectual labor of stepping into this world and experiencing destabilizations of linguistic authority to listen to what these bodies have to say. In this sense, translation thus acts as part of a poetic tactics of "arriving at the truth through inaccuracies, apparent omissions, the propensity to digress, simulation, and constant questioning," which, as Flora María González Mandri argues (borrowing from Lydia Cabrera), are crucial to Afro-Cuban women's cultural self-articulation and diasporic critique (*Guarding Cultural Memory* 1).

This fantasy of a fat black queer woman-ruled nation is part of the song's larger vision of black feminist worldmaking. Odaymar describes their body as both "Redondo como la tierra/ que tantos mítos y leyendas [round like the earth/ like myths and legends]," and as "flotando como mi tierra, Cuba [floating like my homeland, Cuba]." Speaking itself into myth before a backdrop of oversized bowls of rice and beans and colossal loaves of bread, as well as whales, elephants, and images of the earth itself, Odaymar's fat black / queer body creates a new narrative of both diasporic geography and global possibility, each centered on black feminist embodiment and difference. In this narrative, the fat black / queer body becomes both the *site* and the *language* of an origin story: the "myth and legend" of a world in which excesses of black women's embodiment—fatness and queer desire—become the facts on which both Cuba and the world itself are formed.

The visual aesthetics of the video echo this language of bodily excess: in Krudxs Cubensi's visual poetics, the salient facts of blackness and womanhood exist simultaneously in queer proportion to the spectacular presence of sensuality, consumption, desire, and pleasure. The artists' bodies are framed in metonymic relation to the images of food—icons of sensuality and excessive desire—that world the landscape behind them. Verdant lettuce leaves unfold around them as they rhyme about their defiant embodiment; cake wedges twice the size of the rapper's head and cookies wider and rounder than their belly fill the scene as they rhyme "round like the earth, like my homeland, Cuba." By emphasizing the spectacle of fat desire and rendering the perceived objects of

Figure 3.5b. "La Gorda," Las Krudas Cubensi (2009). Courtesy of Krudxs Cubensi.

Figure 3.5c. "La Gorda," Las Krudas Cubensi (2009). Courtesy of Krudxs Cubensi.

that desire (food) on the same visual scale as the image of the earth itself, the video inverts the formal logics of ad campaigns like *Strong4Life*, in which the spectacle of silenced fat black women's bodies is used as a canvas for overlaying rhetorics of pathology, stigma, and state control. It also troubles the logics that animate Wann's "I Stand" project, in which the erasure of black and diasporic bodies limits and delimits the racial parameters of fat freedom; here, the fat blackwoman body is an unavoidable specter of pleasure and desire whose blackness and Cubanness are crucial to its liberatory political work as a worldmaking

Figure 3.5d. "La Gorda," Las Krudas Cubensi (2009). Courtesy of Krudxs Cubensi.

force. The inseparability of blackness, fatness, queerness, and womanhood thus also inverts the formal logics of the "grammars of capture" Spillers discusses, in which black women's bodies and voices are simultaneously evacuated of meaning in the service of colonial power. Here, fat, black / queer Cuban womanhood writes its own language of body and desire and uses that language to imagine both a nation and a world to which both that body and its desires are central.

Yet, "La Gorda's" geopolitical imaginary is not simply a fat black queer utopian fantasy; as much as "La Gorda" imagines a world of fat black / queer pleasure, it also conceives that world as an actively anticolonial project of nation building, labor, and war. Krudxs's body/language situates these individual and subjective experiences of embodiment as a necessary point of entry into the critique and re-creation of national and global politics of diasporic blackness and Afro-Cubanidad. They offer poetic evidence of the extent to which, as Jafari Sinclaire Allen puts it, "gendered, raced, and sexed self-making in Cuba is impelled by interaction with foreigners and global discourses, but most pointedly by individual and group desire for a *larger freedom*" (¡*Venceremos?* 2). Indeed, in the lyrics of "La Gorda," references to decolonization and anticolonial warfare appear nearly as frequently as references to sex, pleasure, and food. Odaymar criticizes the prevalence of "*anorexia en tiempos de Guerra* [anorexia in times of war]" and laments the degree to which "*a quiénes consumen cuerpos colonializados los tienen estresados* [consuming colonized bodies will have you stressed out]." Likewise, the speaker identifies as a "*guerrillera*" or warrior woman, invoking and, again, expanding the image of revolutionary Cubanidad to include the "*gorda, negra, guerrillera* [fat, black, warrior woman]" body. These invocations of war and revolution expand the song's anthem function to a global scale, positioning it as a rallying cry for fat black feminist liberation, but also locating it within a history of diasporic anticolonial struggle to which violences against fat black queer women and nonbinary people are not to be ignored.

Through their body/languages, Shange, Philip, and Krudxs Cubensi create new landscapes of diaspora in which there is, as Las Krudas puts it, "más espacio en el mundo"—more space in the world—for articulations of blackwoman difference. By melding voice and body on the terrains of the page, the stage, and the screen, these writers map global spaces and diasporic relationships as capacious as black women's political subjectivities themselves, visioning worlds of fleshy black voicing in which blackwoman and black / queer embodiment makes room for itself, and for thicker, fuller utterances of black feminist freedom. Through their birthed imperatives, digested narratives, and full-bellied globes of fatness, they forge paths beyond familiar models of blackness, proposing new notions of diasporic belonging defined by the complexity of black women's social, political, and bodily worlds.

# CHAPTER FOUR

# "Languages of Love," "TALK" of Sex

## *Interstitial Idioms of Body and Desire*

The repositioning of women in language occurs when
we interrupt, or dismantle the cultural mythologies that
position women in language . . . when we challenge how
the feminine in language is addressed. It may therefore
include reducing the language to its barest and most
elemental, or it may access other modes of articulating
or even other languages.
—Carole Boyce Davies, *Black Women, Writing, and
Identity: Migrations of the Subject*

. . . [I]dentity is not only a matter of paper and of blood
but also of *language*. And if it seems that language is,
as is so often said, a medium of communication, it is
above all for me, a writer, "a medium of transformation."
—Assia Djebar, "Writing in the Language of the Other"

Is it worth it? Let me work it. I put my thang down,
flip it and reverse it.
—Missy Elliott, "Work It."[1]

Reimagining social and bodily worlds through a poetics of difference requires
imaginative feats of language. Creative, secret, furtive acts of linguistic rein-
vention in African Diaspora women's literature work to inscribe community,
articulate intimacy, and create space for subversive modes of collective engagement through disallowed expressions of the erotic. By "stripping," "flipping,"
"reversing," and "transforming" lexical and grammatical norms of colonial language, black women writers of the diaspora propose collectivities in which the
subversive, erotic, and bodily nuances of blackwoman difference enable radical
modes of intimacy shaped by the unspeakable erotics of the nuantial (Spill-

ers *"Interstices"* 156s). These artists' reimagined languages call for black queer feminist reading strategies that illuminate the nuances of erotic engagement in Afrodiasporic women's literary texts. By inventing "secret" languages of black-woman erotics that must be navigated to access their texts, these artists center interstitial difference as a defining site of blackwoman body, desire, and intimacy for characters and readers alike. Languages reinvented through a poetics of difference reveal the crucial role of black queer feminist reading for exploring the nuances of the erotic in queer and non-queer black women writers' texts.

The archive of invented languages in black women's literature is as expansive as it is undertheorized. While many critics have considered the place of African oral traditions and coded language in African American literature, few have examined the specific place of the invention of language systems in black texts, and none has done so with regard to black women's texts in particular.[2] Yet, from Zora Neale Hurston's use of "Alphabet" as a nickname for her protagonist, Janie, on her quest toward economic, sexual, and emotional self-fulfillment in *Their Eyes Were Watching God*; to Celie's conception of "new" languages in which to talk with her sister across boundaries of nation and sexuality in Alice Walker's *The Color Purple*; to Harryette Mullen's extended poetic excavations of the potentialities of English for critiquing gender, race, and class in her poetry collection *Sleeping with the Dictionary*; to poet M. NourbeSe Philip's recasting of language as "foreign anguish" in *She Tries Her Tongue*, secret languages, new vocabularies, and unthought-of systems of speech figure prominently, if quietly, in black women's anti-oppressive literary critiques.[3]

Across genres and forms, black women writers and artists of the diaspora have invented and reinvented language to articulate unspoken nuances of black women's bodily experience. By speaking difference in new tongues, these artists write, project, image, and imagine the "missing words" of blackwoman difference as a legible, inescapable fact of their texts. In so doing, they expose the hegemonies of dominant language and demonstrate the change-making possibility of black women's creative wordplay, inviting, and in some cases requiring, their readers, viewers, and listeners to play along. By rewriting the grammars of difference in languages of desire, these artists facilitate new means of identification, communication, and intimacy for black women. They expose both the critical possibilities of black women's linguistic imaginations and the theoretical complexities of intersectional experience itself, telling stories of black girl difference in languages that are at once difficult to interpret and impossible to ignore.

Writers such as Walker, Hurston, Mullen, South African-Botswanan writer Bessie Head, Ghanaian writer Ama Ata Aidoo, American writers Suzan-Lori Parks and Toni Morrison, rapper Missy Elliott, and others have all used invented language to explore the queer formal possibilities of intersectionality. These writers use shared invented linguistic systems to highlight and complicate how we conceptualize blackwoman difference and to make space for new models of blackwoman communication, community, and belonging. They construct what Mullen refers to as "a heteroglossia for collaborative reading," in which the presence of multiple speakers, languages, and registers of voice and lyric allows—and *instructs*—readers to make contact with racial and gender alterity through what she terms "the flavor of difference in language" beyond the limits of English (*Recyclopedia* xi).

Reading black women writers' invented languages through a black queer feminist interpretive strategy attuned to the poetics of difference expands important recent discourses on black women's erotic and bodily expression by simultaneously centering queer and diasporic perspectives and examining textual/literary engagement as a site of black feminist erotic praxis. Recent studies of black erotic expression by L. H. Stallings, Amber Jamilla Musser, and others open space for close exploration of the place of language and literary poetics in black sexuality studies and for sustained attention to the diasporic resonances of literary engagements with the erotic. Likewise, explorations of black women's erotic performance by Jennifer Christine Nash, Mireille Miller-Young, Ariane Cruz, and others point to the crucial interventions black women artists make into discourses on race, gender, and erotic specifically through the expressive capacities of the body, and chart pathways for further exploration of the relationships between embodiment and linguistic expression in black feminist conceptions of the erotic on a diasporic stage.

These writers use their invented languages to rewrite what Stallings calls "the enslaved and colonial logics of sexuality," in which the bodily experiences of Afrodiasporic subjects are "assimilated into gender and sexual practices they did not author or narrate in their own tongue." By invoking these languages and requiring their readers to read them, these writers exemplify the processes of "learning and unlearning" that decolonial literacies require (*A Dirty South Manifesto* 16). They exemplify the "alternate language of eroticism and care" that, as Musser argues (drawing on José Esteban Muñoz and Nadia Ellis), emerge from the queer losses and excesses of diaspora and communicate queer modes of "mothering" in diasporic art (Musser 114). Like these "alternate" languages of matrilineal connection and the body/languages Ntozake Shange uses to rewrite Afrodiasporic women's identity through movement, color, and dance in *for colored girls*, the invented languages of interstitial intimacy I explore here offer solutions to the problem of expressing Afrodiasporic women's subjective complexity through black women's nuantial embodiment. Yet, as shared, spoken language systems, the new idioms in these texts also complicate narratives of black multilingualism and address larger social and structural problems of colonial language specifically from diasporic feminist perspectives attuned to the erotic.

Reading black women writers' invented languages for their poetics of difference brings contemporary US-based discourses on black women's erotics into contact with long-standing discussions of linguistic multiplicity and anticoloniality in diasporic literary studies. Ghanaian poet and scholar Abena Busia, Senegalese poet and theorist Léopold Senghor, US writer James Baldwin, Algerian feminist writer Assia Djebar, and Nigerian writer Chinua Achebe are among the many diasporic writers who have debated the functions of colonial language in expressing black identity difference and diasporic connection. Ngùgì Wa Thiong'o argues that colonial language aims, by definition, to "grow on the graveyard of other people's languages," becoming a "language of the world" only through the extermination of the existing languages of "other" worlds and cultures. As he puts it, "an oppressive language invariably carries racist and negative images of the conquered nation . . . and English is no exception" (175). These "racist and negative images," are, of course, marked by hegemonies of gender and sexuality, and endure even in post-colonial and post-emancipation diasporic language systems. As Geneva Smitherman notes, legacies of white/ Western imperialism impact linguistic expression throughout the diaspora, fostering systems of "language oppression," in which Western cultures deny and reject black discursive modes derived from African speech patterns, reinforcing Western visions of gender and sociality through linguistic norms (3). For diasporic women writers, imagining communicative touch beyond language oppression means creating new languages attuned to what Arianne Cruz terms "racial-sexual alterity[:] the perceived entangled racial and sexual otherness that characterizes the lived experience of black womanhood" through "a particular, though neither static nor essential, sociocultural experience of subjectivity—one in which sexual categories of difference are always linked to systems of power and social hierarchies" (33, 34).

Afrodiasporic women writers' poetics of difference have worked to create such languages, addressing the extermination of African languages through enslavement and colonization and the genders, sexualities, and intimacies rendered inarticulable through colonial hierarchies of power and difference. For black feminist writers of the diaspora, linguistic "recovery" takes its place beside the point of the creative process, as even "African" languages carry connections to gender-based hegemonies of their own. For those working in English, navigating language becomes a process of creative memory and narrative visioning, an effort to express the inexpressible in a language that constantly represents loss, liminality, and the systematized silencing of difference. Cultural prohibitions against discussions of sexuality, nonnormative embodiment, and women's erotic desire compound these challenges of language. In a world in which, as Evelynn Hammonds puts it, black women's sexuality is a constant "absence . . . described in metaphors of speechlessness," black women writers are tasked with writing past multiple silencings to articulate their sexual, erotic, and bodily subjectivity ("Black (W)holes" 171). How does one express the already forbidden in a language that cannot, by definition, accommodate one's voice?

Focusing on Morrison's novel *Love* (2003), Parks's play *Fucking A* (2001), Bessie Head's short story "Life" (1981), Ama Ata Aidoo's prosepoem novella, *Our Sister Killjoy* (1977), and Missy Elliott's hip-hop single "Work It" (2002), I argue that invented tongues, recast idioms, and imagined systems of speech enable black women writers and artists to wage important critiques of gender, sexuality, and erotic desire and to mobilize those critiques to define black feminist intimacies rooted in difference. I term these systems *interstitial languages*. I use this to describe invented idioms that provide language for speaking what Hortense Spillers calls "the missing word—the interstice" of black women's sexuality and difference, "which allows us to speak about and that which enables us to speak at all" ("Interstices" 156). Interstitial languages function as invented linguistic systems used by black women writers, artists, and characters to articulate the interconnections and nuances of blackwoman experiences of sexuality, intimacy, embodiment, and desire that are inarticulable in standard English, and to mobilize the site of intersection as a means for creating speaking communities rooted in black blackwoman difference.

I use Spillers's notion of the "interstice" to emphasize the specific silencing of black women's sexuality in particular, even as I also mean to signal its conceptual relation to the trope of the "intersection," through which Kimberlé Crenshaw and many others have read multiplicities of blackwoman difference. As I've argued earlier, the interstice provides a means of theorizing intersectionality specifically through a lens of sexuality and desire as linguistic engagements and returning intersectionality discourse to its proto-discourses in black feminist literary and humanistic studies.

This chapter thus focuses on two major types of interstitial language: (1) those languages that operate at the interstices of English language reading practices and new linguistic forms illegible in terms of standard English morphology; and (2) those that operate at the interstices of the spoken and the silenced within the English language (and/or other dominant Western languages), using the morphologies and vocabularies of those languages in nonnormative ways and explicitly claiming those reconfigurations as "new language."

Through these approaches, interstitial languages extend the narrative and dialogic multiplicities that, as Mae G. Henderson, Dorothy Hale, Dale Peterson, and others have argued, serve pivotal tools in the black women's literary expressions of difference.[4] By inventing new languages for discussing black women's embodiment, black women writers exploit the formal and poetic multiplicities of novelistic dialogism and polyglossia to critique the colonial logics of English, and to interrogate its viability for expressing black women's experiences of difference on both social and bodily planes. Smitherman suggests that "language plays a dominant role in the formation of ideology, consciousness, behavior and social relations; [and] thus contemporary political and social theory must address the role of language in social change." Interstitial language offers a corresponding political possibility for literary studies; by destabilizing dominant language and centering black women's intersectional experience in new languages unfamiliar to standard English readers, these writers "change" the worlds they write about *and* the intellectual landscapes their readers inhabit, challenging readers to navigate multiple forms of alterity in the poetic and linguistic properties of their texts (94).

In approaching this imaginative world-changing through languages of the body in particular, interstitial language instantiates on a linguistic level the radical erotic and bodily "wildness" through which Stallings argues black women's novels and other cultural texts articulate a "self-authored sexual desire and radical black women's sexual subjectivity that purposely incorporates that desire as the context for rebellion from the beginning" (*Mutha Is Half a Word* 3). These languages demonstrate that the textual "beginnings" of rebellious black women's sexual expression can precede even the structures of narrative and genre, often occurring in the very lexicons, grammars, and morphemes through which black women writers set sexuality to speaking. Attention to these nuances of interstitial language allows access to the far reaches of the "sites of suggestive silence" where, according to Aliyyah Abdur-Rahman, "scenes of acknowledged discursive or representational impossibility" reveal "unabashed" and unsanctioned expressions of black sexual life in literature (*Against the Closet* 28). Attention to interstitial languages builds on these and other recent explorations of black women's erotic expressivity by demonstrating black women writers' efforts to subvert hegemonies of language, embodiment, and desire through the poetics of language and creative form. Where Abdur-Rahman analyzes the erotics of silence as resistance in slave narratives, I extend this approach to explore illegibility and untranslatability as modes of both communal pleasure and intersectional critique for black women writers and characters in the twenty-first century.

Each appearing within the first three years of the twenty-first century, the texts by Morrison, Parks, and Elliott use a poetics of interruption consistent with larger trends in twenty-first-century black experimentalism, in which aesthetic variegation complicates the stability of the black subject and emphasizes alterity. As Anthony Reed points out, many black experimental poets of the twenty-first century "use techniques associated with mass media . . . within a dense network of détourned [or reimagined] poetic techniques to trouble and reconceive ideas of voice and identity, emphasizing the moment of self-expression as a moment of self-othering" (98). These writers mobilize this aesthetics of reconceptualization and interruption, tapping into multiplicities of media as well as genre and language. They use these strategies to enact a specifically intersectional "self-othering" that expresses, in Henderson's terms, "the 'other' . . . within" black women's simultaneously racialized, gendered, and erotic selves, and to suggest that those acts of expressive difference can productively re-define and delimit black women's shared and individual experiences of identity in the twenty-first century (24).

For black women writers, the problem of English is the problem of inter-sectionality. Writing in English means creating through, against, and beyond a multilayered discursive system of social and structural silencings—in which normative ideas of "proper" speech coalesce with normative conceptions of blackness, gender, class, and sexuality—rendering black womanhood unspeakable on all fronts. As Spillers, Henderson, and others have pointed out, this erasure is a problem not only of discourse, but of language. Marcyliena Morgan argues that Western culture creates and reifies two key assumptions about the gender dynamics of black speech: first, that the use of "varie[d]," English speech modes (as in code-switching) and the more general ability to demonstrate unfettered verbal self-expression are "linguistically male" phenomena reflective of a specifically patriarchal social power; and, second, that for black women, both speaking multiple languages and speaking *at all* are deviant acts (xiv).[5]

In this context of deviant expressivity, the invention of new languages for articulating black womanhood is an act of both subjective pleasure and political critique. The works of the writers and artists gathered here reveal how black women's interstitial languages reconfigure the landscapes of erotic difference and belonging both within and beyond the text, impact not only the imaginary social world of the characters but also the psychic and intellectual experiences of the reader. Interstitial language operates on affective scales of both sensory pleasure and epistemic discomfort, highlighting black women's erotic difference in different ways, for different audiences. For readers who live and experience the nonnormativities of blackwoman desire, interstitial language occasions familiar interpretive acts that both echo pleasurably the erotics of those desires and confirm them as a set of shared experiences, inscribing characters, authors, and readers in a nonnormative community of blackwoman belonging. Conversely, it challenges those less familiar with ascriptions of deviance to labor through the affective discomfort, intellectual work, and relative powerlessness of illegibility, untranslatability, and unknowing.

Interstitial language is thus crucial for black literary studies not only for what it *means*—that is, for signifying black women artists' critiques of racialized gender, sexuality, and difference—but also for what it *does*. By carving intimate textual space for black women's erotics and requiring others to labor for access to black womanhood, interstitial languages invert long-reigning power paradigms, dislodging linguistic authority from its usual loci and placing it in the hands and mouths of black women and girls.

## "Ush-Hidagay": Interstitial Intimacies in Toni Morrison's *Love*

The play of language in Toni Morrison's *Love* vividly illustrates the potential of invented idioms for facilitating subversive intimacies in black women's fiction and demonstrates the fundamental functions of interstitial language as a means of interrupting interpretive experience across genres and artistic mediums. Published in 2003, *Love* echoes many of Morrison's signature stylistic markers and extends on her long-standing use of form to consider black women's gender and sexuality. Like *The Bluest Eye* (1970), *Beloved* (1987), *Paradise* (1998), *A Mercy* (2008), and *God Help the Child* (2015), the novel explores intricacies of connection among black American women through a heteroglossic narrative structure that moves deftly between characters' interiorities in both first- and third-person narrative. Through this structure, *Love*, like some of these other works, depicts the psychic and interior lives of women learning to live with, relate to, and love one-another in a world in which power is defined exclusively by sexual or hereditary attachment to men, and in which, in either case, "having men mean[s] sharing them" (Morrison 165). Reading this unfolding through a black queer feminist hermeneutic of the interstice reveals how *Love*'s black-girl protagonists use invented idioms to navigate and critique these dynamics, creating space for subversive intimacy and erotic freedom through language.

Despite the identity-defining power of patriarchal affiliation in *Love*, the relationship at the center of the novel's narrative is the lifelong friendship between Heed and Christine Cosey, the wife and granddaughter of Bill Cosey, the patriarch of the black coastal resort town where the novel is set. It is the illicit power of language that facilitates this bond. In the world of the novel, as Morrison's narrator puts it, "language, when it finally comes, has the vigor of a felon pardoned after twenty-one years on hold. Sudden, raw, stripped to its underwear" (184). Heed and Christine's intimacy is rendered through "idagay," a linguistic system the two use throughout their decades-long friendship to communicate only with one another about sex, sexuality, and the erotic capacities of the body. The two develop "idagay" early in girlhood, before the eleven-year-old Heed marries Cosey, Christine's grandfather. The narrator describes "idagay" as their "private code . . . for intimacy, gossip, telling jokes on grown-ups" (188). Through this language, the two create a private space in which to explore themselves, the connections between them, and the world around them as they come of age. "Idagay" resounds with a kind of closeness in which the two girls "shared stomachache laughter, a secret language, and knew as they slept together that one's dreaming was the same as the other one's" (132, 133).

Based in English vocabulary and sentence structure, "idagay" is defined by a reconfigured phonic and syllabic pattern in which English language root syllables are split at the first vowel and appended with the first consonant and the tag "idagay": "rent" becomes "ent-ridagay," "you" becomes "ou-yidagay," and so on (188). "Idagay" adheres to both the formal and sociopolitical properties of what Kyra Gaunt calls "playful speech." While often dismissed as "so-called 'nonsense' language," these forms, which include common forms known as "pig latin" are constantly in conversation with the sociopolitical registers of black girls' lives and experiences (90).[6] In the case of "idagay," the social is indistinguishable from the formal. The disruption of the word and the syllable—and the insertion of black girls' "nonsense" into meaningful language forms—inscribe black girl speakers in a linguistic space designed exclusively for the intimate sharing of "priva[cy]" and "secrets." It creates a space for intimate, autonomous exchange of sensation and information in a larger social landscape in which their bodies are constantly made available for male consumption.

"Idagay" defines this space of black girl "privacy" both through its action on and reconfiguration of standard English morphologies. The language adds three syllables to each English language word ("i-duh-gay"), altering both the word's form and its range of meanings, drawing connections relevant to the novel's critique of racist and sexist sexual mores. For example, "slave" becomes "ave-slidagay" invoking the Latin "ave," or "hail," and places this phoneme "ave" alongside the action of "sliding." Given Morrison's sustained interest in both the aesthetic imprints of biblical narratives on black culture and disallowed modes of black erotic expression, reading through a black queer feminist hermeneutic demonstrates how the "idagay" word for "slave" incorporates into its morphology a direct juxtaposition of languages of religious exaltation and moral descent that echo the norms of gendered ownership and sexual propriety that Morrison's blackgirl protagonists use idagay to grapple with. Here, interstitial language enacts a critique of gender standards in general, and of the conundrums of black womanhood in particular. From a sociolinguistic perspective, these syllables also signal a change in prosody, a hallmark of African American code-switching modes, which, as Karla Scott observes, "involves a culturally-specific contextualization cue, which still allows the one who switches [codes] to embed an in-group message and signal identity" (243). By enacting morphological difference on the English language, "idagay" enables Christine and Heed to think through and bond over the identifications they share (blackness, girlhood / womanhood, and youth).

Yet, as much as it is a language of closeness, "idagay" is also a language of difference—a linguistic means by which power differentials between black women are articulated, reframed, reified, and critiqued. Christine and Heed's coming-of-age stories—and the story of their friendship—are shaped both by shared experiences of gender and race and by defining differences of class and power. By veiling discussions of the women's intimacy and erotic connectedness through interstitial language, Morrison illuminates the interconnectedness of gender, sexuality, and class difference in both their individual development of erotic subjectivity and the experiences of blackwoman deviance and desire they share.

The most meaningful difference between Heed and Christine is that of class status—a difference that, in the novel, operates most directly through its place in the sexual economies of marriage. While Christine is born heiress to Cosey's earnings, Heed comes from the poor "Up Beach" section of the town, where "every woman's obituary could have read 'Death by Children'" (104). The eleven-year-old Heed's marriage to Bill Cosey thus marks a substantial class ascendancy and a prepubescent entry into both sexual objectification and sexual experience at once. Christine, in particular, imagines the two women's class differences in terms of language, constantly using her command of grammar as a means of asserting power and primacy over Heed, particularly in contests for Cosey's affections (134).

The novel's third-person narrator further emphasizes this linkage of language, class, and sexual deviance in each girl's characterization. Heed is described as a "born . . . liar" whose verbal duplicity, like her poverty and perceived lasciviousness, seems congenital, or is at least inherited through social rituals of "upbeach" culture (145). Similarly, Christine flaunts grammatical correctness as evidence of her social superiority and can only question the value of normative language later in adulthood, once her own marriage begins to fail. For her, securing class superiority means entry into the "organization with the least privacy, the most rules, and the fewest choices: the biggest, totally male entity in the world"—heterosexual marriage (92). Once her marriage falls apart and her status becomes uncertain, Christine understands the failure of marriage as a failure of expressive capacity. She describes the pain of the split as a "hyphenating" of her lungs, reworking English to articulate the socioeconomic trauma of marriage and its failures as both bodily and linguistic rupture (161).

For both Christine and Heed, class differences also mean differing relationships to sex, sexuality, and marriage, a nexus of new and diverging experiences of power and embodiment that can only be articulated through languages made different as well. "Idagay" thus serves a dual function. It acts as a metaphorical system of opposition to the legal and social schemas of heteropatriarchal marriage, offering young black women both, as the novel puts it, "privacy" and "choices" with which to express the fullness of self and sexuality in a specifically nonmasculinist linguistic context and providing a space for intimate, autonomous exchange of sensation and information in a larger social landscape in which their bodies are constantly made available for male consumption. Yet, "idagay" also enables Christine and Heed to create a space in which differences *between* black womanhoods may be voiced with the direct precision of a whisper.

We see this differentiating function of "idagay" most clearly at the midpoint of the novel, when the two girls slip into it during an argument over Cosey's affections. Refusing to accept Heed's complicity in her newly consummated marriage to Cosey, the 12-year-old Christine shouts: "Ou-yidagay a ave-slidagay! E-hidagay ought-bidagay ou-yidagay ith-widagay a ear's-yidaga ent-redagay an-didagay a andy-cidagy ar-bidagay!" ("You a slave! He bought you with a year's rent and a candy bar!") (129). Here, Christine mobilizes discourses of race, gender, sexuality, and class simultaneously, using "idagay" both to critique hegemonic structures of enslavement and child sexual abuse and to designate Heed as deviant on all fronts. "Idagay" thus mediates a fraught in-group critique of black women's sexuality and power. Christine has internalized patriarchal codes of sociality in which women bear responsibility for various forms of abuse. This, along with a received cultural logic that resorts to, as Morrison's narrator puts it, "blaming a child for a grown man's interest in her," render Christine unable to dislodge Heed's status as Cosey's juvenile sexual property from her perceived sexual deviance and availability as a poor Up Beach girl (145).

By presenting this argument through dialogue in "idagay," Morrison calls on her reader to navigate difference as her characters experience it, introducing Christine and Heed's raced, classed, and gendered experiences of sexuality through an epistemic struggle with the alien technologies of interstitial language. "Idagay" is legible enough so that the reader can make meaning; phonetically; however, its syllables are just dissonant enough within the context of the novel's English language narrative to require a concerted effort on the part of the reader. Morrison asks readers to assume what Algerian feminist writer Djebar, in her important essay, "Writing in the Language of the Other," calls a "mnemonic responsibility," through which engaging with the language of the other involves "not merely being able to cross the threshold of the other"; it also requires an intimate engagement with the history, context, and lineages of the speaking others' experiences (317). This engagement is not only historical but also cognitive and affective; the reader's experience of the text shifts to accommodate the mnemonic unfamiliarity of the black girls' self-created language of difference and perform the intellectual labor of attempting to understand black girlhood both *on* and *in* its own terms. That this attempt is necessarily incomplete echoes the constantly frustrated nature of the aims of idagay itself; just as the language cannot create a secure and permanent space of power and self-definition for the girls, the reader can access only the language's epistemic signification—never the experiences that give those significations their meanings, textures, and social weight.

This attempt at translation is necessarily fraught and incomplete. Neither Morrison's characters nor her narrator translates "idagay" when it is first presented in the novel; translation is constantly deferred and embedded within Morrison's often cavernous narrative. For example, although Christine calls Heed "a ave-slidagay," near the midpoint of the novel, it is not until the novel's close that Heed partially translates Christine's exclamation, saying "Ave-slidagay. That hurt, Christine . . . Calling me a slave" (188). By refusing to translate the rest of Christine's insult ("He bought you with a year's rent and a candy bar"), Morrison leaves readers to develop their own literacy through which to grasp the relationship between enslavement and the class status and girlhood that the "year's rent" and "candy bar," respectively, signal.

Rather than provide direct and complete translations of her characters' idiom of difference, Morrison weaves the experience and meanings of difference into the structure of her narrative, developing a poetics in which interconnectedness of different bodies and voices echoes the interconnectedness of sexual experience and class difference. At the close of the novel, when Christine and Heed lay near death in the ruins of the Cosey resort, "idagay" expands from dialogic idiom to narrative strategy, as their bodies and voices merge in contemplation of the multiple forms of ownership, oppression, and alterity they experience:

> Well, it's like we started out being sold, got free of it, then sold ourselves to the highest bidder.
> Who you mean "we"? Black people? Women? You mean me and you?
> I don't know what I mean. Christine touches Heed's ankle. The unswollen one.
> Sssss.
> Sorry. [ . . . ]
> Hold my . . . my hand.
> He took all my childhood away from me, girl.
> He took all of you away from me.
> The sky, remember? When the sun went down?
> Sand. It turned pale blue. [ . . . ]
> Pretty. So so pretty.
> Love. I really do.
> Ush-hidagay. Ush-hidagay (185–195).

"Idagay" joins with Morrison's expressive embodiments and her heteroglossic narrative structure to convey black women's subjective and relational complexity. The pain Heed feels in her ankle becomes part of Morrison's polyglossia, represented in the onomatopoeic sound "sssss," the sibilance of which links the physical experience of pain to the aural/oral soundscape of the narrative. Christine's hesitation in asking Heed to touch her and her repetition of the word "my" in that request foreground the importance of comfort and sensual pleasure in this embodied language of intimacy. The deferred request for touch gestures to the various tensions and desires that will find fulfillment in the women's simultaneous physical and verbal embrace.

As dialogue tags and attributions disappear, Morrison exploits the full narrative potential of "idagay" as an idiom of blackwoman difference. As Heed and Christine discuss the interconnectedness and indistinguishability of raced and gendered structures of human ownership in their lives, their voices, too, become entangled inextricably. The distinctions between black and woman, wife and child, narrator and character, girlhood friendship and queer love are all effaced as Morrison's poetics lead the reader to decipher a new idiom of difference. The reader thus experiences both Christine's confusion and Heed's pain while working to piece together a narrative of the countless identifications that have joined and distanced them, an effort which the narrator at once echoes and dismisses with the intimately coded imperative to "ush-hidagay." In *Love*'s language, the narrative informs us, black women's intimacy, like difference itself, will not yield to normative grammars. Only in the spaces between recognizable sounds—in the imaginative territories of language remade—can the "missing word[s]" of black womanhood find expression.

## "TALK of Sex": Parks's *Fucking A*

Suzan-Lori Parks's *Red Letter Plays* (2001) takes up this notion of black women's bodies as subversive text in quite literal, material ways. The collection's final play, *Fucking A*, in particular, demonstrates the potential of interstitial language to center black women's erotic and bodily difference not only in the psychic experience of the reader, as Morrison does, but also on the material space of both the stage and the text. Parks configures the body itself as a material through which invented languages of sexual deviance are created. *Fucking A* and its sister play, *In the Blood*, feature two versions of Hester, a woman character living in undefined geographical and temporal context(s). The social landscape(s) of this setting evoke a constant sense of political upheaval, particularly in relation to cultural logics and state race, gender, and sexuality. Like Nathaniel Hawthorne's Hester Prynne, Parks's Hesters are emblems of women's deviant sexual autonomy and crucial figures in structuring public discourses on deviance. They insert into that discourse the state's "divergent fantasies" of what Lauren Berlant, in her reading of Hawthorne, calls "the Utopian promises of collective identity" based in spontaneous, ubiquitous virtue on one hand, and, on the other hand, the enticing regulatory powers of the law (Berlant 115, 61). And like Hawthorne's Hester, Parks's protagonists bear these public signs of gendered deviance materially—in the form of graffiti and other textual markings on Hester's home in *In the Blood*; and in the form of a letter "A"—for "Abortionist"—seared on her chest in "Fucking A."

This linguistic branding symbolizes the constant connections between sexual deviance, bodily autonomy, and language in *Fucking A*, first produced in 2000 and published in 2001. In the play, language written *on* the deviant body becomes language written *for and through* the deviant body in "TALK," a coded, non-English linguistic system used by the characters exclusively to describe issues of women's sexuality, desire, sexual violence, reproduction, and embodiment. TALK incorporates elements of nine spoken languages, including English, Spanish, French, and German, as well as some not readily associated with any spoken language. Glossed in the back matter of the text version of *Fucking A* and often projected onto the stage or distributed in pamphlet form during live productions, TALK requires the reader/viewer to constantly engage sexual and gender difference, as well as how language polices those differences.[7] Reading *Fucking A* through a black queer feminist interpretive strategy demonstrates how TALK facilitates subversive modes of blackwoman intimacy, connection, and erotic and reproductive autonomy within the text, and trains readers and viewers to navigate multiple structures of power in order to access the play's intersectional critique.

By engaging in these acts of translation directly, Parks's audience negotiates, in Djebar's phrase, "the threshold of the other" through multiple reading and viewing technologies (317). Yet, the "otherness" that TALK invokes is not merely the diasporic oral and linguistic multiplicity broadly associated with black diasporic vernacular dialogic traditions. TALK is a specifically gendered, often erotic linguistic methodology, reserved for what Hester's friend Canary calls "[w]omen things. Private women's things. Motherhood things. Things like that" (213). These "private women's things" span a range of topics pertaining to blackwoman corporeality, sexuality, and femininity. Discussing the power-hungry white First Lady's inability to bear children, for example, Hester and Canary depart from the play's standard vernacular English, concurring, in TALK, "*Falltima Ovo ella greek Tragedy woah-ya*" (124). By translating this phrase as "When her period comes she is in hysterics," Parks's glossary implicates the First Lady in a mocking critique of privileged femininities in which encounters with the body's uncontrollability constitute epic drama (223). Likewise, when Hester approaches a worker from the agency from which she must buy her incarcerated son's release from prison, the worker uses TALK to extend her role in the town's civic disciplinary structures to a disciplining of sexuality and black motherhood. She refuses Hester's request, switching from English to TALK to condemn Hester as one of the town's many women who "*Tee tee kop fuh Binah Zoo*"—"open their legs for everybody" (132, 223).

TALK also expresses women's sexual desire and critiques the stigmas that it sometimes articulates. Only through TALK, for example, can the First Lady boast, *"meh Kazo-say greengrass ee-sunny skies ee"*—"my vagina is nice and pleasant" (128, 223). TALK, too, enables Hester to speak out against state-sanctioned sexual violence against women, chastising one of the hunters tasked with apprehending and killing escaped convicts: *"Le doe-dunk eyesee Frahla ehle dunk sehh Frala ah ma, Mister Hunter"*—"you force yrself on yr wife and then you send her to me, Mister Hunter" (146, 224).[8] These dual valences of TALK—as a hegemonic language for removing undesirable elements of women's sexuality from public discourse and as a radical mode of speaking back to gender and sexual normativity and reproductive and sexual violence—reflect Hester's ambivalence toward difference and echo the broader conundrum of writing through the intersectional experience.

For contemporary black women writers, the critical question in the development of a new poetics is how to create languages that fold the experience of multiple forms of oppression into the practice of cultural consumption without either overwriting or understating the limiting as well as liberatory properties of difference. For Parks, the solution is to allow both black *women* to speak and the black women's *bodies* to speak, and to do so in a new language invented specifically for those purposes. The body does the work that voice alone cannot, making clear the traumas and distortions that difference enacts on black womanhood in normative spaces. Through this invented language, Parks's characters expand the potentials of language to express blackwoman sexuality by accessing the expressive technologies of the body. TALK allows Parks's women to complicate difference by speaking, as Hester puts it, *"Woah-yah dateh"*—"as if their vaginas were their mouths" (132, 225).

TALK is thus both a means of disciplining public discourse about women's sexuality *and* of creating transgressive intimacies and communities rooted in women's sexual deviance. TALK serves the populace of Parks's town as a sanitizing idiom, relegating discussion of women's anatomy, sexuality, gender, and desire to the private realm; it also produces a community of linguistic insiders defined by difference and gives otherwise silenced voices a forum in which to speak their difference freely and to critique the discursive structures that silence them. The visual dissonance of the projected translations on stage and the intellectual rupture produced by the manual turn from text to glossary reinforce the duality of TALK, requiring that the reader/viewer actively navigate this collectivizing line in expressly bodily ways. The reader/viewer is called constantly to traverse the space between inside and outside, shifting their gaze up and down, turning the page back and forth, as Parks's characters "talk" their difference onto stage and text.

This transformation of space—of both the stage and the printed text—is crucial to the ways in which Parks's interstitial language helps us reconceive diasporic space, creating communities and worlds of blackwoman sexual and erotic difference. As Spillers points out, expressions of the interstice (like the interstitial language, TALK) must, by definition "share . . . a common border with another country of symbols—the iconographic" (156). The stage projections and appended glossaries of TALK perform this iconographic work as dramaturgical/textual analogs of Hester's A-shaped wound. TALK functions as an antinormative language through which Parks's characters may forge a boundary-traversing linguistic community of difference. For Parks, these boundaries map directly onto lived, geographical space. As she states, "[p]lays are about space, and [about] . . . strange people not connected to any one backdrop" (309). The text and stage directions of play act as "the map of a piece of land. And what [Parks tries] to do is say there are 10 roads, 20, 50 roads—take one" (Jiggetts 312). Parks's conception of the "space" of the stage resonates deeply with contemporary conceptions of Afro-diaspora. Her stage is both a complex geographical terrain defined by its innumerable paths to meaning and a gathering place of "[dis]connected" subjects defined by "strange[ness]" and a shared experience of difference. And, significantly, in *Fucking A*, TALK does this work on explicitly woman-centered, sexually deviant terms. If the world of the play is one in which women express their sexuality "as if their vaginas were their mouths," TALK mobilizes this gendered self-expression toward the articulation of a diaspora based in women's sexual difference (Parks 224).[9]

In this difference-based space, TALK presents a language of intimacy and alliance among women. The subversive and collectivizing functions of Parks's interstitial language are, perhaps, most apparent in the final scene, where Monster (Boy's adult manifestation) comes to Hester for refuge, claiming to be a friend of Boy's from prison there to deliver his belongings. Following his departure, Hester talks with Canary and the Butcher, Hester's male love interest, who "couldn't speak TALK to save [his] life" (225). The Butcher's complete lack of access to the TALK enables Canary to perform intimacy in the safe space of coded language:

| | |
|---|---|
| CANARY: *Jamah, Hester, jamah?* | Hester, what's the matter? |
| HESTER: *Doht.* | Nothing. |
| CANARY: *Jamah?* | What is it?[10] |

Initially, Hester resists Canary's prodding, describing only vaguely her interaction with Monster in English. Yet when Canary inquires about Boy's belongings, Hester invokes the subversive potential of polyglossia, responding first in English, then rerouting the conversation into TALK:

HESTER: *Le traja Scrapeahdepth woah-ya, C-Mary*  A friend of his brought them by. He had a very odd-looking scar.
CANARY: *Scrapeahdepth?*  An odd-looking scar?
HESTER: *Di.*  Yeah.

Hester and Canary can thus articulate the kinship ties broken by both the town's penal system and the larger historical structures of difference-based oppression (most prominently, New World enslavement) that system reproduces. By omitting the abbreviation of Canary Mary's name ("C-Mary") in the translation, Parks emphasizes the intimacy of TALK, especially its ability to create and facilitate difference-based bonds untranslatable in English.

While TALK touches on English vocabularies, it does so primarily to highlight the failures of English and to gesture toward new possibilities for communicating black women's sexual difference at the levels of lexicon and morphology. TALK provides multiple words and phrases for describing sexual anatomy, including "woah-ya," and "kazo," both of which the glossary translates as "vagina." "Woah-ya" itself has several meanings, also signifying "period" and "very" depending on its context. TALK thus constitutes Karla Scott's sense of "formulaic speech," through which black women speakers in particular "mark . . . identity with culturally-specific contextualization cues" (241). According to the *Dictionary of Linguistics and Phonetics*, these utterances are identifiable by their resistance to "normal syntactic or morphological characteristics" in both "individual utterances [and] larger spoken or written events." "Formulaic" speech serves an explicitly "social purpose, such as greeting exchanges, skipping rhymes or the words of a marriage ceremony" ("Formulaic Language"). In its formulaic qualities, TALK articulates group identifications by orchestrating dialogic situations in which "specific cultural knowledge is required for reference and understanding" blackwoman sexuality and sexual deviance ("Formulaic Language").

Like Morrison's "idagay," TALK also performs larger identifying functions by emphasizing difference as a matter of group membership and belonging both within and beyond the bounds of the play. While some of TALK's modalities may sound familiar to outsiders, the act of TALKing with fluency is possible only for characters whose subject position outside of normative gender and sexuality enable them to fully "understand" or readers and viewers who engage the appended glossary and projected translations rigorously, and in this way iteratively rigorously encounter difference.

This engagement marks the radical potential of interstitial language for the "social change" that Smitherman names as a central function of language (94). Where Morrison leaves "idagay" untranslated but provides sufficient syntactic and phonetic cues so that her reader glean each phrase's most basic meaning, Parks endows her interstitial language with a metatextual reach, requiring the reader temporarily to forgo linguistic privilege and engage in the epistemic and physical labor of language acquisition to begin to "understand" her characters, their relationships, and the experiences of difference that define their stories.

The full effects of Parks's translation are most apparent in the play's final scene, following Monster's final return. This scene presents the play's most extended dialogue in TALK, with seven consecutive lines delivered in the interstitial language, broken up only briefly by English phrases. This fluid transition to TALK reflects a climactic shift in the interpretive techniques that the text requires of readers and viewers. By presenting an extended dialogic exchange almost entirely in her invented language of women's sexual difference, Parks calls on the reader/viewer to apply the nuantial hermeneutics of the interstice in which the text has trained her. The constant grappling with multiple difference imposed on the reader/viewer through the disparate media of the projection and the forced manual turn to the glossary now give way to a sustained engagement with the social dislocations, intimacies, and "scars" that difference has worked to speak. Here, the dissonance of polyglossia dissolves into the sustained translation of difference through interstitial language, suggesting that Parks's poetics has prepared the reading outsider to navigate the "bad and good and good and bad" of difference alongside—and, indeed, in conversation with—her characters (153).

## "Fuck-about" Shorthand and Irruptive "Languages of Love": Bessie Head's "Life" and Ama Ata Aidoo's *Our Sister Killjoy*

This effort to convey the complexity of difference through reformulated language is central to both African American women's writing and to women's literature of the African diaspora. African women writers' linguistic engagements with difference take on particularly anticolonial dimensions as they negotiate the links between familiar "mother tongues" and the vocabularies of colonialism. For contemporary African women writers, escaping what Smitherman calls "language oppression" means not only creating new means of expressing black womanhood and sexuality, but also directly and explicitly interrogating colonial languages such that their structural "element[s]," as Davies terms them, may be reconfigured to accommodate complex postcolonial women's subjectivity (Smitherman 3; Davies 163). For many of these writers, interstitial language thus becomes less a development of new, assimilable, and teachable languages and more a radical rewriting of existing colonial languages. It is not by the morphological structures of these African women writers' interstitial languages that the interstices of blackness, womanhood, and sexuality are made apparent; rather, it is in the *effects* of these new idioms on both characters and text through which African women writers lay difference and desire bare.

Bessie Head's short story "Life" (pronounced "Lee-fay") and Ama Ata Aidoo's prosepoem novella *Our Sister Killjoy* exemplify the uses of interstitial language in expressing African women's sexuality and multiple difference. In each of these texts, a young woman protagonist uses colonial language to develop "a language of her own" through which she may articulate and claim her sexuality and her interstitial difference (Head 40). While these languages are morphologically indistinguishable from the European/colonial languages the narrator/speakers speak (English in "Life" and both English and German in *Our Sister Killjoy*), they have their formal effects on the level of syntax and genre. They require an interstitial hermeneutics that does not translate words or phrases from an othered language, but that works to identify the other *within* the familiar language. In so doing, they force readers to interrogate identity in a familiar idiom and to consider their role in both "language oppression" and the multiple other oppressions it facilitates (Smitherman 3). Reading "Life" from a black queer feminist hermeneutic of the interstice demonstrates how these idioms recast colonial language to critique the racial, sexual, and economic impacts of language oppression, enabling black women to forge subversive sexual economies and erotic connections inarticulable in colonial English.

In her national identifications and her relationship to her sexuality, Life, the protagonist of Head's story, reflects the veiled difference that defines the story's interstitial English. Like Head herself, Life is born in South Africa and emigrates to Botswana, developing identificatory ties to both nations. The narrative frames Life as a modern woman for whom changed economic circumstances mean a return to unexplored, provincial roots. Her unknown relatives greet her as "our daughter," yet she is soon revealed as an anomaly in the village's social milieu. Head's third-person narrator figures Life's foreignness in terms of a socioeconomics directly related to sexuality. Having been, as the narrator explains "a singer, beauty queen, advertising model, and prostitute," in Johannesburg, Life is unable to accept the limited career options available to her in the village, which include "for the illiterate women . . . farming and housework; for the literate, nursing, teaching, and clerical work" (39, 40). Life thus becomes the first sex worker in the village, a decision that causes a scandal not because it reflects sexual lasciviousness, but because Life uses sex to provide herself with a means of financial self-sustenance that exempts her from economic dependence on marriage. In the village, the narrator notes, "[p]eople's attitude to sex was broad and generous—it was recognized . . . that it ought to be available whenever possible like food and water, or else one's life would be extinguished or one would get dreadfully ill" (39). Yet, in this cultural logic, sex is acceptable only when it does not undermine gendered economic relationships. In Life's new community, "men and women generally had quite a lot of sex but on a respectable and human level, with financial considerations coming in as an afterthought" (39). As a woman who has sex to gain financial independence, Life is cast out of the realm of the "respectable and human," and is branded "a terrible fuck-about" (42).

Life renegotiates English to express her sexual difference, incorporating this "fuck-about" identity into her speech. She develops what the narrator describes as "a language of her own," which she uses in discussions of money and gender, highlighting the ways in which both are constantly inflected with deviant sexuality. When her Botswanan women friends comment on the amount and quality of the food she offers them, she replies "in a carefree, off-hand way: 'I'm used to handling big money.'" Similarly, though her physique and beauty are constantly remarked upon by the women of the community, Life's only direct comment on beauty is her "motto . . . : live fast, die young, and have a good-looking corpse" (39). The narrator offers these lines as examples of Life's "own" language, even as these utterances are rendered in a standard English, readily intelligible by the reader.[11] The only salient difference marking Life's language is the quality of its delivery: she explains these and other life philosophies in an axiomatic prose, "with the bold, free joy of a woman who had broken all the social taboos" (Head 40).[12]

This tone of subtle insurgency is reflected in the structure of Life's interstitial language. She speaks an English organized around and attuned to irony, sarcasm, and frankness, and uses it to express her irreverent sexuality as a central component of "free" womanhood. The syntax of Life's idiom features short sentences, single-word interrogatives, and a lexicon of monosyllabic nouns and pronouns, often without joining verbs or adjectival embellishment. Just as Life's "free[dom]" from stigmas around sex prompt her to speak in direct, "bold" English constructions, her male clients "quickly got to the stage where they communicated with Life in shorthand language: 'When?' And she would reply: 'Ten o'clock'" (Head 40, 41). The efficiency of the language mirrors Life's clear attitude toward sex as both pleasure and capital.

Head's shorthand language has communitivizing effects as well. While Life's candor about sex scandalizes most of the women in the community, it "attracts" the village's women beer brewers, "a gay and lovable crowd who had emancipated themselves some time ago. They were drunk every day and could be seen staggering around the village, usually with a wide-eyed illegitimate baby hitched on their hips." Like Life, the beer-brewing women "talked and laughed loudly . . . and had developed a language all their own." And, like Life's language, the beer-brewers' proprietary speech is characterized not by new words or syllables, but by a syntactic directness that reflects a sexual "emancipat[ion]" and economic autonomy accessed outside of marriage. Thus, when male lovers aim to exploit their financial resources under the guise of affection, they retort curtly, "Love is love and money is money. You owe me money" (40). In providing an example of their unique language, the narrative quotes: "'Boyfriends, yes. Husbands, uh, uh, no. Do this! Do that! We want to rule ourselves" (Head 39).

Though legible and ostensibly accessible without translation, the Englishes spoken by Life and the beer brewers bear crucial grammatical markers of difference. Smitherman argues that, "not only is the pernicious use of language evident in words, qua words, but also in syntactical contouring and discourse style we can witness evidence of language to conceal, obfuscate and distort reality. Yes, syntax can code a world view" (98). We see this in the English through which Head's "fuck-about" women discuss sexual autonomy that serves as a counter-discourse to language oppression. Her characters use subversive syntaxes to undo both silence and stigma around women's sexual desire and to link that desire explicitly to economic and social freedoms.

On a structural level, Head's sexual shorthand, like Parks's TALK, and Morrison's "idagay," functions as what Scott terms a "formulaic language"—a language that allows speakers articulate belonging in opposition to an externally defined norm ("Crossing Cultural Borders" 241). Yet, while TALK and "idagay" perform "in-group identity" through a system of "utterances which lack normal . . . morphological characteristics," this shorthand or formulaic language does so by subverting "normal syntactic" structures (Scott 241). Life and the beer brewers speak primarily in brief, mono-phrasal sentences that depart from standard English grammars, rejecting the primacy of the verb almost entirely. By de-prioritizing verbs in communications around sex, this shorthand positions the women's speech in either an immediate present tense, unfettered by the details of conjugation and temporality, or a constant imperative tense, in which they have full linguistic control over their negotiations of desire and its fulfillment. For these women, sexual *doing* and *action* are not in question, but are simply functions of what "is" (Head 40).

In addition to inscribing community through formulaic speech, Head's interstitial language also constitutes what sociolinguist Terry Meier calls "oppositional talk," a system of verbal patterns in which black women renegotiate social relationships by opposing and "play[ing] off" other speakers' "utterance[s] in strategic and creative ways" ("Stand Up and Speak Out" 247). When Head's woman deviants do speak in grammatically complete sentences, their language is used either in axiomatic renderings of their worldviews or in commands that impel outsiders to acquiesce to their perspectives; this is oppositional talk. For example, when the beer-brewing women's male sex partners ask for financial assistance in return for love, saying "you help me and I'll help you," the women respond with the dictum that "love is love and money is money" (38). They repeat the syllabic and rhythmic patterns of the request in order to obliterate its logic, staking sole claim over their sexual and financial lives and assuming full authority over the definitions of both.

Through the "formulaic" and oppositional qualities of her interstitial language, Head applies a feminist ethos to what Achebe sees as a chief task of African writers: "to use English in a way that brings out [their] message best without altering the language to the extent that its value as a medium of intercultural exchange will be lost" and thus to "aim at fashioning out an English which is at once universal and able to carry [their] peculiar experience" (198). These characters use the "universal" aspects of their English-derived language in much the same way as other black women writers' use their counter-generic poetics of difference—they adapt dominant expressive forms both to inscribe and examine difference within and for their identity groups, *and* to announce their understandings of their interstitial differences to larger publics. "For 'Life's' blackwoman deviants, verbal "bold[ness]" and directness constitute a non-normative language in which the connections among gender, sexuality, and economic autonomy may be expressed. In their "own" interstitial languages, Head's characters redefine their community's dominant sexual economy. They establish their "want[s]" and imperatives as central to sexual culture; they rework English to support this new structure and teach their male sex partners, their women interlocutors, and Head's undefined body of readers to do the same.

Where Head uses her "peculiar" English to communicate black women's sexual deviance through her characters' speech in dialogue, Aidoo's *Our Sister Killjoy* reveals the possibilities of such an interstitial language for reconfiguring genre. For Aidoo, rewriting "the missing word[s]" of black women's difference means negotiating dominant language through both the polyglossias inherent in Afrodiasporic expression and the generic subversion accessed through a poetics of difference (Spillers "Interstices" 115). *Our Sister Killjoy* uses interstitial language as a narrative strategy, extracting from it a set of patterns, rules, and craft choices through which Aidoo subverts conventions of prose and poetry to express her protagonist's desire and difference in normative spaces.

Through this language, Aidoo's speaker/protagonist explores her gender and sexuality as a black Ghanaian woman in multiple racial, social, and national contexts, creating the mixed-genre text as a unique space in which these identities may find full expression.

Published as a novel, *Our Sister Killjoy* shares characteristics with both the novella and the prosepoem. It contains full sections of narrative and lengthy interjections of free verse; even within sections of prose and verse, the speaker/narrator's poetics of difference operates through polyglossia; it delivers the interior monologue and dialogue of both Sissie and the racial/gender/ethnic others she encounters in English, French, German, and Afrikaans. Fully titled *Our Sister Killjoy: Reflections from a Black-Eyed Squint*, the text shifts between first- and third-person perspectives, following the sometimes-protagonist, sometimes-speaker Sissie, as she emigrates from Ghana to Europe on an academic scholarship, recording her negotiations of her racial, national, gender, and sexual difference in new geographical contexts and synthesizing those observations through a heteroglossic form. As the title suggests, Sissie is a "killjoy," a relentlessly critical figure for whom acquiescing to comfortable notions of normalcy and dominant power structures is impossible, and whom, as Sara Ahmed puts it, "gets in the way" of organic social accord (*The Promise of Happiness* 213). As a narrator and speaker, Sissie inserts her difference into accepted social discourses through a heterogeneous narrative structure and a nonnormative point of view. Through her critically perceptive and willfully expressive "squint," Sissie articulates her positionality as a young black Ghanaian woman transcending class boundaries and exploring gender and sexuality in elite European contexts. By offering her critique in a decidedly anti-normative form, she obstructs readers' views about Africanness, womanhood, sexuality, immigrant identity, and the connections of these differences in black women's lives.

Aidoo's reformulation of genre in *Our Sister Killjoy* is part of a tradition of generic innovation with roots in both feminist ideologies and African literary practices. Thérèse Migraine-George argues in her analysis of Aidoo's stage work that "the thematic and formal innovations of postcolonial African literature . . . not only participate in the aesthetics and ideology of postmodernity but also open up new horizons by challenging the limitations of Western aesthetic categories" and extend "the tight connection between aesthetics and politics that has traditionally characterized African cultures" (84). This culturally rooted formal innovation takes on new resonances in the context of Aidoo's feminist perspective. Susan Stanford Friedman notes that post-structuralist feminist literature challenges traditionally gendered visions of genre, in which the lyric/poetic is associated with that which is repressed, feminine, maternal, pre-oedipal, and the narrative with the masculine, paternal (*Mappings* 229). Conversely, Aidoo's poetics presents Sissie as sexually fluid and explicitly resistant to conventional models of a static, stable femininity. Moreover, while the text's narrative prose account of Sissie's responds, in part, to what Friedman identifies as "a need for narrative based in traditional western exclusions of women from subjectivity and from the discourses of both myth and history," by constantly interspersing its narrative prose with various forms of poetry, Aidoo enacts a revision of narrative through which Sissie can not only access the exclusive authority of narrative on behalf of *women's* experience, she can also redefine that authority through the formal and linguistic heterogeneities central to Afrodiasporic identity and cultural expression (Mappings 230).[13]

Sissie is acutely aware of the intrinsic inability of standard English to articulate this experience, and of the need for a new language more capable of expressing her complex subjectivity. In the final section of the text, titled "A Love Letter," she addresses her male lover, still in Ghana, declaring abstractly: "My Precious

Something,/ First of all, there is this language. This language." In the "letter," Sissie goes on to describe her frustration with the feeling that she "cannot give voice to [her] soul and still have her heard . . . [s]ince so far," she continues, "I have only been able to use a language that enslaved me, and therefore, the messengers of my mind always come shackled" (112). In response to this dilemma, she proposes a "language of love . . . beyond Akan or Ewe, English or French" (113). This invented "language of love" thus holds the potential not only to express Sissie's own complex "soul" in colonial spaces but can also facilitate communication among nonnormative subjectivities across diasporic space. It serves as a creative response to the dilemmas of diasporic language that Busia, Djebar, Senghor, Achebe, Thiong'o, Baldwin, and others have debated. Through its roots in "love," it accesses the ubiquity and universality for which Senghor values colonial language; yet, in moving "beyond" both colonial and African languages alike, it articulates the particularities and nuances of black subjectivity that each of those languages is structurally unequipped to express.

For Aidoo, interstitial language is a means of renegotiating Western parlances (as Head does), but it is also a means of reconfiguring dominant generic forms to express "the missing word[s]" of blackwoman difference, identity, and desire. From Sissie's perspective, in both colonial and indigenous linguistic systems, black diasporic subjects "cannot write to one another, or speak across the talking cables or converse as [they] travel on a bus or a train or anywhere . . . without feeling inhibited because [they] suspect that someone is listening" (115). Communication in the "language of love," however, can effectively express black subjectivity across diasporic space precisely because it "does not have to be audible"; rather, it can make meaning on the level of genre, and through epistemic engagement with structure and form (113). The "language of love" enacts what Ahmed calls the "willfulness" of the feminist killjoy on the level of verbal language systems. It signals a "willing[ness] to cause . . . obstruction" to normative language and to reroute language around a body that deliberately and emphatically "get[s] in the way" of dominant processes of communication and identification ("Feminist Killjoys"; *The Promise of Happiness* 67). It is this "language of love" in which *Our Sister Killjoy* is written and according to which the logic of its generic heterogeneity functions. Funneled through this language, Sissie's "black-eyed" perspective speaks, having its radical effects not in "audible" acts of voice in dialogue but, in the critical strain of a squinting eye, the unsettling beak of a prosepoetic line.

In Aidoo's text, interstitial language is inextricably linked to the body, which is figured as a primary site from which poetic voice and narrative point of view issue. Just as Parks uses the sexualized breast and vagina as sites through which to write her interstitial language of deviance, Aidoo stresses the possibilities of blackwoman perceptory anatomy in rewriting languages of genre and form. As the text's title indicates, Aidoo locates both Sissie's critical stance and her creative "reflections" on identity at the site of the eye. For the college-age Sissie, the "squint"—and the "black" eyes through which it is configured—signal both her developing critical perspective on the world of difference, which she encounters outside of her home community in Ghana, and the perceptive mechanisms through which she is able to view, consider, and "reflect" on her own identity. As a crucial part of her own perceptive anatomy, Sissie's "eye" reveals key dynamics of her squint as a structuring tool of her poetic narrative of multiple difference. Marlon Ross points out that the elements of the face both constitute an "aspect (a word that means that which we can look at) of a human body," and function as, "if not the key to the soul, at least a locked door whose keyhole we can peep through to glimpse the messy inner life of an individual as specimen of the group of identifications that she or he has internalized" (Ross "Pleasuring Identity" 828).[14] Accessing the eye's capacity for illuminating "messy" interiority and complex identity, Aidoo thus troubles Shange's model of visuality. As discussed in Chapter 2, Shange's *for colored girls* opens with a crucial failure of recognition, in which her protagonists are unable to "see" one another because they cannot access one another's voice; in Shange's model, then, "being seen" both acknowledges a vulnerability to an othering gaze and indicates the possibility of empowering recognition among blackwoman subjects.[15] From Sissie's perspective, however, *vision*, rather than visibility, is the most important function of the ocular; blackwoman subjectivity may be fully seen only through the black woman subject's own critical, self-reflective perspective. Sissie's squint thus articulates the perceptory dimensions of the "facial stunting" techniques Miller-Young names, through which black women performers' pointed facial expressions critique the ways in which they and their performances are read (*A Taste for Brown Sugar* 63). The squint serves as both a visible critique, and, more importantly, a crucial focusing of her own field of vision to center her critical perspective.

In Sissie's world, as in Life's, the body is not simply a metaphor for black women's perspectives on sociality in new national contexts; nor does it serve exclusively as a vessel for representing racial "black[ness]." The body, in these texts, is a dynamic perceptive tool for synthesizing and expressing information about identity. It spans the figurative and physiological poles of perception, allowing Sissie to understand the new modes of identification she encounters abroad and to "reflect" physically her own complex location within those identifications. For Aidoo, writing "from the black-eyed squint" means writing from the critical vantage point of the interstice and using her poetics of difference to articulate black women's subjective complexity through the novelistic, narrative, and poetic elements of the text. For Sissie, "*reflecting* from" the squint means both expressing her interstitial identity as a black Ghanaian woman coming into self-awareness in Europe, and absorbing, processing, and re-projecting the image her "black" body produces in the worlds she moves in. The "black-eyed squint" is both a critical transformative gesture of blackwoman corporeality and a radical epistemological point of view through which Sissie expresses her own experience of difference.

Sissie's first form-altering encounter with her complex "black[ness]" occurs early in the text, when she is forced to encounter her race and color for the first time on the streets of Germany. The third-person speaker describes Sissie's experience "feasting her village eyes" on the sights, smells, and sounds of this new environment.[16]

> Cloths. Perfume. Flowers. Fruits . . . Music. Sounds. Noises.
> So many different noises mixed together (12).
> Sissie's reflections are interrupted when she overhears a woman pointing
> her out to a young girl with the words
> **"Ja, das Schwartze Mädchen."**
> Sissie deduces from her limited knowledge of German that this means "black
> girl."
> She was somewhat puzzled.
> Black girl? Black girl?
> She looked around her, really well this time (12–13).

Sissie's experience of cultural difference—both her own and those of the unfamiliar surroundings of Germany—is symbolized by effects of sound and gendered objects related to the body. The nearly overwhelming experience of difference in Europe is echoed in the speaker's attempts to catalogue the "many different" sounds and bodily implements Sissie encounters and to reflect this collision with difference in the poetic form of the text. The speaker departs from third-person narrative poetry to access Sissie's interior monologue, articulating both her impressions of the "many different noises" she encounters and her startled efforts to identify the "Black girl" the German woman hails, both of which are described in sentence fragments that depart from the speakers' dominant narrative prosepoetic syntax. The appearance of the phrase "'Ja, das Schwartz Mädchen'" extends this vocal embodiment of difference. It enacts a transition between English and German to evoke both the unintelligibility of racial difference for Sissie and the efforts she must employ to understand the meanings of her "black girl" body in this new environment. Navigating the multiple shifts between prose and verse, the reader must join Sissy in looking "really well" for the locations of difference. The text reflects on a linguistic level the impact of white/colonial contact on African identity. As 'Molara Ogundipe-Leslie points out, the representation of colonial speech in African-authored texts reconstitutes the speaker herself as a "different person or persona" ("The Bilingual" 106). In this way, in translating the bolded "'Ja, das Schwartze Mädchen'" into the English "Black girl? Black girl?" Aidoo emphasizes the foreignness of this conception of her race, gender, and sex. Through her black-eyed squint, Sissie is forced to translate both her "Black Girl" subjectivity and the body through which that subjectivity is read into a language she can effectively speak and understand.

The implications of Aidoo's "language of love" expand as Sissie explores her sexuality abroad. Sissie's most prominent same-gender relationship in the text—and the relationship through which she most explicitly examines sexual desire—is her relationship with Marija, a German woman she meets through a chance encounter in the streets of Frankfurt. Sissie and Marija develop a fast but uneasy friendship marked by a series of verbal miscommunications and corporeal misreadings. At their first meeting, for example, Marija is unable to understand Sissie as black. Having no frame of reference for Ghana or even Africa, Marija understands dark-skinned racial others only in terms of "ze two Indians who verkt in ze supermarket" she frequented years before Sissie's arrival (24).

Despite Marija's exaggerated inability to understand race, Sissie finds grounds for connection in this ignorance, too, remarking to herself: "IT CANNOT BE NORMAL/ for a young/ Hausfrau to/ Like/Two Indians/ Who work in/ Supermarkets" (23). Sissie's typography and her departure from the narrative prose in which this free verse section is couched suggest her attempts to understand Marija's racial misrecognition as evidence of a nonnormativity parallel to the multiple difference she reflects through her own form-altering perspective. Still developing her critical perspective on identity—and the language with which to express it—Sissie suspends the critical impulse of her squint here and continues to build a friendship with Marija.

Forged in ethnic and racial difference, this relationship with Marija forces Sissie to interrogate her notions of desire and intimacy. When Marija makes a sexual advance toward Sissie, the gesture not only unsettles Sissie's understandings of her gender and her sexuality, but also undermines the structural coherence of both Sissie's body and the text. Rejected, Marija begins to display jealousy, showing her emotional investment in the relationship, at which point, the narrator states, "Sissie felt like a bastard. Not a bitch. A bastard" (75). Sissie's confrontation with the instability of gender through this relationship begins to unsettle the coherence of her corporeality within the narrative. As Marija's complaints continue, the narrator describes, "Suddenly, something exploded in Sissie like fire. She did not know exactly what it was. It was not painful. . . . It was a pleasurable heat" (ibid.). For Sissie, the presence of queer desire thus occurs first as a destabilization of gender, then soon results in a disconnection of the body and the psyche in which she is unable to articulate even the most "explosive" presences of feeling inside her. Her surprise at the interplay of pleasure and shame she experiences with Marija is echoed in the form of this section of the narrative, as the third-person narrator registers the surprise and suddenness of Sissie's physical experience of "pleasure" in short, anaphoric prose sentences (as in "It was not painful" and "It was a pleasurable heat").

This struggle to negotiate gender and sexuality through the sensations of an alienated body quickly causes a series of like destabilizations of form in the scene. Sissie delivers her initial response to Marija's advance in prose:

> One evening the woman seizes you in her embrace, her cold fingers on your breasts, warm tears on your face, hot lips on your lips, do you go back to your village in Africa and say . . . what do you say even from the beginning of your story that you met a married woman? No, it would not be easy to talk about this white woman to just anyone at home. . . . Look at how pale she suddenly is as she moves shakily, looking lost in her own house. (65)

The rushing interior monologue here suggests a panic at the thought of a queer relationship; moreover, the ellipses elide the possibility of any discussion of Sissie's desire in the scene. Here, same-sex desire is immediately elided by the concerns of race, gender, and nation; Marija's whiteness and her status as a married woman eclipse the homoerotics of the two womens' relationship. While the timber of the interior monologue during this prose section bars full exploration of Sissie's sexuality and desire, Aidoo's poetics of difference once again makes recourse to both physical and textual bodies to express what Sissie cannot articulate in either standard English prose or recognizable poetic structures alone. Through her differentiating "black-eyed squint," Sissie observes as Marija cries. Her attention to the eye intensifies as she notices "a tear streaming out of one of her eyes. The tear was coming out of the left eye only. The right eye was completely dry." The narrator describes Sissie's "pain at the sight of that one tear. That forever tear out of one eye" (65).

> L
> O
> N
> E
> L
> I
> N
> E
> S
> S
> Forever falling like a tear out of a woman's eye. (65)

The erotic "heat" between the two women becomes a multilayered synesthetic experience in which Sissie feels Marija's "pain," at first psychic and emotional, now located, like Sissie's interstitial difference, at the corporeal site of the eye. The text replicates this exchange, as the vertical positioning of "LONELINESS" renders the tear at the center of the page in a ten-line departure from prose. While Sissie aims to contextualize Marija's desire as a result of loneliness within her heterosexual marriage, her efforts to distance herself and Marija from the possibility of queer desire are belied by the form of text. Marija's feelings cannot be subsumed entirely into a normative model of heterosexual "LONELINESS" if Sissie herself experiences that loneliness as a shared pain and expresses it through the same poetic strategies she uses to describe her own multiple difference. Marija's "lonely," queer eye thus becomes a "reflection" of Sissie's own interstitial subject position and is used to inscribe the sexually deviant body through the heterogeneous corpus of the text.

Aidoo's interstitial "language of love" requires of its reader several queer hermeneutic interventions. Aidoo's generic multiplicity is crucial not only to her expression of difference but also to the interpretive technologies the reader must develop in order to make meaning in *Our Sister Killjoy*. The merging of poetic and narrative forms emphasizes the effect of such heterogeneities on readers. In *Legba's Crossing*, Heather Russell argues that the disruption of narrative holds the potential "to so discomfit readers that they have no choice but to self-reflexively attend to their desires for linearity, clarity, causality, and coherent meaning . . . the frustrated reader becomes in this instant an imaginative agent, and an anxious talisman toward new identities" (143). William Andrews usefully frames this process as an entry into "a living contract with unfinished, still-evolving contemporary reality" as reflected in the "indeterminacy" of hybrid texts (*To Tell a Free Story* 272). This process of navigating the affective and intellectual discomfort of rupture is a key aspect of black queer feminist reading.

Black queer feminist reading brings the reader in contact with multiple "realities" of difference and power as Sissy experiences them. Generic hybridity thus holds the power to draw readers into a "contract" in which they agree to engage new models of identity. For Aidoo, this contract bids readers to reconsider coherent distinctions between self and other, and between normative and nonnormative experience. If, as Russell suggests, "to interrupt narratology is to productively unsettle the readerly enterprise; to disrupt narratology is to self-consciously thwart readerly expectation; [and] to erupt narratology is to fully explode the readerly process," Aidoo's partly narrative prosepoem novella may be said to *irrupt* readerly practice, literally *breaking into* readers' intellectual conceptions of racial, national, gender, and sexual identity so that they may be dismantled and reconstituted anew (143). This is a decidedly "killjoy" endeavor and is the project of Aidoo's interstitial "language of love": to offer both internal "reflect[ions]" *on* and irruptive "reflect[ions]" *of* complex black-woman identity. Aidoo willfully demonstrates the multiplicity of black women's experience in diaspora and forces the reader to engage that experience through language and form.

This act of poetic irruption into dominant discourse furthers Sissie's understanding of her difference in its larger social contexts. The process of translating her raced and gendered body through interstitial language allows Sissie to see and articulate the connections between her race, her gender, her sexuality, and their connections to larger global systems. It also enables her narrator/speaker to impel readers to do the same. As Sissie is newly confronted with difference, the text breaks form again. It shifts into free verse as the speaker describes Sissie's internal experience at "this moment when she was made to notice differences in human colouring" (12–13). The experience prompts lifelong "regret" that registers in Sissie's body, as the narrator/speaker states:

> Power, Child, Power.
> For this is all anything is about. Power to decide
> Who is to live, Who is to die, (13)

Here, the text stops mid-sentence with a comma, leaving the rest of the page in whitespace. On each of the three pages that follow, only a single word appears: "Where," "When," and "How." Each of these is separated by a page break and surrounded entirely by whitespace; the reader must turn the page to complete the sentence (14-16).

By switching from narrative prosepoetry to free verse, Aidoo's speaker/narrator reflects on a formal level the relationships between the German mother's racialist articulation of Sissie's black womanhood and larger power structures that define other kinds of oppressions. The narrator's efforts to write a coherent narrative of race and gender difference disintegrate as she considers the matrix of "Power" in which those differences are mobilized. Her discussion of the "someone" who perpetrates racism as "meanness" concludes in an end-stopped line, suggesting once again her struggle to contain difference within the confines of a manageable, familiar syntax; yet the absence of phrasal lines in the verse that follows—and those lines' dependence on the prosepoem's discussion of that same dominant "someone" for their meaning—suggest a clear continuity between the life-defining and life-taking "Power[s]" that Sissie's experiences as a black Ghanaian immigrant woman from a working-class family and the various dominant "someone[s]" Sissie encounters throughout the story.

This disintegration of coherent narratives of identity finds its full formal expression in the final pages and lines of this, the novella's first section. The speaker concludes Sissie's traumatic first critical engagements with difference with three single-word pages of text, demanding that the reader engage with the "Where," "When," and "How," of a "Power" all too easily attributed to the unnamed, disidentificatiory mechanism of "someone" else.

In extending the logic of interstitial language to the level of genre, Aidoo circumvents the issues of translation that Morrison's and Parks's texts introduce.

By linking the logics of oppression with the technologies of reading themselves, Aidoo's speaker disables any disidentification with the multifaceted "power," she critiques. Instead, writing in her "language of love," Aidoo forces the reader to confront difference as inseparable from the experience of reading, and to identify with multiple oppressions through an act as meaningful and as mundane as the turning of the page.

## Flip It and Reverse It: The Poetics of Reversal in Missy Elliott's "Work It"

This use of invented, recoded language to articulate black women's sexuality and bodily desire carries across literary and artistic forms. While Aidoo, Morrison, Parks, and Head use interstitial language to reframe interpretive experiences of black women's erotics in textual and performative space, examining invented linguistic codes in hip-hop music offers insight into how interstitial language shapes identification with, and interpretation of, black women's desire in racialized and gendered public social spaces defined by eroticism and affect, such as dance clubs. In these spaces, both black bodies and the interstitial languages they enable delimit modes of collectivity defined by subversive engagements with the erotic.

In twenty-first-century black women's artistic cultures, hip-hop emerges as an important form for exploring the place of linguistic innovation in gender and sexual critique. In diasporic women's hip-hop, interstitial language emerges as a crucial tool for expressing and critiquing models of race, sexuality, and embodiment and proposing subversive models of feminist collectivity. In his study of black poetics, Anthony Reed notes that important links exist between contemporary black poetic experimentalism and hip-hop culture (98). In the early 2000s in particular, as commercial hip-hop moved away from both the linear narrative storytelling modes that characterized much popular rap of the 1980s and the deep regional identificatory emphases and sampling aesthetics of 1990s commercial hip-hop, both of which tended to privilege masculine sexuality and coming-of-age, the genre's poetics undergo a shift that makes space for both new aesthetic practices and new articulations of black women's sexuality. Rapper Missy Elliott's work in the first years of the twenty-first century represent such a shift, demonstrating the place of interstitial language in reshaping interpretive and identificatory experiences with black women's eroticism through hip-hop.[17]

Though twenty-first-century hip-hop puts a premium on rigorous wordcraft that might seem to render invented language gimmicky, women rappers have consistently incorporated coded idioms and deviant Englishes into their poetics, particularly in discussions of sex. Elliott is one of the contemporary women rappers best known for such linguistic play. Her 2002 single, "Work It," exemplifies how invented language expresses and complicates black women's sexuality in hip-hop. Reading "Work It" through a black queer feminist hermeneutic of the interstice highlights how Elliott's interstitial language critiques normative proscriptions of sexuality and uses those critiques to inscribe collectivity grounded in subversive erotics.

The lead single from her double-platinum fourth studio album, *Under Construction*, "Work It" is a bass-heavy dance tune about black women's sexuality and embodiment; it touches on the place of black women's erotics in sexual and intimate relationships. Using a direct, imperative tone and language as explicit as that of Parks's characters in TALK, Missy Elliott, as speaker, instructs an imagined lover as to how to please and fulfill her. Elliott delivers the first two of the song's three verses primarily in the imperative form, making explicit erotic demands of both the ungendered sexual partners the speaker refers to and, by extension, the listener, who is indirectly positioned as a figure in the narrative. She states:

> Gimme all your numbers so I can phone ya
> Your girl acting stank than call me over
> Not on the bed, lay me on your sofa
> Call before you come, I need to shave my chocha
> You do or you don't or you will or you won't ya
> Go downtown and eat it like a vulture. . . .
> If you're a fly gyal, then get your nails done
> Get a pedicure, get your hair did. ("Work It")[18]

Elliott devotes the majority of her verses to establishing an authoritative voice through which she stakes claim over her own sexuality and encourages women listeners to take up her conception of "fly" black femininity. Her use of the imperative command form throughout indicates the importance of communication in this effort: she is not simply speaking about sex but is speaking *to* an audience and demanding to be heard and understood. Intermittently throughout the verses, Elliott's mode of communication morphs as her address reaches full affective and sensory effects on the listener:

> This the kinda beat that go bha ta
> Sex me so good I say blah blah blah . . .
> Listen up close while I take you backwards
> *(Played in reverse): Watch the way Missy like to take it backwards*
> I'm not a prostitute but I can give you what you want. [ . . . ]
> Is it worth it? Let me work it. I put my thang down, flip it, and reverse it.
> *(Played in reverse): I Put my thang down, flip it and reverse it.*
> I put my thang down, flip it and reverse it.

Elliott eschews standard English and recognizable black dialects, instead reconfiguring language to demand both sexual pleasure from the figure the speaker addresses and "close" attentive hearing from her listener. She first develops an onomatopoeic linguistic form to connect the quality of the "beat" to her own expressions of sexual pleasure, heard in the rhyming echo of the "bah ta" of the beat and the "blah blah blah" of the speaker's expression of erotic satisfaction. This language then gives way to an auditory morphological system unintelligible for the English-speaking listener, as the line "watch the way Missy like to take it backwards" is heard in reverse, a strategy later repeated in the hook's closing line: "I put my thing down, flip it and reverse it."

This signifying practice is particularly meaningful given the substantial speculations around Elliott's sexuality, and the rapper's general refusal to disclose her sexual identification. Often rumored to be lesbian in hip-hop magazines and blogs, and linked romantically to women artists including Keri Hilson and rapper Sharaya J, Elliott has long been the subject of what cultural theorist C. Riley Snorton terms "rumormongering about black celebrity sexuality [that] evinces a set of logics that presume that one can apprehend the 'truth' of identity through the visual and thus that increased surveillance of a public figure will bear more accurate results" (*Nobody Is Supposed to Know* 135).[19] By referring to "the way Missy like to take it backwards" in reversed sound, Elliott sidesteps the visual hegemonies of sexual surveillance by expressing "backwards" desire and pleasure through reconfigurations of sound. She both encodes and draws attention to her (or her speaker's) relationship to a complex, potentially multidirectional sexual pleasure, and she links it to the sonic complexity and linguistic multiplicity of her music. As the speaker issues explicit commands regarding her sexual pleasure, the phrase "I put my thing down, flip it, and reverse it" is played repeatedly both forward and backward, requiring listeners to adapt new listening technologies as they engage the song's transgression of appropriate female sexuality. "Backwards" sexual pleasures and sonic/erotic "reversal" converge, signaling a broad range of potential erotic differences and sexual deviations that may be viewed as backward or perverse, including queer and anal sex, along with broader social "reversals" intrinsic to the sonic event of a black woman speaking in tongues as she commands her own pleasure.

By reversing the reader's listening practices, Elliott trains her audience to listen for—and experience—the difference in her erotic self-expression. Elliott's interstitial language of reversal constitutes a linguistic and lyrical instantiation of what Stallings thinks of as black women's literary tradition of "trickster-troping," or a "non-heteronormative act of tactically joining orality and sexuality. . . . To create a folk-based discourse of desire" (*Mutha Is Half a Word* 10). For Elliott, while the facts and objects of sexual desire can be communicated in legible

English, the contours of queerness and the feel of desire defined by deviance cannot. Elliott's linguistic play of queer commands, sexual flipping, and erotic reversals emphasizes experiences of difference on various levels; in the midst of the song's otherwise highly singable hook and verses, groups of listeners must pause in the middle of the hook, unable to sing the line that completes the chorus's foundational rhyme scheme.

This tactical trickery has different effects on different listeners. Elliott's interstitial language of reversal emphasizes difference as part of the listening experience and thus stimulates corresponding sets of affects for her listener, according to their relationships to the black women's erotic difference voiced in the song. For some listeners in public or club settings, the dissonance between familiar and unfamiliar linguistic modes highlights the experience of outsider status, requiring them either to perform the intellectual labor of researching the song's lyrics to translate the reversed lines or to navigate their estrangement and the relative powerless of unknowing. Yet for groups of listeners familiar with Elliott's erotics and hip-hop poetics more broadly, this interruption of rhythm and rhyme creates dissonance and collective experience of pleasure—a shared laugh at the illegibility of the line, the impossibility of singing the rhyme or translating it into recognizable language, and shared communal recognition of Elliott's creative genius as the dance, the beat, and the instrumental qualities of the lyrics themselves communicate more about the "worth," the "work," and the transgressive multidirectionalities of black women's sex than standard English ever could.

By critiquing sexual politics through the sensory and structural modalities of invented linguistic systems, interstitial languages emphasize the bodily and erotic complexities of black women's sexual acts and experiences; they also emphasize the affective and sensual registers of black women's creative expression and textuality and emphasize the erotic dimensions of language itself. Through their invented lexicons, Aidoo, Parks, Morrison, Head, and Elliott provide new linguistic means of overwriting the grammars of racism, sexism, and heterosexism, reconfiguring the languages in which stories of black womanhood can be told, and provoking the world to listen.

# Speech between Silence
## *Distance, Difference, and the Queer Poetics of Blackwoman Living*

In a feminist utopia we'd dance together, make a gleeful
exit, and seek satisfaction with stacks of Denny's buttermilk
pancakes. Instead, she seemed to stand in judgment. . . .
She knew I knew that all it'd take to shatter my fragile
normality as another pretty girl in a club was a whisper.
The last thing I wanted that night was for her to speak.

—Janet Mock, *Surpassing Certainty: What My Twenties
  Taught Me*

silence is
silence is
silence is
the sound, the very sound; between the words
in the interstices of time divided by the word
between
outer and inner
space /silence
is
the boundary

—M. NourbeSe Philip, "*Dis Place* the Space Between"

In the opening scenes of her second memoir, *Surpassing Certainty*, black feminist
writer and trans activist Janet Mock describes a crucial moment of fracture and
(mis)recognition between herself and another woman in a Waikiki, Hawaii,
night club. The woman, described as "tall, olive-skinned, and dark eyed" (bodily
markers that also fit Mock herself) is someone Mock recognizes from the school
she attended during the early moments of her transition—a fact that the woman
discloses, unprompted, to a suitor Mock meets at the club that evening. The
outing is a quiet act of violence; the suitor recounts the conversation incredu-
lously to Mock, who laughs it off with feigned confidence, and the two head

to the beach for a late-night swim. There is no spoken confrontation with the classmate, and the suitor continues his pursuit. Yet, even in the absence of verbal or physical conflict, the narrative reveals an important psychic shift, a rupture to which Mock returns regularly throughout the text: "Forced disclosure always shook me," she says, "leaving me in a frightening place where my body served as proof of my realness. The need to prove myself valid was never-ending in its plea to affirm, connect, deny, and erase. I aspired daily to be like Toni Morrison's Sula, a woman who shuns the demands placed on her by her watchful community, a woman who lacks ego, a woman OK in her otherness. She feels no pressure to verify herself. . . . On that beach, I was far from that place" (3).

Mock's encounter with the woman at the nightclub—and the transition into interior narration that that encounter provokes—reveals the multiple functions of silence in black feminist literature and discourse. On one hand, the woman's silence is a boundary for Mock, a gesture of disidentification and a marker of how far her reality lies from the "feminist utopia" of shared enjoyment and identification that she imagines having with a ciswoman friend. On the other hand, silence offers her protection and a retreat to the black feminist literary interior—a space where she can be with blackwoman fictional icons like Morrison's Sula, with whom she can identify freely without interrogation, castigation, and demands for bodily proof of her womanhood.

This polysemous silencing reveals important limits of black feminist identification and introduces urgent questions facing contemporary black feminist theorizing and the languages in which that theorizing takes place. What are black feminism's objects and subjects of study? What are our available languages for discussing black feminist genders, and what better languages can we create? How do the categories of "black woman" and "black female" cohere beyond frameworks of legible "realness" and bodily "proof," frameworks which, we know, have historically been used violently to erase, commodify, and destroy blackwoman subjects? What nuances do these terms silence—borrowed as they are from colonial languages unequipped to think diasporic genders? What interstitial silences do these phrases leave intact? What boundaries do these words create?

Attention to black feminist discourse as an artistic enterprise, as I have attempted to show, demonstrates that the grounds on which black women's identities are written, read, and contested are constantly shaped by difference and by structural and linguistic silencings. Black women writers have mobilized formal and poetic difference as a tool for rethinking identity, precisely because of difference's insistence on eluding language as we know it.

I have argued here that women writers and artists from various African diaspora locales have made queer creative use of the blackwoman nuantial to speak from the silenced interstitial spaces of blackwoman experience. From these unmapped sites, they invent biomythic histories, choreopoetic embodiments, interstitial languages, and nuantial globalities that tap into the perpetual unwieldiness that difference poses, honing it as a tool for forwarding complex, antinormative models of black womanhood that critique multiple power structures and interpretive conventions at once. In doing so, these writers and artists queer difference, showing through their poetics that to name a single set of differences is to silence innumerable others, while failing to name difference at all silences subjectivities, identities, communities, and lives.

By writing through the unheard interstices of identity, Afrodiasporic women writers and artists recalibrate such silences to rearticulate the conceptual limits of the self. In the hands of Audre Lorde, Dionne Brand, Zanele Muholi, Ntozake Shange, Toni Morrison, Suzan-Lori Parks, Ama Ata Aidoo, Bessie Head, Lxs Krudxs Cubensi, and the others gathered here, silence becomes a tool not only for undoing black women's erasure from discussions of racial, gender, and sexual alterity, but also for remapping the boundaries of subjectivity to illuminate the many differences that operate among black womanhoods. Reading Afrodiasporic women writers' formal choices through a black queer feminist analytic illustrates the challenges that Afrodiasporic women writers issue to queer studies, Africana studies, feminist studies, and other related critiques of identity. These writers and artists join theorists from each of these discourses in interrogating institutional silencings on the grounds of race, gender, class, nation, and sexuality, and they do so through an explicitly anti-normative perspective that exposes the power dynamics that shape black women's experiences within each of these identity groups.

By insisting on silence as, in M. NourbeSe Philip's phrasing, "the sound between the words" that shape identity discourse, these writers and artists invite new modes of listening, hearing, learning, and reading—a set of interstitial hermeneutics attuned to the silenced nuances of blackwoman subjectivity. These writers' poetics of difference work to construct feminist and queer instantiations of what Fred Moten terms "new universalities held within the difference/s of phonic substance" (*In The Break* 198), situating queer and feminist readings of the interstice as the vital wave of diasporic connection, and a crucial means of learning for non-diasporic subjects.

Yet, Mock's nightclub confrontation and her recourse to the blackwoman literary interior also highlight the distancing, fragmenting, and distinguishing effects of difference in black women's experience. They speak to the need for further exploration of the poetic effects of distancing as black queer feminist critique. For Mock, complete black feminist connection is a utopian fantasy available not through shared voicing, but through quiet engagement of the literary imagination. Even as black women writers interrogate the viability of shared experience as a means of re-creating connection, difference remains crucial in expressing the gaps and distances that separate Afrodiasporic womanhoods, and the ways in which power mediates how black women treat, care for, and engage each other. The specific place- and language-based differences that shape individual women writers' poetics of difference in specific temporal, geographical, and political contexts—and that concern specific modes of gender, womanhood, and embodiment—are important in understanding how identity is contested through black women's formal work and play.

Future work on black women's poetics of difference might examine these distancing functions of difference within and between Afrodiasporic women writers' poetic approaches. Already we see this in Mock's shifting narrative interiorities in her two memoirs, *Redefining Realness* (2014) and *Surpassing Certainty* (2017), both of which highlight the tensions between embodiment, womanhood, and feminist identification in black trans experience. Edwidge Danticat's invocation of Haitian storytelling paradigms in the structure of her short story collection *Krik?Krak!* (1995) provides models of gender and sexual identity critique deeply conversant with the specific histories of Haitian colonization, emigration, and global politics not easily legible through US-centric interpretive frames. Michelle Cliff's *No Telephone to Heaven* (1987) highlights gender fluidity as a metaphor for instabilities of blackness within Jamaican nationalist identity discourses through the narrative and dialogic speech of Cliff's transgender secondary character. Likewise, Zadie Smith's *On Beauty* (2005) uses characters' English-language accents to articulate key tensions between gendered identifications of blackness in British and US contexts.

These works illustrate the ways in which the specific bodily experiences, gender identities, multilingualisms, social structures, and political concerns of various African, Caribbean, African American, and Afro-European cultures influence black women's poetics of difference in various African diaspora settings. They demonstrate how difference reconfigures collective definitions of blackness and black womanhood while also emphasizing the specific timbres of difference that distinguish articulations of black womanhood across locations, genres, and texts.

Black women's poetics of difference map these specificities along genre lines as well. Shange's choreopoem, for example, is linked to a tradition that includes Julie Dash's impressionistic historiographic film *Daughters of the Dust* (1991), in which Dash uses vocal and visual heterogeneities to forward a woman-centered cinematic diaspora rooted specifically in the Gullah culture of the American South. Similarly, the choreopoem's focus on black women's body/language as a means of rearticulating diaspora provides a context for reading Nikki Finney's 2003 poetry collection, *The World Is Round*, in which Finney's formal strategy positions black American women's bodies as synecdoches for global life and experience. These texts emphasize the distancing functions of Afrodiasporic women's counter-genre poetics of difference, signaling the extent to which black women's genre subversions articulate disparate aspects of nuantial subjectivity in response to the black feminist concerns of specific temporal and geographic contexts.

Even within the lives of particular blackwoman-authored literary texts, the distancing functions of difference are at play. My exploration of cross-genre adaptations of Shange's *for colored girls* (including its 1982 telefilm and 2010 feature film versions) reveals the need for similar exploration of other important adaptations of black feminist literary texts, such as those of Zora Neale Hurston's 1937 novel *Their Eyes Were Watching God* (adapted as a telefilm in 2005); Gloria Naylor's 1982 novel *The Women of Brewster Place* (aired as a television miniseries in 1989); Alice Walker's 1982 novel *The Color Purple* (adapted to film in 1985 and for Broadway in 2005); Toni Morrison's 1987 novel *Beloved* (adapted to film in 1998); Sapphire's 1996 novel *Push* (adapted as the feature film *Precious: Based on the Novel Push by Sapphire* in 2009); and Chimamanda Ngozi Adichie's 2006 novel *Half of a Yellow Sun* (adapted to film in 2013). These adaptations call attention to the ways in which black women's poetics of difference both enable and resist translation across genres and highlight the various and often contradictory meanings of black feminist difference, particularly when deployed for broader audiences through feature-length film. Exploring such adaptations through a nuantial hermeneutic of the interstice might enrich recent critiques of black feminism by calling more squarely into question the issues of socioeconomic access, cultural scope, and audience that subtend debates on both the interdisciplinary reach of black feminist theory and the representational universality of blackwoman life.

Through further attention to these distancing mechanisms of difference, future studies of black queer feminist poetics can also examine the intertextual legacies of the explicit genre subversions that texts such as Shange's choreopoem, Lorde's biomythography, and Aidoo's prosepoem novella introduce, and the ways in which these texts mobilize difference not only to problematize discourses of identity, but to challenge and expand black feminism itself. For example, poet Kamilah Aishah Moon uses the genre of the "biomythography" to locate her 2014 poetry collection, *She Has a Name*, incorporating into Lorde's black feminist poetics of difference the collection's core themes of autism, (dis)ability, neurodiversity, and black family life (2014). Trans nonbinary Nigerian author Akwaeke Emezi's multisubjective, mixed-genre young adult novel *Freshwater* (2018) extends heteroglossic fictional and poetic techniques such as those we see in Aidoo and Brand, shaping them around the novel's subversion of spiritual ontology and binary gender as tropes of coming-of-age. Likewise, rapper/singer Janelle Monáe's hybrid, multi-platform "emotion picture" *Dirty Computer* (2018) points to the possibilities of choreopoetics for exploring expressive black/queer sexual bodies in Afrofuturist digital forms.

Together, the works of these writers and artists point to numerous paths of counter-genre thinking that extend the works of Lorde, Shange, Aidoo, and others gathered here. In their choreopoetic embodiments, their biomythic temporalities, and their nuantial visions of identity, these artists insist upon the queer poetics of blackwoman living. Writing new and nuanced genres of and for black womanhood, they reimagine our histories, our presents, our futures, and the queer languages in which we might convey them. In so doing, they illuminate the crucial poetic functions of difference, and form rich ground for the continued life of black queer feminist thought.

# Notes

## Introduction

1. Earlier in *Zami*, Lorde describes her experience "growing up fat, black, nearly blind and ambidextrous in a West Indian Household," foregrounding corporeal differences, differences of (dis)ability, and ethnicity alongside her racial difference. (24). Similarly, in "Age, Race, Class, and Sex: Women Redefining Difference," Lorde identifies herself as "a forty-nine-year-old Black lesbian feminist socialist mother of two, including one boy and a member of an interracial couple," emphasizing differences of political perspective and other experiential circumstances as central to her identity (114).

2. See Nash, *Black Feminism Reimagined*; and Cho, Crenshaw, and McCall, "Toward a Field of Intersectionality Studies" (785–810).

3. See Henderson, "Speaking in Tongues; Alexander, "'Coming Out Blackened and Whole'" (695–715); Holloway's analysis of black women's "plurisignant texts" in "Revision and (Re)membrance (617–631); Pinto, *Difficult Diasporas*; Peterson, "Response and Call" (761–775); and Hale, "Bakhtin in African American Literary Theory" (445–471). A number of these studies have applied Bakhtinian notions of dialogism to black women's prose, focusing primarily on the textures of black women characters' voices in dialogue, and, to a lesser extent, on instabilities of genre. In "Speaking in Tongues," Henderson uses the theory of dialogism to read the "inner speech" represented in Morrison's *Sula* and *Their Eyes Were Watching God*, arguing that vocal shifts in these texts work by "privileging (rather than repressing) 'the other in ourselves'" (19). Henderson's focus on characters' speech in dialogue prevents her from readings of the larger narrative structures of her chosen texts. Similarly, Alexander identifies Lorde's "new collaged genre," the biomythography, as an effort to create the "hybrid language" required to articulate her complex subjectivity ("Coming out Blackened and Whole" 696). Yet in focusing on biomythography as a metaphor for *embodied* blackwoman subjectivity, this reading does not take up the full range of vocal and narrative modes at play in Lorde's "collage" and the specific poetic strategies Lorde employs in developing her discourse of difference.

4. See Brown, *Writing the Black Revolutionary Diva*; Rojas, *Women of Color and Feminism*; and Hong, *Death beyond Disavowal.*

5. See Nash, *Black Feminism Reimagined* and "Practicing Love"; and Puar "'I would rather be a cyborg than a goddess,'" (49–66). For a broad discussion of recent debates on intersectionality, see Cho, Crenshaw, and McCall, "Toward a Field of Intersectionality Studies" (785–810).

6. Jacques Derrida describes this phenomenon as *différance*, which he defines as "the displaced and equivocal passage of one different thing to another, from one term of an opposition to another." Différance, for Derrida, takes on the "complex structure of a weaving, an interlacing which permits the different threads and different lines of meaning" to converge and diverge, and through which "one could reconsider all the pairs of opposites on which philosophy is constructed and on which our discourse lives, not in order to see opposition erase itself but to see what indicates that each of the terms must appear as the *différance* of the other" (*Margins of Philosophy* 16, 3).

7. I use the term *black/queer* here to indicate the simultaneity of blackness and queerness—and of racist and heterosexist oppressions—as they shape black feminist poetics. I use this term primarily as an adjective to name certain concepts and experiences relevant to the lives of black queer people, rather than to describe black queer people themselves. I expand on this term in Chapter 1: "Biomythic Times: Voice, Genre, and the Invention of Black/Queer History."

8. As a critical practice simultaneously focused on feminist and antiracist perspectives, Crenshaw's intersectionality issues an important answer to Lorde's call. Yet, by focusing her analysis on what she terms as the "primary" confluences of race and gender and introducing the related issues of "class, sexual orientation, age, and color" identification only in a footnote to a later essay ("Mapping the Margins" 1243–1244 n9), Crenshaw's originary model of intersectionality leaves space for fuller interrogations of hierarchical constructions of difference, even as it remains central to feminist scholarship.

9. See Zeleza, "Rewriting the African Diaspora" (35–68); Davies and Ogundipe-Leslie, *Moving beyond Boundaries*; and Manning, *The African Diaspora.*

10. The texts I explore operationalize what Judith Butler, in *Gender Trouble*, terms the "embarrassed etcetera," with which neoliberal references to multiple difference often end (for example, "race, gender, class, sexuality, etc."). She reads this "etc." as evidence of "the illimitable process of signification itself" and of "exhaustion," presumably on the part of those privileged with the option not to consider multiple forms of difference. Yet, Butler acknowledges, "This illimitable *et cetera . . .* offers itself as a new departure for feminist political theorizing" (182). Reading for the poetics of difference reveals how black women artists have led such departures and have theorized illimitable difference for decades. See Butler, *Gender Trouble.*

11. These writers and artists destabilize binary gender in their lives and work. For example, Lorde's understanding of her "woman" gender incorporates "both man and woman" (Zami 7). Similarly, Krudxs Cubensi uses a range of language to describe themself, including both "feminine" and gender neutral Spanish language adjectives, and, in English, "boy. . . girl. . . man. . . woman. . . both and none of them" ("Who We Are"). I use the term "women" as inclusive of the trans and nonbinary artists gathered

here who have used this language to describe their own identities, as well as the genders of the characters, speakers, and subjects their work centers. In addition, because of my specific interest in poetic and formal manipulations of language, I have chosen to center this study on Anglophone texts to best draw out common poetic and linguistic strategies and to consider these writers' creative strategies apart from the dialogism that attends acts of translation, except in the case of texts that use multiple spoken languages and thus mobilize translation and untranslatability as poetic devices within the texts themselves.

12. Harryette Mullen, excerpt from "Preface: 'Recycle this Book'" from Recyclopedia: Trimmings, S*PeRM**K*T, and Muse & Drudge. Copyright © 2006 by Harryette Mullen. Reprinted with the permission of The Permissions Company, LLC on behalf of Graywolf Press, graywolfpress.org.

13. This is not to suggest that such generic hybridity does not occur before this period. Texts as early as Mary Prince's eighteenth-century slave narrative *The History of Mary Prince* suggest a dialogism that prefigures the formal strategies of the texts I consider.

14. For an analysis of the marginalization of women writers during the black arts movement, see Clarke, *After Mecca*.

15. The development of internationally focused black liberation organizations in the United States, including the TransAfrica organization in Washington D.C. (founded in 1977) and Maulana Karenga's Us Organization (founded in 1965); the dissemination of the Pan-Africanist ideologies of Ghanaian president Kwame Nkrumah (1952–1966), Kenyan President Jomo Kenyatta (1964–1978), and Haile Selassie, Emperor of Ethiopia (1930–1974); the publication and popular reception of Afrocentrist texts such as Molefi Kete Asante's *Afrocentricity* (1980) in the United States, and the international popular reception of transnational black liberation ideologies through both political figures such as Kenyatta, Selassie, and Malcolm X, and cultural figures (including Nigerian-born musician Fela Kuti, Jamaican-born musician Bob Marley, and others) suggest the scale of and scope of diasporic-leaning black thought during this part of the twentieth century. Many of these ideologies (particularly those originating in the United States) extend from the thinking of late-nineteenth- and early-twentieth-century figures, including Marcus Garvey, W. E. B. DuBois, and Edward Wilmot Blyden. See Adi and Sherwood *Pan-African History*; Manning, *The African Diaspora*; and Okpewho, Davies, and Mazrui, *The African Diaspora*. For an important exploration of feminist critiques of black nationalist ideologies, see Farmer, *Re-Thinking Black Power*.

16. Shange's use of "voice" also provides an important critical alternative to tropes of "representation" to describe the presence of blackwoman subjectivities in literature. As Shange, Cornell West, Kara Keeling, and others point out, "representation" as an imperative of black cultural production can have grossly limiting effects, privileging those black subjectivities that can be read as constituting "positive" representations and excluding those that might be read as "negative," including those marked with sexual, corporeal, or other stigmatized intra-racial differences. See Keeling, "Joining the Lesbians," in Johnson and Henderson, *Black Queer Studies*; and West, "The New Cultural Politics of Difference" (93–109).

17. For an analysis of Shange's diasporic consciousness, see Clarke, *After Mecca*.

Shange's diasporic poetics is explored further in Chapter Three: Feeling Colors and Seeing Speech: Body/Language and Black Women's Diasporas of Difference."

18. Shange's vocal "singularity" applies an intersectional and Afrodiasporic framework to Roland Barthes's notion of "the grain" of musical voice. Barthes, like Shange, observes that musical voice reveals important information about the social functions of the voice as a socially contextualizable "body." However, Barthes's argument that "the voice is not personal: it expresses nothing of the cantor, of his soul; it is not original" fails to account for the imperatives of cultural representation and the subversive potential of "original" voicing for non-Western subjectivities (180–182). See Barthes, "The Grain of Voice" (179–189).

19. See, for example, Washington, "'Taming All That Anger Down'"; Christian, "Nuance and the Novella"; Frazier, "Domestic Epic Warfare in *Maud Martha*" (133–141); and Rugoff, "The Historical and Social Context of Gwendolyn Brooks's Poetry."

20. *Trinbagonian* is a term used by Philip and others to signal the peoples, histories, and cultures of Trinidad and Tobago. Philip, "Fugues, Fragments, and Fissures" (1–15).

21. Lorde attributes this power to what she calls the "mythical norm"—the rhetorical image of the "white, thin, male, young, heterosexual, christian, and financially secure" icon around which Western standards of normalcy are set and through which privilege and power allocated ("Age, Race, Class and Sex" 116). Queer theorist Michael Warner states that "to be fully normal is, strictly speaking, impossible. Everyone deviates from the norm in some way. Even if one belongs to the statistical majority in age group, race, height, weight, frequency of orgasm, gender of sexual partners, and annual income, then simply by virtue of this unlikely combination of normalcies one's profile would already depart from the norm. . . . The problem, always, is that embracing this standard [of normalcy] merely throws shame on those who stand farther down the ladder of respectability. . . . It does not seem possible to think of oneself as normal without thinking that some other kind of person as pathological." See Warner, *The Trouble with Normal*.

22. Christian's *Black Feminist Criticism*; Evelyn Hammonds' "Black (W)holes and the Geometry of Black Female Sexuality": and Wahneema Lubiano's "Shuckin' Off the African-American Native Other" are part of an important body of black feminist scholarship that explores the nexus of race- and gender-based oppression explicitly in terms of silence and speech. Christian's observation that "to use the range of one's voice, to attempt to express the totality of the self" is the central priority of black women's writing illustrates the place of voice in black feminist theorizing (172). See Christian, *Black Feminist Criticism*, and Christian, "The Race for Theory"; Hammonds, "Black (W)holes and the Geometry of Black Female Sexuality"; and Lubiano, "Shuckin' Off the African-American Native Other" (149–186).

23. Collins's "black feminist standpoint" is in dialogue with other feminist standpoint theorists of the 1980s and 1990s, including Sara Ruddick, Susan Heckman, Donna Haraway, and others. See Collins, *Black Feminist Thought* and "Comment on Heckman's 'Truth and Method.'"

24. Xekatwane, "Conquering Fears of Queerness."

25. Here, I invoke Cathy Cohen's vision of queerness as a complex alignment of radical anti-normativities, in which "the nonnormative and marginal position of punks, bull-

daggers and welfare queens," emblems of racial, class, and other differences concurrent with sexual difference, form "the basis for progressive transformative coalition" (22). See Cohen, "Punks, Bulldaggers and Welfare Queens."

26. The poetics of difference expands W. E. B. Du Bois's notion of "double-consciousness," which describes the inescapable duality of black American subjects' worldviews as a result of concurrent experiences of blackness and locatedness in white-dominated social contexts. Du Bois's choice to articulate this positionality in his hybrid text *The Souls of Black Folk (1903)* illustrates the capacity of generic subversion for articulating such heterogeneous worldviews. Afrodiasporic women's subversive poetics emphasize the simultaneous effects of multiple differences on these perspectives and the various ways in which such perspectives may be expressed through literary form. See Du Bois, *The Souls of Black Folk (1903)* (1996).

27. See Lillvis, *Posthuman Blackness*; Keeling, *Queer Times, Black Futures*; Weheliye, *Habeas Viscus*; and Nyong'o, *Afro-Fabulations*.

## Chapter One. Biomythic Times

1. I borrow this notion of black linguistic "retool[ing]" from Hortense Spillers, who writes that "Black writers, whatever their location and by whatever projects and allegiances they are compelled, must retool the language(s) that they inherit." See Spillers, "Introduction: Peter's Pans" 4.

2. In black studies scholarship, this axiom is often linked to the Ghanaian Adinkra symbol "Sankofa," the meaning of which is translated as "return and fetch it" or "Learn from your past." See Kwami, *Adinkra*.

3. Foundational among this line of anti-relational and anti-futurist thinking is Leo Bersani's argument in his 1995 text *Homos*. Bersani argues that queer identity signals "a potentially revolutionary inaptitude . . . for sociality as it is known." See Bersani, *Homos* 76. The question of *who knows* these unuseful socialities—or which racial, ethnic, gender, and class communities are allowed to define "known" forms of sociality—remains unanswered in Bersani's text. The implicit Anglo-normative, middle-class, and often male-centered underpinnings of anti-relational and anti-futurist discourses have been debated by several scholars and are important to the project of queer of color critique. As José Esteban Muñoz notes, arguments for queer anti-relationality spring from a resistance to acknowledge the relatedness of queer studies and other identity discourses; see Muñoz, *Cruising Utopia* 11. Rejecting relationality also allows white queer studies to reject of the project of intersectionality, and to dismiss the interrelatedness of oppressions on which black feminism has insisted for decades.

4. In a footnote to his introduction, Edelman anticipates critiques of this argument as inflected by his privilege as a white, middle-class male, a complaint for which, he states, he has little "sympathy," because "many of those proposing this reading will themselves be 'white,' 'middle-class,' 'academic,' or 'gay male'" (*No Future* n19). Yet a black queer feminist reading of queer literary temporalities cannot avoid such a critique, and the breach between this anti-futurist counter-ideal and the experiences of Afrodiasporic queer people (and particularly Afrodiasporic queer women) cannot be overstated.

5. This is not to say that reflections on and expressions of experiences of abjection are not useful or important for black/queer subjects. As the works of Scott, Aaliyyah I. Abdur-Rahman, and others suggest, such reflections are crucial for black/queer possibility. I am arguing that while expressing and exploring abject states is crucial, the nearly ineluctable location of abjection itself—being and feeling abject as a black/queer person—is most readily useful as a political tool (rather than a fact of black/queer life) when deployed in critique of the structural circumstances of black/queer abjection (Abdur-Rahman "The Black Ecstatic" 343–365).

6. The published forum response to the 2005 MLA panel "The Antisocial Thesis in Queer Theory" represents several pivotal critiques of Edelman's anti-futurism. In it, Jack Halberstam questions the gay male focus of Edelman's archive, as well as his inattention to patriarchy's role in queer women's experiences of abjection. Halberstam argues that the inclusion of "[d]yke anger, anticolonial despair, racial rage, counterhegemonic violence [and] punk pugilism" is crucial to a politically useful theory of queer anti-sociality (824). Muñoz, in his response, highlights the roles of anti-futurist and antisocial paradigms in defining queerness as a white male province. Rejecting relationality, he argues "distances queerness from what some theorists seem to think of as contamination by race, gender, or other partcularities that taint the plurality of sexuality as a singular trope of difference" (825). See Halberstam, "The Politics of Negativity"; and Muñoz, "Thinking beyond Antirelationality" 823–826.

7. The namelessness of Verlia's uncle reflects the woman-centered genealogy operative on the island of Nowhere, and elsewhere in Brand's work. As Garvey points out ("The Place She Miss," Brand's woman-centered lineages in *At the Full and Change of the Moon*, "push [male protagonists] to the sidelines" (494).

8. The inclusion of vocalist Nina Simone, in particular, signals an attentiveness to blackwoman political difference and the ways in which it can be mobilized through heteroglossic creative expression. See, for example, Nina Simone's "Four Women" (1966) and Michelle Russell's "Slave Codes and Liner Notes."

9. Edelman views the abstract symbol of the "the Child" as a specter of "the whole network of Symbolic relations and the future that serves as its prop." For him, the Symbolic child is an icon to which queer anti-futurism should respond "with violent force" (29).

10. "Ossuary XI," "Ossuary I," "Ossuary II," "Ossuary V," "Ossuary VI," and "Ossuary XIII" from OSSUARIES by Dionne Brand, Copyright © 2010 Dionne Brand. Reprinted by permission of McClelland & Stewart, a division of Penguin Random House Canada Limited. All rights reserved. World: Extracts from OSSUARIES by Dionne Brand. Copyright © 2010 by Dionne Brand, used by permission of The Wylie Agency LLC.

11. Verlia, too, enacts a certain black queer self-exploration through subversive naming and unnaming. Upon reaching Toronto, Verlia is immediately assured that her "brothers and sisters" in the Movement will also "find [her] a new name soon" (Brand *In Another Place* 171). While she is most frequently hailed as Verlia by the novel's characters and narrators, she is also sporadically hailed as "Vee," and as "sister" (1, 158). In the novel, the term *sister* is polysemous, referring also to Abena, Verlia's comrade and lover in Toronto, and to Elizette, for whom the term carries an explicitly erotic resonance (14).

12. I use the term *yonic* here as a corollary to *phallic*. Yonic, in its adjectival form, is defined as of or relating to "a figure or symbol of the female organ of generation as an object of veneration" ("Yonic" OED).

13. Here, Elizette's historiography mirrors Lorde's "Biomythic" history once again. By pairing erotic desire with domestic labor, she locates herself within a history of "women who work together as friends and lovers" (*Zami* 255).

14. This scene illustrates the narrative possibilities of what Elizabeth Freeman terms *erotohistoriography*, in which the carnal, the pleasurable, and the erotic provide radical pathways to engaging with the past and to structuring queer socialities. See Freeman, *Time Binds*.

15. This linking of queer desire and history through voice is reinforced by Elizette's erotic evocation of Moriah; as the mythical land to which Adela disappears, and as the site of Isaac's sacrificial blinding in the bible's book of Genesis, Moriah signals both a lost, unlocatable past and the freedom of an imagined future, as well as a move away from the technologies of visuality and, potentially, toward other means of understanding (Kalimi, "The Land of Moriah" 347, 348; Brand *In Another Place* 23).

16. Elizette's attraction to Verlia occurs through voice before the two have any sustained visual or physical contact. In their first interaction, Verlia's "look" is off-putting to Elizette, yet when Verlia calls her "sister," Elizette's response is erotic and immediate. The sound of the word, she remarks, "feel like rum going through my throat . . . it surprise me how I want to touch she teeth and hold she mouth on that word" (*In Another Place* 15).

17. While Juani is twenty-four at the start of *Memory Mambo*—significantly older than a traditional bildungsroman protagonist—this expanded temporal frame is characteristic of what Rita Felski terms the *feminist Bildungsroman*, in which it is only after the dissolution of a significant adult relationship (most typically a marriage), that "the heroine is able to see through and reject the seductive myth of romance as the key to female self-identity" (Felski "The Novel of Self-Discovery" 137, 138).

18. Jiménez Román and Flores helpfully introduce the term *Afrolatin@* to signal the gender nuances of Afrolatino and Afrolatina identities, and to acknowledge the role of gender and gendered language in discussions of Afrolatinidad. Here, I use Afrolatina rather than Afrolatin@ or Afrolatinx in order to highlight the role of gendered language in both shaping and contesting diasporic identification within feminist poetics of difference.

19. Juani's belief in objective history filters into her self-construction as well. She attributes her decision to come out as a lack of sufficient "patience, or maybe the brains, to lie, to dodge the truth," even as she acknowledges its disruptive effects on her homophobic family, for which it is "vital . . . that [she] not be provoked into the truth" (*Obejas* 78, 80).

20. Jed Esty offers an important analysis of the impacts of critiques of empire and interrogations of white bourgeoise values on bildungsroman forms of the late nineteenth and early twentieth centuries. See Esty *Unseasonable Youth*.

21. Moretti organizes the modern bildungsroman according to two thematic categories—those novels predominantly concerned with the protagonist's "transformation" on one hand, and those that chart processes of "classification" on the other. Novels of

the first type, he argues, privilege "dynamism" and internal change, while novels of "classification" build toward the establishment of a "definitive" conception of identity, particularly in relation to larger social bodies (556).

22. Felski, for example, points out the ways in which postmodern women's bildungs-roman depart from eighteenth-century male-centered generic norms by privileging a movement away from the domesticity and heterosexual marriage—rather than toward it—as a climactic act of liberation and empowerment (138).

23. This homophobic outcasting from the novel's Cuban immigrant community is personified through Juani's machisto cousin-in-law, Jimmy, who refers derogatorily to all of Juani's friends as a "gaggle of tortilleras" (17).

24. If, as critic Katharine Sugg suggests, we can read Juani's violent aggression in this scene as a masculinist or machista attempt to "legitimat[e] a national discourse of Cubanidad" (468), then this fight scene also highlights different performances of gender between the two, as Juani's performance of masculinity is added to the nexus of interconnected differences "captured" in Juani's voice.

25. Titi's name, too, positions her as an ancestral figure. In many Spanish-speaking communities, "Titi" is an affectionate shorthand for "tia," literally translated as "aunt" but also applicable to older maternal figures regardless of blood relation.

26. The image of the "sealed island" also invokes Guantanamo Bay. By emphasizing the tensions between US and Cuban national politics as a metaphor for the conflicts between national and ethnic identifications in Afrocubans in the United States, this iconography further illuminates Juani's longing for radical cross-temporal and cross-geographical identification through difference.

27. "Need" functions similarly in much of Audre Lorde's work, in which it signals both queer erotic desire and several other forms of potential empowerment as well. Lorde's piece "Need: A Chorale or Black Women's Voices" serves as an example of a text that subverts generic norms (here blending poetry and drama) in an explication of the multiple forms of need experienced by black women.

28. The marks Juani scribbles on the napkin mirror the series of scattered markings that delineate the section breaks within each chapter. Juani's narrative parallels Lorde's in that it seeks to construct an interstitial history located within the object of the book itself.

29. See Smiley, "LGBT Suicides"; "Raymond Chase Commits Suicide, Fifth Gay Youth to Take Life in Three Weeks," Huffington Post. www.huffingtonpost.com. October 1, 2010; Dominus, "A Suicide More Complex than a Slogan"; "Sakia Gunn," The LGBT Hate Crimes Project. www.lgbthatecrimes.org; "Michael Sandy," The LGBT Hate Crimes Project. www.lgbthatecrimes.org; and O'Donnell et al., "Increased Risk of Suicide Attempts."

30. Activist works such as Alexis Pauline Gumbs's "Mobile Homecoming Project" and publisher Lisa C. Moore and filmmaker Tiona McClodden's "Untitled Black Lesbian Elders Project" signal a move among contemporary black queer activists and artists to begin documenting black queer histories. To date, however, none of these efforts has been documented in a book-length study, and none has taken up the specific roles of creative voice in the production of these histories.

31. The works of Heather Love, Carolyn Dinshaw, Jeffrey Weeks, and David Halperin among others take up important discussions of queer history and historiography; Siobhan Somerville, too, is among those examining the history of sexuality in terms of race. Still, to my knowledge, few book-length studies have examined the specific place of history and historiography in black queer women's experiences.

32. Alicia Garza, "A Herstory of the #Black Lives Matter Movement."

33. In the opening text of its #SayHerName media guide, the African American Policy Forum states: "Say Her Name begins to shine a light on the ways that Black women are policed in ways that are similar to other members of our communities—whether it's police killings, "stop and frisk," "broken windows policing," or the "war on drugs." It also pushes open the frame to include other forms and contexts of police violence, such as sexual assault by police; police abuse of pregnant women; profiling and abusive treatment specifically of lesbian, bisexual, trans, and gender nonconforming Black women; and police brutality in the context of responses to state and other forms of violence—all of which bring Black women's experiences into even sharper focus. See "#SAYHERNAME: Resisting Police Brutality against Black Women: A Social Media Guide." African American Policy Forum (www.aapf.org). See also and Crenshaw and Ritchie with Anspach, Gilmer, and Harris, *Say Her Name.*

34. Toni Morrison's first of two published short stories, "Recitatif," functions in much the same way, using a first-person narrator who gains varying levels of access to the motivations and interiority of her white female friend over the course of the story, marking linguistic and rhythmic shifts in the texture of the narrative. Through this bending of narrative form, Morrison provides a narrative backstory for the connections and dissonances that mark American race and gender relations during the time of public school integration and the landmark *Brown v. Board of Education of Topeka* Supreme Court decision of 1954, which established racial segregation in public schools as unconstitutional. See Morrison, "Recitatif." *Norton Anthology of American Literature*, Vol 2, (1998): 2078–2092.

35. "A Litany for Survival". Copyright © 1978 by Audre Lorde, from *The Collected Poems of Audre Lorde* by Audre Lorde. Used by permission of W. W. Norton & Company, Inc.

## Chapter Two. "walkin on the edges of the galaxy"

1. Excerpts from Akilah Oliver, *the she said dialogues: flesh memory* reprinted by permission of Night Boat Books.

2. In a 2010 study of forty-two major US- and UK-based literary publications, the independent organization VIDA: Women in the Literary Arts found that all but two reviewed, published, and interviewed significantly more male authors than female authors in 2010. The margin of this discrepancy ranged from 12.5 percent (the percentage of women authors interviewed in *The Paris Review*) to 38.4 percent+ (the percentage of interviews conducted by women in *Tin House*). See "The Count 2010." http://vidaweb.org/the-count-2010.

3. This situation persists for more recent black women playwrights as well. As Dana A. Williams observes, the "patriarchal mindset of those who determine the American

drama canon" at the turn of the twenty-first century, and the underrepresentation of black women–authored dramatic texts on college drama, literature, and African American literature syllabi continue to result in a situation in which "many published black female playwrights go unnoticed, unpublished, and unproduced" (xx, xv). See Williams, *Contemporary African American Women Playwrights*. Theatre organizations such as the National Black Theatre Festival and the African-American Theatre Festival in Boston have worked to produce and call attention to the works of black women playwrights. See Brown, "African-American Theater Festival."

4. See Stallings, "Funking Machine," and Simmons, "A State of Rage."

5. See, for example, Hobson, *Venus in the Dark*; Wright and Schuhmann, *Blackness and Sexualities*; Spillers, "Mama's Baby, Papa's Maybe."

6. Evidence of Shange's engagement with this contradictory ethos may be seen in her designation of her protagonists as "ladies," rather than as "women." As Dickerson points out, the former term connotes a femininity historically inaccessible yet tacitly desirable for black women well into the latter parts of the twentieth century. See Dickerson, "The Cult of True Womanhood," 178–187.

7. Canonical black feminist scholars such as Patricia Hill Collins, bell hooks, Michelle Wallace, and many others have explored the significance of stereotyping in understanding black female voicing. Melissa V. Harris-Perry, too, draws on Shange's work to frame her interrogation of black female identity and voicing, subtitling her text, "For Colored Girls Who've Considered Politics When Being Strong Is Enuf." See Harris-Perry, *Sister Citizen*.

8. The expressive technologies of color are central to Shange's body/language as well. As Cheryl Clarke and others have pointed out, "color" functions in the choreopoem version of *for colored girls* as a crucial signifier of ethnic and racial difference within women's communities. See Clarke, *After Mecca* 98.

9. The composition of this sketch also evokes the iconic cover illustration of the Scribner edition of the choreopoem, painted by Paul Davis.

10. Poem appears courtesy of Pam Dlungwana.

11. See Holibaugh and Moraga, "What We're Rollin' Around in Bed With," and Lorde, "Uses of the Erotic."

12. In 2006, Muholi created the queer activism and digital media organization Inkanyiso to address the erasure of queer and LGBTI people from media in South Africa and beyond, providing media, video activism, and visual literacy training to black queer and LGBTI South African youth. Inkanyiso's site includes a broad and rich archive of narrative and video documenting black lesbian experiences with HIV and AIDS in South Africa, including video of a vigil for black lesbian HIV/AIDS activist Buhle Msibi and Busisiwe Sigasa, the lesbian Soweto-born poet, photographer, and blogger who died of AIDS-related illnesses in 2007. See http://inkanyiso.org/category/black-lesbians-and -hiv-aids-in-south-africa/.

13. From *for colored girls who have considered suicide / when the rainbow is enuf (Play)* by Ntozake Shange. Copyright © 1975, 1976, 1977, 2010 by Ntozake Shange. Reprinted with the permission of Scribner, a division of Simon & Schuster, Inc. All rights reserved. Reprinted by the permission of Russell & Volkening as agents for Ntozake Shange, copyright ©1983, 1991, 1992 by Ntozake Shange.

14. Importantly, stage productions of *Cornered in the Dark* have used multicultural casting approaches. For Moise, Shange's vision of black feminist healing becomes a useful modality for exploring queer pleasure and sexual trauma in a multiracial context.

15. *Cornered in the Dark*, copyright © 2002 by Lenelle Moïse. Excerpts used by permission.

16. "Burlesque Top 50." 21st *Century Burlesque Magazine*, https://21stcenturyburlesque .com/burlesque-top-50–2019/.

17. McDaniel, "Photo Essay."

18. Lyndsey, "The Burlesque Booty Queen: Interview with JanTina." See also Parker, "Silhouettes." https://academicworks.cuny.edu/cc_etds_theses/445.

19. Notably, burlesque is also an important form within Shange's choreopoem. The 1983 PBS Telefilm version of *for colored girls* depicts the text's character Sechita as a burlesque dancer harassed by male audience members who violently "aim . . . quarters between her thighs." This scene emphasizes the violence to which black women's performances of the erotic are vulnerable in masculinist performance spaces, and it issues a quiet call for the kinds of blackwoman-centered spaces of erotic expression like those Tate and other burlesque figures create (*for colored girls who have considered suicide/when the rainbow is enuf* 1983).

20. Tate does not use languages of "queer," "heterosexual," or other identificatory phrases to describe her own individual sexuality. I use the term "queer" here to describe the radical erotic subversion and subjective complexity at the core of "Evil Beautiful Sunshine" and its capacity for creating black/queer community.

21. "I Want to Be Evil" lyrics by Lester Judson and Raymond Taylor and published by Songs of Universal. Used by permission of Hal Leonard, LLC.

22. McDaniel, "Photo Essay."

23. Mecca Jamilah Sullivan and Chicava HoneyChild Tate: Interview with Chicava HoneyChild Tate, September 26, 2015. (Unpublished).

## Chapter Three. Feeling Colors and Seeing Speech

1. Excerpts from *A Daughter's Geography*, *Nappy Edges*, *See No Evil*, *three pieces*, and *for colored girls who have considered suicide/ when the rainbow is enuf*: Reprinted by the permission of Russell & Volkening as agents for Ntozake Shange. Copyright © 1983, 1991, 1992 by Ntozake Shange.

2. From a methodological standpoint, diasporas of difference reconfigure Arjun Appadurai's model of "differential diaspora," which takes into account the specific ethnic, technological, economic, social, and ideological dimensions of transgeographical diaspora. Diasporas of difference add to this list the crucial category of narrative/poetic expression (what might be referred to as "cultural representation") and highlight the entanglements of each of these categories with the innumerable differences and identifications that define blackness in various diaspora locales (33–34). In diasporas of difference, geographic space becomes, in part, a metaphor for imagining the spatial terrain and boundaries of subjectivity, while race takes on additional meaning as a riff on the body's various mechanisms for communicating difference. See Appadurai, "Disjuncture and Difference in the Global Cultural Economy."

3. Drawing from the French definitions of *décalage* as a "'gap,' 'discrepancy,' 'time lag,' or 'interval,'" Edwards defines the term as "the re-establishment of a prior unevenness or diversity," reflecting multiple levels of "unevenness in the African Diaspora" (*The Practice of Diaspora* 6).

4. Foundational works by Brent Edwards and Paul Gilroy illustrate the ways in which many theories of diaspora, while hugely important in its mappings of diasporic subjectivity, have yet to articulate the mutual imbrications and simultaneities of difference central to black women's lives. Edwards positions "nation, class, gender, sexuality, and language" as categories that "internally . . . fracture" black racial identity just as "external" geographic dispersal differentiates global blacknesses according to experiences of transnationalism and migration (*The Practice of Diaspora* 12). Gilroy likewise imagines "class, sexuality, gender, age, ethnicity, economics, and political consciousness" as "internal" divisions of "black particularity" independent of, if related to, diaspora's geographical "relational network . . . produced through forced dispersal and reluctant scattering" (*The Black Atlantic* 32; *Against Race* 123). For both thinkers, framing diaspora in terms of "internal" and "external" differences imposes false distinctions among the various components of diasporic identity and tacitly privileges race as a singular defining component of black diasporic experience. The result is a missed opportunity to consider the full implications of what V. Y. Mudimbe calls "the points of conversion, complementarities, and contestation" that define black diasporic identifications and cultural expressions *across* lines of gender, sexuality, nationality, ethnicity, and language (*The Idea of Africa* 49).

5. For more on queer diasporas, see Fortier, "Queer Diaspora"; Walcott, "Outside in Black Studies"; Gopinath, *Impossible Desires*; and Eng, *The Feeling of Kinship*. I borrow the term *transDiaspora* from Jackson-Opoku, who uses it to describe the connections between imperial and contemporary African diaspora experiences; see "Out beyond Our Borders." Neferti Xina M. Tadiar uses the term *Personal Diasporas* to describe links among affective ties to multiple communities. See Tadiar, "Personal Diaspora."

6. Saussure describes "la langue" as "a social product of the faculty of speech and a collection of necessary conventions that have been adopted by the social body to permit individuals to exercise this faculty," and he describes "la langage," as the "many-sided and heterogeneous" cultural product resulting from this system of codes and the specific utterances it produces in the social world. As such, "la langage" straddles "several areas simultaneously—physical, physiological, and psychological—it belongs both to the individual and to society." See de Saussure, *Course in General Linguistics* 9.

7. Through her poetics of difference, Shange thus provides a bold, declarative answer to Kenneth Warren's much-debated question, "What Was African American Literature?" in which he questions what the speaking subject of African American literature could be—and therefore, what a coherent black racial difference could be—as the structures of American racism change in the twenty-first century (5). Shange's global black feminist poetics moves us past this question, demonstrating the ways in which black women's literature has been vulnerable to erasure *not* because of any incoherence or irrelevance in contemporary political or interpretive landscapes, but because of a critical refusal on the part of dominant scholarship to learn to read black women's texts. See Warren. *What Was African American Literature?*

8. For US-born black women writers since the latter half of the twentieth century, the possibility of an Afrodiasporic community rooted in black womanhood has been a major creative concern. The centrality of African and diasporic spiritual traditions to community building in Toni Cade Bambara's *The Salt Eaters* (1980); Paule Marshall's evocation of symbolic diasporic content as crucial for black American women's psychic healing in *Praisesong for the Widow* (1983); and Alice Walker's narrative investigation of black womanhood in several diasporic locales in *The Temple of My Familiar* (1989) as well as her interrogation of African cultural practices surrounding gender in *Possessing the Secret of Joy* (1992) all indicate black America women writers' investments in creating black feminist diasporas through literature. These diasporas aim to access the transnational black empowerment of Pan-Africanism and Afrocentrism but also include women's multiple and differing experiences of black alterity in the African diaspora.

9. For a discussion of the place of gender in major Pan-Africanist movements of the twentieth century, see Reddock, "Gender Equality," 255–267.

10. Overwhelmingly, both critical and creative efforts to undermine notions of diasporic racial sameness occur at the level of voice. Foundational twentieth-century models of diaspora foreground voice as a vehicle for communication and mobilization of African subjectivities of the past. Édouard Glissant, for example, imagines the African figure of the griot as a formative factor in New World poetics. For Glissant, "[t]he voice of the griot rises out of Africa. Slowly it frees itself; finally we hear it. We now distinguish his part in our voice. We hear the explanation of origins, the wanderings of our ancestors, our separation from the elements." See Glissant, *Caribbean Discourse* 391. Yet, as Edwards and others emphasize, the "wanderings" of black diasporic voices cannot be conceived as unidirectional movement of a single voice from the "origin" of an African past to the present tense of the black New World. In reading black diasporic voice, it is crucial, as Ato Quayson puts it, to "read for the signs of multivocality and disjuncture that lie within it." As he observes, the relationship between a black-authored text's locus of production and the Africa with which its voices converse is "always variegated, heterogeneous and processual" ("Incessant Particularities" 130). Diaspora, in other words, is continuously written in difference.

11. In the poetry collection version of *A Daughter's Geography*, the text of the piece remains unchanged, but all scene numbers are omitted and the designation of the speaker as the piece's "character" does not appear. Shang's use of "bocas," Spanish for "mouths" echoes her persistent inclusion of Afrolatin cultures in her models of blackness and indicates her investment in specifically Afrodiasporic geographies.

12. See the following scenes of the stage version of *A Daughter's Geography*: Scene 2, "Tween Itaparica & Itapuã"; Scene 5, "A Black Night in Haiti, Palais National, Port-au-Prince"; and Scene 7, "About Atlanta."

13. This list includes some locations (for example, Manila and Palestine) not generally included within traditional conceptions of Afrodiaspora. These locations do, however, have important historical ties with Afrodiasporic people on the grounds of anti-oppressive struggle. The historic presence of African American "Buffalo" soldiers during the Philippine-American War for independence at the turn of the twentieth century and frequent public comparisons between the Israeli occupation of Palestine and the South

African system of apartheid signal the logic by which Shange includes these locales in her diaspora of difference.

14. Because the marker "/" often appears in each of Shange's texts as a formal device which does not, most often, indicate a line break, I use the marker "[]" to indicate line breaks and/or whitespace between characters as needed. Shange's typography serves as further reflection of her investment in using form to express difference. Shange offers insight into the "emotional" motivations of her typographic system and its relation to black subjectivity in "Ntozake Shange," in Tate, *Black Women Writers at Work.*

15. For example, in "The Ontological Imperative for the New African Diaspora," Yoruba philosopher Adeolu Ademoyo articulates a common suspicion of diaspora theories that overemphasize the subjectiveness of diasporic identity and ignore the historical realities of Afrodiasporic experience (500). Yet, the title of Ademoyo's essay illustrates the ways in which such a critique fails to question the place of a static, monolithic racial "ontology" in diaspora identifications. See "The Ontological Imperative."

16. In this way, Shange's diasporas move, as Brent Edwards puts it in his 2007 essay, "Langston Hughes and the Futures of Diaspora": "away from an understanding of the movement of groups as discrete or self-contained, and toward a focus on the ways that the movements of groups always necessarily intersect, leading to exchange, assimilation, expropriation, coalition, or dissension" (691). Through the poetics of difference, black women writers dramatize these movements on and across the representational spaces of text and stage.

17. This typographic rupture echoes the Lady in Blue's typographic shift in the choreo-poem version of *for colored girls*, in which the capitalization of her speech emphasizes her assumption of a violent masculinity.

18. Images of the jíbaro and the jibarita are often pictured dancing in Puerto Rican novelties, alternately emblematizing a nostalgic or sentimentalist vision of the freedom and sensuousness of rural life or satirical critiques of such sentimental iconography. The image of "La Jibarita" also figures prominently in Puerto Rican musical traditions, particularly that of Johnny Rodriguez, a pioneer of salsa music. Other definitions of Jíbaro include *vendedroga* or *pusher*, signaling the socioeconomic dimensions of the term (Jíbaro, *Concise Oxford Spanish Dictionary*).

19. I use the term *African American* here (rather than *black*) to distinguish between the black American and black Puerto Rican identities that the Lady in Blue performs in this scene.

20. The Lady in Green gives a similar performance through dance, becoming "Sechita," whose name invokes the same investment in representations of Afrolatina identity as Graciela's, but whom the Lady in Green describes as both a "quadroon," and an "Egyptian goddess" with a "face like Nefertiti" (24).

21. This is much in line with Stuart Hall's use of "home" as a metaphor for the failures of origin- and arrival-based models of diaspora. For Hall, the adage "'you can't go home again' . . . [expresses] exactly the diasporic experience, far away enough to experience the sense of exile and loss, close enough to understand the enigma of an always-postponed 'arrival.'" See Hall, *Critical Dialogues in Cultural Studies* 490.

22. This logic is inflected by the logic of the modern European bildungsroman, in

which the white male protagonist inherits his freedom, independence, and full adult subjectivity through rituals of travel and access to space. See, for example, Moretti, *The Way of the World*.

23. This reconfiguration of diasporic space within black female "homeplaces" is evidenced in Shange's 1985 novel, *Betsey Brown*, in which the black American middle-class child protagonist re-creates domestic space to allow her simultaneous access to the reaches of her individuality as well as to a larger world. Betsey uses imagined companions and "made up stories" to "fashion . . . parameters of her own for the house she share[d] with everyone else." thus empowering herself to re-create domestic identificatory space in order to "take . . . in *the world* all on her own." See Shange, *Betsy Brown* 6; emphasis added.

24. This is seen most clearly in Perry's adaptation of the famous scene in the choreopoem in which the colored girls affirm their capacity for intimacy by offering various descriptions of "[their] love," descriptions that the stage directions suggest prompt their physical "com[ing] to life" In Perry's film, Loretta Divine's character, Juanita (whose lines are drawn mostly from the Lady in Brown's) is a social worker who proposes the chorus as an exercise for her women's group, which sits in a circle and utters the choreopoem's lines. The exercise is aimed toward psychological healing through voice, yet its depiction in the film is divorced from the movement and embodiment through which the choreopoem dramatizes black female self-affirmation and community.

25. Toussaint's transition through death not only allows him to be reborn as a ("meta") physical icon of diaspora, but also allows the Lady in Brown access to the subjective complexity and transmutation that death affords. By linking her to what Sharon Holland refers to as the "genderless space" of death, L'Ouverture's transition to embodiment prepares the Lady in Brown, too, to transcend normative conceptions of body and identity. It is this transition, arguably, that allows her to "become . . . [a] man" later in the text (Holland 6; Shange 36).

26. In her 1983 definition of "womanist" from *In Search of our Mothers' Gardens: Womanist Prose*, Walker defines a womanist as "A black feminist or feminist of color," and as someone who is "Committed to survival and wholeness of entire people, male *and* female. Not a separatist, except periodically, for health." Similarly, the Combahee River Collective's "Black Feminist Statement" notes: "we reject the stance of Lesbian separatism because it is not a viable political analysis or strategy for us. It leaves out far too much and far too many people, particularly Black men, women, and children" (214).

27. See Godard's "Rape by Grammar"; Fumagalli's *Caribbean Perspectives on Modernity*; and Carr's "To 'Heal the Word Wounded,'" 793.

28. Philip's engagements with sound echo this multi-vocal structure in readings of the piece. In "Notes on the completion of potentiality," she describes one reading in which she agreed to read from "she tries her tongue" aloud only if a student were to read with her. See "Recordings," http://www.nourbese.com/poetry/she-tries-her-tongue/.

29. See Eimil, "Krudas Cubensi" and Lima, "Krudas Cubensi."

30. Though the group's members Odaymar Cuesta ("Pasa Kruda"), Olivikrude Prendes ("Pelusa/x Kruda"), and original member Odalys Cuesta ("Wanda Kruda"), reflect a range of skin tones perhaps not immediately legible through US-centric schemas of

racial blackness, the group's self-acknowledged blackness and their emphasis on black feminist critique speak to the complexities of blackness in Cuba and in Afrodiaspora more broadly.

31. See Wilson's "Widening the Dialogue" and Hughes's "Soul, Black Women, and Food." While these essays offer helpful analyses of cultural links between fatness and black womanhood, they stop short of addressing black fatness, gender, and sexuality in broader contexts.

32. Somerville's groundbreaking text *Queering the Color Line* examines the historical links between scientific discourses of race and the institutionalization of homosexual identity in American social culture. Holland's recent work *The Erotic Life of Racism* continues this inquiry, examining the place of race and quotidian racism in contemporary experiences of choice and desire.

33. In March 2012, the People of Color Caucus of fat activist group NOLOSE published an open letter critiquing the "I Stand" campaign and the racism of the white fat activist and fat justice movements more broadly. Following such critiques, Wann expanded efforts to increase representation of people of color in the "I Stand" campaign. See NOLOSE (March 2012).

34. This distinction is further emphasized by the choice to use "llego" rather than the past perfect "ha llegado [has arrived]," which, in addition to being a more formal and perhaps more awkward formulation, fails to convey the acute focus on the specific moment of the fat blackwoman body's intervention into hegemonic and normative psychic and interpretive spaces.

35. "La Gorda" lyrics appear courtesy of Las Krudas Cubensi.

## Chapter Four. "Languages of Love"

1. "Work It" lyrics by Joseph Simmons, Missy Elliott, Paul Simon, Debbie Harry, Christopher Stein, and Darryl McDaniels and published by the Universal Music Publishing Group and Paul Simon Music. Used by permission of Hal Leonard, LLC.

2. Canonical studies such as Henry Louis Gates's *The Signifying Monkey: A Theory of Afro-American Literary Criticism*, Barbara Christian's *Black Feminist Criticism: Perspectives on Black Women Writers*, and Fred Moten's *In the Break: The Aesthetics of the Black Radical Tradition* provide key discussions of linguistic innovation and code switching in African American Literature, yet none of these takes up instantiations of invented, spoken linguistic systems in black women's literature.

3. This moment, though overlooked in the ample critical engagement with Walker's works, is especially important given the queer diasporic dynamics of the novel. Celie's invocation of a "new" language as the only means of contact with her sister—from whom she has been separated by both Afrodiasporic space and by the patriarchal rule of her husband in the midst of her own queer erotic development—points to the role of invented language in facilitating disallowed intimacies in even the most familiar of black feminist literary texts.

4. See Henderson, "Speaking in Tongues"; Peterson, "Response and Call"; and Hale, "Bakhtin in African American Literary Theory."

5. In prevailing Western cultural logics, as in dominant sociolinguistic discourse, black women are, as Marcyliena Morgan argues "viewed as linguistically male in terms of outspokenness, dialect variety etc. . . . [which has] led to the argument that the speech of the 'regular' [black] male is the same as the 'regular' [black] female . . . who had no virtue" (xvi). The notion of a black women's language system is thus doubly deviant, first in its expression of a "virtue[less]" identity, and second, in its explicit distinctness from what is accepted as 'regular' black [male] speech. See Morgan, "Just Take Me as I Am."

6. In her analysis of the popular black girls' hand-clapping game "eeny meeny pepsa-dini," Gaunt translates the refrain "atchi catchi liberatchi" as a phonetic reconfiguration of "education liberation," reflecting black girls' absorption of rhetorics of black sociopolitical reform of the 1980s and their rearticulation of those discourses through their own creative linguistic systems (90, 92). The popularization of black-male-authored pig latins (as in rapper Snoop Dogg's late 1990s tag phrase "fa shizzle, my nizzle"), and the commercial cooptation of such idioms by white media and corporations (such as Wrigley's, which used the term *fa shizzle* in its 2002 Eclipse gum campaign) indicate the various usages of black-invented idioms in both the negotiation of the politics of black self-expression and in the commercial marketing of blackness. See Gaunt, *Games Black Girls Play*.

7. Parks's stage directions call for "nonaudible simultaneous English translation" of TALK (115). The appendix of *Fucking A* also includes the lyrics and sheet music to several original songs that appear throughout the play. These songs constitute another important level of the play's heteroglossia.

8. TALK also bears some morphological resemblance to German. "The abortion," for example, is translated as "die Abah-nazip" (Parks *Red Letter Plays* 17). This syllabic parallel between homonymic relationship between Parks's "die" and the German word for "the" render the TALK phrase at least partially legible to English speakers with any basic familiarity with German language. Similarly, the capitalized "A" of "Abah-nazip" further conveys the term's meaning, and hails the polysemous "A" marking Hester's body.

9. Parks's English dialect, too, redefines the stage as a space defined by multiplicities of black female difference. Parks omits linguistic signifiers of possession, replacing them with signifiers of plurality, such that "Hester's Home" reads instead as "Hesters Home," and "Hester's place" becomes "Hesters place" (157, 205). Here, Parks's polyglossia revises historical languages of both race- and gender-based oppressions with the same sort of complex social poetics through which TALK wages its critique.

10. Excerpts from *The Red Letter Plays: In The Blood and Fucking A* (New York: Theatre Communications Group, 2001) used by permission of Creative Artists Agency.

11. The ViVa Books Well Known Stories edition of "Life," adapted by Ivan Vladisavic and published in 1993, emphasizes the functions of the story's English in conveying messages about sexuality. In its back matter, the text notes that "VivaBooks publishes books that teach and entertain." Appended to the story is a "word list," in which words like "prostitute," "carefree," and "respectable" are defined in English. This strategy prepares readers to better understand the valences of Head's English and the place of sexuality in Life's interstitial language. See Bessie Head, *Life*.

12. Eve Kosofsky Sedgwick's notion of the "axiomatic" as a means of creating narratives about sexuality and its larger relations to identification is pertinent here. In keeping

with Sedgwick's logic, these "bold" declarations of "philosoph[ies]" on sexuality may be seen as counter-discourses to the Western cultural axioms Sedgwick critiques. See Sedgwick, *Epistemology of the Closet.*

13. Aidoo exploits the already marginal, feminized genre of the contemporary novella to wage her critique of genre. As Joanna Sullivan argues, African "novellas" or "novelettes" authors in particular are vulnerable to critique and marginalization, as "the term itself, with its diminutive "a/ette" ending carries the potential weight of pejorative criticism," distinguishing it from a "'real' novel" (185). See Sullivan, "Redefining the Novel in Africa."

14. The eye has a crucial function for troubling identity in Head's "Life" as well. Head's narrator dismisses the beer brewers' claims of a love that nullifies the women's disproportionate financial contributions as "so much eye-wash" (Head 39). The eye thus serves as a site at which the sexual dynamics of heterosexual economic engagement may either be illuminated or obfuscated.

15. This trope is carried through elsewhere in Shange's work. See, for example, *Sassafrass, Cypress, and Indigo* in which Indigo states that "the stars that fall from between [her] legs can only be seen by boys who are pure of mind and strong of body" (22). Also see *From Okra to Greens*, in which the female Okra hyperbolizes her love for the male Greens through a metaphor of the "crests of waves of slaves who cd not move without being seen" (16).

16. As Esther Pujolràs Noguer points out, this is a misspelling. See Pujolràs Noguer, *An African (Auto)biography.*

17. Hip-hop culture serves as a symbol of public deviance in Morrison's and Parks's texts as well. Morrison's narrator describes gender dynamics in contemporary African American culture as a landscape of women "straddling a chair or dancing half naked on TV," invoking hip-hop videos to paint a world in which contemporary black women have, as she puts it, no "secrets," either "to hold" or "to tell" (4, 3). Parks similarly invokes hip-hop culture as public transgression, offering a list of criminal offenses punishable in *Fucking A*'s fictional setting that includes "playing loud music" and "fighting the power," a reference to rap group Public Enemy's controversial 1990 song, "Fight the Power," which critiqued police and state violence (160).

18. "Gyal" signals Elliott's affectation of a Caribbean accent in this line. "Chocha" likewise tags Spanish-language slang for vagina. Here, Elliott further complicates black female gender by briefly invoking feminine attractiveness in specifically Caribbean diasporic contexts.

19. See Starbury, "Keri Hilson, Missy Elliott Rebuke," and Magget, "Miss Elliott Gay Wedding 2013."

# Works Cited


Abdur-Rahman, Aliyyah I. *Against the Closet: Black Political Longing and the Erotics of Race*. Durham: Duke University Press, 2012.

——. "The Black Ecstatic." *GLQ: A Journal of Lesbian and Gay Studies* 24, no. 2–3 (June 2018): 343–365.

Achebe, Chinua. "The African Writer and the English Language." In *Switching Languages: Translingual Writers Reflect on Their Craft*, edited by Steven G. Kellman, 191–200. Lincoln: University of Nebraska Press, 2003.

Ademoyo, Adeolu. "The Ontological Imperative for the New African Diaspora." In *The New African Diaspora*, edited by Isidore Okpewho and Nkiru Nzegwu, 500–517. Bloomington: Indiana University Press, 2009.

Adi, Hakim, and Marika Sherwood, eds. *Pan-African History: Political Figures from Africa and the Diaspora since 1787.* London: Routledge, 2003.

Adichie, Chimamanda Ngozi. *Half of a Yellow Sun*. London: Fourth Estate, 2006.

——. "You in America." In *Discovering Home: A Selection of Writings from the 2002 Caine Prize for African Writing*, 27–34. Bellevue, South Africa: Jacana, 2003.

African American Policy Forum (AAPF) and Center for Intersectionality and Social Policy Studies at Columbia Law School (CISPES). (2015) *#SayHerName: Resisting Police Brutality against Black Women: A Social Media Guide*. www.aapf.org/publications.

Ahmed, Sarah. "Feminist Killjoys (And Other Willful Subjects)." *Scholar and Feminist Online* 8, no. 3 (Summer 2010). www.barnard.edu/sfonline.

——. *The Promise of Happiness*. Durham: Duke University Press, 2010.

Aidoo, Ama Ata. *Our Sister Killjoy*. New York: Longman, 1977.

Alexander, Elizabeth. "'Coming Out Blackened and Whole': Fragmentation and Reintegration in Audre Lorde's *Zami* and *The Cancer Journals*." *American Literary History* 6, no. 4 (Winter 1994): 695–715.

Alexander, M. Jacqui. "Erotic Autonomy as Decolonization: An Anatomy of Feminist and State Practice in Bahamas Tourism." In *Feminist Genealogies, Colonial Legacies, Democratic Futures*, edited by M. Jacqui Alexander and Chandra T. Mohanty, 63–100. New York: Routledge, 1997.

———. "Not Just (Any) Body Can Be a Citizen: The Politics of Law, Sexuality, and Post-coloniality in Trinidad and Tobago and the Bahamas." *Feminist Review* 48 (Autumn 1994): 5–23.

Allen, Jafari Sinclaire. ¡*Venceremos?: The Erotics of Black Self-making in Cuba*. Durham: Duke University Press, 2011.

Anderlini, Serina. "Drama or Performance Art? An Interview with Ntozake Shange." *Journal of Dramatic Theory and Criticism* (Fall 1991): 85–97.

Anderson, Benedict. *Imagined Communities: Reflections on the Origin and Spread of Nationalism*. London: Verso, 1991.

Andrews, William. *To Tell a Free Story: The First Century of Afro-American Autobiography, 1760–1865* (Urbana: University of Illinois Press, 1986), quoted in Helen Larsen, *Legba's Crossing: Narratology in the African Atlantic*. Athens: University of Georgia Press, 2009.

Appadurai, Arjun. "Disjuncture and Difference in the Global Cultural Economy." In *Theorizing Diaspora*, edited by Jana Evans Braziel and Anita Mannur, 25–48. Oxford: Blackwell Publishers, 2003.

Appiah, Kwame Anthony. *Cosmopolitanism: Ethics in a World of Strangers*. New York: W.W. Norton & Co., 2006.

Avilez, GerShun. *Radical Aesthetics and Modern Black Nationalism*. Urbana: University of Illinois Press, 2016.

Baker, Houston A. *Turning South Again: Re-Thinking Modernism/Re-Reading Booker T*. Durham: Duke University Press, 2001.

Bakhtin, Mikhail. *The Dialogic Imagination*. Austin: University of Texas Press, 1981.

Balogun, F. Odun. "Self, Place, and Identity in Two Generations of West African Immigrant Women Memoirs: Emcheta's Head above Water and Danquah's Willow Weep for Me." In *The New African Diaspora*, edited by Isidore Okpewho and Nkiru Nzegwu, 442–458. Bloomington: Indiana University Press, 2009.

Bambara, Toni Cade. *The Salt Eaters*. New York: Vintage-Random House, 1980.

Banfield, Ann. "From *Unspeakable Sentences*." In *Theory of the Novel: A Historical Approach*, edited by Michael McKeon, 515–536. Baltimore: Johns Hopkins University Press, 2000.

———. *Unspeakable Sentences: Narration and Representation in the Language of Fiction*. Boston: Routledge, 1982.

Barriteau, Eudene. "Theorizing Gender Systems and the Project of Modernity in the Twentieth-Century Caribbean." *Feminist Review* 59 (Summer 1998): 186–201.

Barthes, Roland. "The Grain of Voice" in *Image, Music, Text*. New York: MacMillan, 1977.

Bergson, Howard H. *Palindromes and Anagrams*. UK: Constable & Company, Ltd., 1973.

Berlant, Lauren. *The Anatomy of National Fantasy: Hawthorne, Utopia, and Everyday Life*. Chicago: University of Chicago Press, 1991.

Bersani, Leo. *Homos*. Cambridge: Harvard University Press, 1995.

Bethlehem, Louise Shabat. "Strange Loops and Writes-of-Passage: Double-Crossing Diaspora." *South Atlantic Quarterly* (Winter/Spring 1999): 255–266.

Bhabha, Homi. "Interrogating Identity," quoted in Busia, Abena. "Languages of the

Self" in *Theorizing Black Feminisms: The Visionary Pragmatism of Black Women.* New York: Routledge, 1993.

———. *The Location of Culture.* New York: Routledge, 1994.

———. "Of Mimicry and Man: The Ambivalence of Colonial Discourse." *October* 28 (Spring 1984): 125–137.

Body Ecology. "Choreopoetic Aesthetics." Ritual Theatre & Choreopoem Aesthetics Performance Residency Workshop, Medgar Evers College. October 3, 2011.

Boykin, Keith, ed. *For Colored Boys Who Have Considered Suicide When the Rainbow Is Still Not Enough.* New York: Magnus Books, 2012.

Branch, Jerome C. *The Poetics and Politics of Diaspora: Transatlantic Musings.* New York: Routledge, 2015.

Brand, Dionne. *At the Full and Change of the Moon.* New York: Grove Press, 2000.

———. *In Another Place, Not Here.* Toronto: Knopf Canada, 1996.

———. *Ossuaries.* Toronto: McClelland and Stewart, 2010.

Brathwaite, Kamau. *History of the Voice: The Development of Nation Language in Anglophone Caribbean Poetry.* London: New Beacon Books, 1984.

Brody, Jennifer DeVere. *Punctuation: Art, Politics, and Play.* Durham: Duke University Press, 2008.

Brown, Joel. "African-American Theatre Festival Focuses on the Lives of Women, Girls." *Boston Globe* online. www.boston.com. May 29, 2009.

Brown, Kimberly Nichele. *Writing the Black Revolutionary Diva: Women's Subjectivity and the Decolonizing Text.* Bloomington: Indiana University Press, 2010.

BrownGirls Burlesque. "Evil Beautiful Sunshine." Youtube video by Chicava HoneyChild, uploaded July 2, 2008. https://www.youtube.com/watch?v=yTzbOuDmId4.

Bucholtz, Mary, and Qiuana Lopez. "Performing Blackness, Forming Whiteness: Linguistic Minstrelsy in Hollywood Film." *Journal of Sociolinguistics* 15, no. 5 (2011): 680–706.

Busia, Abena P. A. "Languages of the Self." In *Theorizing Black Feminisms: The Visionary Pragmatism of Black Women*, edited by Stanlie M. James and Abena P. A. Busia, 205. New York: Routledge 1993.

———. "What Is Africa to Me? Knowledge Possession, Knowledge Production, and the Health of Our Bodies Politic in Africa and the Africa Diaspora." *African Studies Review* 49, no. 1 (2006): 15–30.

Butler, Judith. *Gender Trouble: Feminism and the Subversion of Identity.* New York: Routledge, 1990.

———. *Undoing Gender.* New York: Routledge, 2004.

Campt, Tina M. *Listening to Images.* Durham: Duke University Press, 2017.

Carpenter, Faedra Chatard. "Robert O'Hara's Insurrection: 'Que(e)rying History.'" In *Black Queer Studies*, edited by E. Patrick Johnson and Mae Henderson, 323–348. Durham: Duke University Press, 2005.

Carr, Brenda. "To 'Heal the Word Wounded': Agency and the Materiality of Language and Form in M. NourbeSe Philip's *She Tries Her Tongue, Her Silence Softly Breaks.*" *Studies in Canadian Literature* 19, no. 1 (1994): 72–93.

Chen, Kuan-Hsing. "Cultural Studies and the Politics of Internationalization: An Interview with Stuart Hall." In *Stuart Hall: Critical Dialogues in Cultural Studies*, edited by David Morely and Kuan-Hsing Chen, 309–325. London: Routledge, 1996.

Cho, Sumi, Kimberlé Williams Crenshaw, and Leslie McCall. "Toward a Field of Intersectionality Studies: Theory, Applications, and Praxis," *Signs* 38, no. 4 (Summer 2013): 785–810.

Christian, Barbara. *Black Feminist Criticism: Perspectives on Black Women Writers*. New York: Teachers College Press, 1985.

———. "Nuance and the Novella: A Study of Gwendolyn Brooks's *Maud Martha*." In *A Life Distilled: Gwendolyn Brooks, Her Poetry and Fiction*, edited by Maria K. Mootry and Gary Smith. Urbana: University of Illinois Press, 1987.

———. "The Race for Theory." *Cultural Critique* 6 (1987): 51–63.

Cixous, Hélène, Keith Cohen, and Paula Cohen. "The Laugh of the Medusa." *Signs* 1, no. 4 (Summer 1976): 875–893.

Clarke, Cheryl. *After Mecca: Women Poets and the Black Arts Movement*. New Brunswick: Rutgers University Press, 2004.

Clarke, Kamari Maxine, and Deborah A. Thomas, eds. *Globalization and Race: Transformations in the Cultural Production of Blackness*. Durham: Duke University Press, 2006.

Cliff, Michelle. *No Telephone to Heaven*. Boston: Dutton Adult, 1987.

Cohen, Cathy. "Punks, Bulldaggers and Welfare Queens: The Radical Potential of Queer Politics?" In *Black Queer Studies*, edited by E. Patrick Johnson and Mae G. Henderson, 21–50. Durham: Duke University Press, 2005.

Collins, Patricia Hill. *Black Feminist Thought: Knowledge, Consciousness, and the Politics of Empowerment*. New York: Routledge, 2000.

———. "Comment on Heckman's 'Truth and Method: Feminist Standpoint Theory Revisited': Where's the Power?" In *Provoking Feminisms*, edited by Carolyn Allen and Judith A. Howard. Chicago: University of Chicago Press, 2000.

Combahee River Collective. "Combahee River Collective Statement." In *Home Girls: A Black Feminist Anthology*, edited by Barbara Smith, 272–282. New York: Kitchen Table Women of Color Press, 1983.

Coopan, Vilashini. *Worlds Within: National Narratives and Global Connections in Postcolonial Women's Writing*. Stanford: Stanford University Press, 2009.

Crenshaw, Kimberlé. "Demarginalizing the Intersection of Race and Sex: A Black Feminist Critique of Antidiscrimination Doctrine, Feminist Theory and Antiracist Politics." *University of Chicago Legal Forum* (1989): 139–168.

———. "Kimberlé Crenshaw on Intersectionality, More than Two Decades Later." Columbia Law School. June 8, 2017. https://www.law.columbia.edu/pt-br/news/2017/06/kimberle-crenshaw-intersectionality.

———. "Mapping the Margins: Intersectionality, Identity Politics, and Violence against Women of Color." *Stanford Law Review* 43 (1991): 1241–1299.

Crenshaw, Kimberlé Williams, and Andrea J. Ritchie with Rachel Anspach, Rachel Glimer, and Luke Harris. *SayHerName: Resisting Police Brutality against Black Women*. New York: African American Policy Forum and Center for Intersectionality and Social Policy Studies at Columbia Law School (CISPES), 2015. http://www.aapf.org/sayhernamereport/.

Cruz, Arianne. *The Color of Kink: Black Women, BDSM, and Pornography*. New York: New York University Press, 2016.

Danticat, Edwidge. *The Dew Breaker*. New York: Vintage Books, 2005.

———. Krik?*Krak!* New York: Soho Press, 1995.

*Daughters of the Dust*. Directed by Julie Dash. American Playhouse, Geechee Girls, and WMG Film, 1991.

Davies, Carole Boyce. *Black Women, Writing and Identity: Migrations of the Subject*. New York: Routledge, 1994.

Davies, Carole Boyce, and Leslie Molara Ogundipe, eds. *Moving beyond Boundaries: Volume 2 Black Women's Diasporas*. New York: New York University Press, 1995.

DeFrantz, Thomas F., and Anita Gonzales, eds. *Black Performance Theory*. Durham: Duke University Press, 2014.

Delany, Samuel R. *The Motion of Light in Water: Sex and Science Fiction Writing in the East Village, 1957–1965*. New York: Arbor House, 1988.

Delgado, Richard. *Critical Race Theory an Introduction*. New York: New York University Press, 2012.

Derrida, Jacques. *Margins of Philosophy*. Trans. Alan Bass. Chicago: University of Chicago Press, 1982.

Dickerson, Glenda. "The Cult of True Womanhood: Toward a Womanist Attitude in African-American Theatre." *Theatre Journal* (May 1988): 178–187.

———. "Transforming through Performing: Oral History, African-American Women's Voices and the Power of Theater." Address at the University of Michigan, 2002. http://hdl.handle.net.

*Dictionary of Linguistics and Phonetics*. Oxford: Blackwell Publishers, 2003. Credo Reference. Web. April 28, 2011.

Dinshaw, Carolyn. *How Soon Is Now? Medieval Texts, Amateur Readers, and the Queerness of Time*. Durham: Duke University Press, 2012.

Djebar, Assia. "Writing in the Language of the Other." In *Switching Languages: Translingual Writers Reflect on Their Craft*, edited by Steven G. Kellman, 311–318. Lincoln: University of Nebraska Press, 2003.

Dominus, Susan. "A Suicide More Complex than a Slogan." *New York Times*, November 5, 2010.

Du Bois, W. E. B. *The Souls of Black Folk (1903)*. New York: Penguin Classics, 1996.

Durrow, Heidi W. *The Girl Who Fell from the Sky*. Chapel Hill: Algonquin Books, 2010.

Edelman, Lee. *No Future: Queer Theory and the Death Drive*. Durham: Duke University Press, 2004.

Edwards, Brent Hayes. "Langston Hughes and the Futures of Diaspora." *American Literary History* 19, no. 3 (Fall 2007): 689–711.

———. *The Practice of Diaspora: Literature, Translation, and the Rise of Black Internationalism*. Cambridge: Harvard University Press, 2003.

———. "The Uses of Diaspora." *Social Text* 19, no. 1 (2001): 45–73.

Eimil, Ernesto. "Krudas Cubensi: Vivir en Resistencia," AMPM: Descarga Música Cubana. https://www.magazineampm.com/krudas-cubensi-vivir-en-resisrwnce/. November 27, 2020.

Elliott, Missy. *Under Construction*. Elektra Records, 2002.

Emezi, Akwaeke. *Freshwater*. New York: Grove Press, 2018.

Eng, David. *The Feeling of Kinship: Queer Liberalism and the Racialization of Intimacy*. Durham: Duke University Press, 2010.

Esty, Jed. *Unseasonable Youth: Modernism, Colonialism, and the Fiction of Development*. London: Oxford University Press, 2011.

Euripides III. *Hecuba, Andromache, The Trojan Women, Ion*. New York: CreateSpace, 2009.

Farmer, Ashley. *Re-Thinking Black Power: How Black Women Transformed an Era*. Durham: University of North Carolina Press, 2017.

Farrell, Amy Erdman. *Fat Shame: Stigma and the Fat Body on American Culture*. New York: New York University Press, 2011.

Faucheux, Amandine H. "Race and Sexuality in Nalo Hopkinson's Oeuvre; or, Queer Afrofuturism." *Science Fiction Studies* 44, no. 3 (2017): 563–580.

Felski, Rita. "The Novel of Self-Discovery: A Necessary Fiction?" *Southern Review* 19 (1986): 131–148.

Ferguson, Moira. "A Lot of Memory: An Interview with Jamaica Kincaid." *Kenyon Review* 16, no. 1 (Winter 1994): 163–188.

Fernandez, June. "Cuerpos Feministas: Krudas Cubensi: Raperas que Cantan a las Negras, a las Pobres, a las Gordas." Mari Kazetari: Periodismo de Gafas Violeta. http://gentedigital.es/comunidad/june/. March 26, 2012.

Finney, Nikki. *The World Is Round*. Evanston: TriQuarterly Books/Northwestern University Press, 2003.

Fleetwood, Nicole R. *Troubling Vision: Performance, Visuality and Blackness*. Chicago: University of Chicago Press, 2011.

Forbes, Curdella. "Fracturing Subjectivities: International Space and the Discourse of Individualism in Colin Channer's *Waiting in Vain* and Jamaica Kincaid's *Mr. Potter*." *Small Axe: A Caribbean Journal of Criticism* 12, no. 1 (February 2008): 16–37.

*For Colored Girls*. Directed by Tyler Perry. Lion's Gate Entertainment, 2010.

*for colored girls who have considered suicide/when the rainbow is enuf*. Directed by Oz Scott. Thirteen/WNET. New York: American Playhouse, 1982.

Fortier, Anne-Marie. "Queer Diaspora." In *Handbook of Lesbian and Gay Studies*, edited by Diane Richardson and Steven Seidman, 183–198. London: Sage, 2002.

Foucault, Michel. *The History of Sexuality Vol. 1: An Introduction*. London: Penguin, 1976.

———. "Nietzsche, Genealogy, History." In *Language, Counter-Memory, Practice: Selected Essays and Interviews*, edited by D. F. Bouchard. Ithaca: Cornell University Press, 1977.

Frazier, Valerie. "Domestic Epic Warfare in *Maud Martha*." *African American Review* 39, no. 1/2 (2005): 133–141.

Freeman, Elizabeth. *Time Binds: Queer Temporalities, Queer Histories*. Durham: Duke University Press, 2010.

Friedman, Susan Stanford. "Bodies on the Move: A Poetics of Home and Diaspora." *Tulsa Studies in Women's Literature* 23, no. 2 (Fall 2004): 189–212.

———. *Mappings: Feminism and the Cultural Geographies of Encounter*. Princeton, NJ: Princeton University Press, 1998.

Fumagalli, Maria Christina. *Caribbean Perspectives on Modernity: Returning Medusa's Gaze*. Charlottesville: University of Virginia Press, 2009.

Garvey, Johanna X. K. "'The Place She Miss': Exile, Memory, and Resistance in Dionne Brand's Fiction." *Callaloo* 26, no. 2 (2003): 486–503.

Garza, Alicia. "A Herstory of the #Black Lives Matter Movement by Alicia Garza." *The Feminist Wire*, October 7, 2014.

Gates, Henry Louis, Jr. *Figures in Black: Words, Signs, and the "Racial" Self*. New York: Oxford University Press, 1989.

———. *The Signifying Monkey: A Theory of Afro-American Literary Criticism*. New York: Oxford University Press, 1988.

Gaunt, Kyra. *Games Black Girls Play: Learning the Ropes from Double-Dutch to Hip-Hop*. New York: New York University Press, 2006.

George-Graves, Nadine. *Urban Bush Women: Twenty Years of Dance Theatre, Community Engagement, and Working It Out*. Madison: University of Wisconsin Press, 2010.

Gerrey, Alta, and Irene Reti. *Alta and the History of Shameless Hussy Press, 1969–1989*. Transcript and recording, University of California, Santa Cruz, University Library. https://escholarship.org/uc/item/1fx8d588.

Gilroy, Paul. *Against Race: Imagining Political Culture beyond the Color Line*. Cambridge: Harvard University Press, 2001.

———. *The Black Atlantic: Modernity and Double Consciousness*. Cambridge: Harvard University Press, 1993.

Glissant, Édouard. *Caribbean Discourse: Selected Essays*. Charlottesville: University of Virginia Press, 1999.

Godard, Barbara. "Rape by Grammar: Marlene NourbeSe Philip's *Hyphenated Tongue* or Writing the Caribbean Demotic between Africa and the Artic." In *Contemporary Women Writing in the Other Americas: Contemporary Women Writing in Canada and Quebec, Vol. 3*, edited by Georgiana M. M. Colvile. New York: Edward Mellen Press, 1996.

Goffman, Erving. *Stigma: Notes on the Management of Spoiled Identity*. New York: Penguin Books, 1963.

Gopinath, Gayatri. *Impossible Desires: Queer Diasporas and South Asian Public Cultures*. Durham: Duke University Press, 2005.

Gumbs, Alexis Pauline. "Mobile Homecoming Project." www.mobilehomecoming.wordpress.com.

Hada, Kenneth. "The Power to Undo Sin: Race, History and Literary Blackness in Rilla Askew's 'Fire in Beulah.'" *College Literature* 34, no. 4 (Fall 2007): 166–189.

Halberstam, Judith. "Mackdaddy, Superfly, Rapper: Gender, Race, and Masculinity in the Drag King Scene." *Social Text* 52/53 (Winter 1997): 104–131.

———. "The Politics of Negativity in Recent Queer Theory," in "The Anti-Social Thesis in Queer Theory" in "Forum: Conference Debates: The Anti-Social Thesis in Queer Theory." *PMLA* 121, no. 3 (2006): 823–824.

Hale, Dorothy J. "Bakhtin in African American Literary Theory." *English Literary Theory* 61, no. 2 (1994): 445–471.

Hall, Stuart. *Critical Dialogues in Cultural Studies*. New York: Routledge, 1996.

———. "The Question of Cultural Identity." In *Modernity and Its Futures*, edited by Stuart Hall, David Held, and Tony McGrew. Cambridge: Polity Press, 1992.

Halperin, David. *How to Do the History of Homosexuality*. Chicago: University of Chicago Press, 2002.

Hammonds, Evelynn. "Black (W)holes and the Geometry of Black Female Sexuality." In *African American Literary Theory: A Reader*, edited by Winston Napier, 482–497. New York: New York University Press, 2000.

———. "Toward a Genealogy of Black Female Sexuality: The Problematic of Silence." In *Feminist Genealogies, Colonial Legacies, Democratic Futures*, edited by M. Jacqui Alexander and Chandra T. Mohanty, 170–182. New York: Routledge, 1997.

Harris-Perry, Melissa V. *Sister Citizen: Shame, Stereotypes and Black Women in America*. New Haven: Yale University Press, 2011.

Hartman, Saidiya. "Venus in Two Acts." *Small Axe: A Caribbean Journal of Criticism* 12, no. 2 (2008): 1–14.

Hartsock, Nancy C. M. *Money, Sex, and Power: Toward a Feminist Historical Materialism*. New York: Longman, 1983.

Hawthorne, Nathaniel. *The Scarlet Letter*. 1850. New York: Bantam, 1981.

Head, Bessie. *The Collector of Treasures: and Other Botswana Tales*. Portsmouth, NH: Heinemann, Publishing, 1989.

———. *Life*. Kensington, SA: ViVa Books, 1993.

Heckman, Susan. "Truth and Method: Feminist Standpoint Theory Revisited" in *Provoking Feminisms*, edited by Carolyn Allen and Judith A. Howard. Chicago: University of Chicago Press, 2000.

Hemphill, Essex. *Brother to Brother: New Writing by Black Gay Men*. Los Angeles, Alyson Books: 1991.

Henderson, Mae G. "Speaking in Tongues: Dialogics, Dialectics, and the African American Woman's Literary Tradition." In *Changing Our Own Words: Essays on Criticism, Theory, and Writing by Black Women*, edited by Cheryl Wall. New Brunswick: Rutgers University Press, 1989.

Higashida, Cheryl. *Black Internationalist Feminism: Women Writers of the Black Left, 1945–1995*. Urbana: University of Illinois Press, 2011.

Hobson, Janelle. *Venus in the Dark: Blackness and Beauty in Popular Culture*. New York: Routledge, 2005.

Holibaugh, Amber, and Cherrie Moraga, "What We're Rollin' Around in Bed With." In *Sexual Revolution*, edited by Jeffrey Escoffier, 538–535. New York: Thunder's Mouth Press, 2003.

Holland, Sharon Patricia. *The Erotic Life of Racism*. Durham: Duke University Press, 2012.

———. *Raising the Dead: Readings of Death and (Black) Subjectivity*. Durham: Duke University Press, 2000.

Honey, Maureen. "A Sensibility of Struggle and Hope." *Prairie Schooner* 58, no. 4 (Winter 1984): 111–112.

Hong, Grace Kyungwon. *Death beyond Disavowal: The Impossible Politics of Difference*. Minneapolis: University of Minnesota Press, 2015.

hooks, bell. *Belonging: A Culture of Place*. New York: Routledge, 2009.

———. "Homeplace: A Site of Resistance." In *Yearning: Race, Gender, and Cultural Politics*. Boston: South End Press, 1990.

———. *Talking Back: Thinking Feminist, Thinking Black*. Boston: South End Press, 1989.

———. "Writing Autobiography." In *Talking Back: Thinking Feminist, Thinking Black*. Boston: South End Press, 1989.

Huffington Post. "Raymond Chase Commits Suicide, Fifth Gay Youth to Take Life in Three Weeks," Huffington Post. www.huffingtonpost.com. October 1, 2010.

Hughes, Marvalene H. "Soul, Black Women, and Food." In *Food and Culture: A Reader*. New York: Routledge, 1997.

Humphries, Jill M. "Resisting 'Race': Organizing African Transnational Identities in the United States." In *The New African Diaspora*, edited by Isidore Okpewho and Nkiru Nzegwu, 272–300. Bloomington: Indiana University Press, 2009.

Hurston, Zora Neale. *Their Eyes Were Watching God* (1937). New York: Harper, 1990.

Jackson-Opoku, Sandra. "Out beyond Our Borders: Literary Travelers of the TransDiaspora." In *The New African Diaspora*, edited by Isidore Okpewho and Nkiru Nzegwu, 476–482. Bloomington: Indiana University Press, 2009.

Jaji, Tsitsi Ella. *Africa in Stereo: Modernism, Music, and Pan-African Solidarity*. New York: Oxford University Press, 2014.

"jíbaro1." *The Concise Oxford Spanish Dictionary*, edited by Nicholas Rollin. Oxford University Press, 1998. Oxford Reference Online. Oxford University Press. University of Pennsylvania. March 2. 2011. http://www.oxfordreference.com/views/ENTRY.html?subview=Main&entry=t67a.e18024.

"jíbaro2." *The Concise Oxford Spanish Dictionary*, edited by Nicholas Rollin. Oxford University Press, 1998. Oxford Reference Online. Oxford University Press. University of Pennsylvania. March 2, 2011. http://www.oxfordreference.com/views/ENTRY.html?subview=Main&entry=t67a.e18025.

Jiggetts, Shelby. "An Interview with Suzan-Lori Parks." *Callaloo* 19, no. 2 (Spring 1996): 309–317.

Johnson, E. Patrick. "Feeling the Spirit in the Dark: Expanding Notions of the Sacred in the African American Gay Community." *Callaloo* 21, no. 2 (Winter/Spring 1998): 399–416.

Jones, Gayle. *Corregidora*. New York: Random House, 1975.

Jones, Meta DuEwa. *The Muse Is Music: Jazz Poetry from the Harlem Renaissance to Spoken Word*. Urbana: University of Illinois Press, 2012.

Kalimi, Isaac. "The Land of Moriah, Mount Moriah and the Site of Solomon's Temple in Biblical Historiography." *Harvard Theological Review* 83 (1990): 345–362.

Keeling, Kara. "Joining the Lesbians: Cinematic Regimes of Lesbian Visibility." In *Black Queer Studies*, edited by E. Patrick Johnson and Mae G. Henderson, 213–227. Durham: Duke University Press, 2005.

———. *Queer Times, Black Futures*. New York: New York University Press, 2019.

———. *Sexing the Caribbean: Gender, Race, and Sexual Labor*. New York: Routledge, 2009.

———. *The Witch's Flight: The Cinematic, the Black Femme, and the Image of Common Sense*. Durham: Duke University Press, 2007.

Kenan, Randall. *Let the Dead Bury Their Dead and Other Stories*. New York: Harcourt, 1992.

Kincaid, Jamaica. *Annie John*. New York: Farrar, Strauss & Giroux, 1985.

———. *At the Bottom of the River*. New York: Farrar, Strauss & Giroux, 1983.

———. *The Autobiography of My Mother*. New York: Farrar, Strauss & Giroux, 1996.

———. Kelly Writers' House Fellows Reading. University of Pennsylvania, Philadelphia. March 18, 2007.

———. *Lucy*. New York: Plume, 1991.

———. *Mr. Potter*. New York: Farrar, Strauss & Giroux, 2002.

King, Rosamond S. *Island Bodies: Transgressive Sexualities in the Caribbean Imagination*. Gainesville: University of Florida Press, 2014.

Kitt, Eartha. "I Want to Be Evil." Lyrics by Lester Judson and Raymond Taylor. *The Wicked Eartha Kitt*. RCA Recordings, 1953.

Klein, Reisa. "Laughing It Off: Neo-burlesque Striptease and the Case of the Sexual Overtones as a Theatre of Resistance." *Revista Científica de Informacion y Comunicación* (2014): 245–265.

Kraidy, Marwan M. *Hybridity, or the Cultural Logic of Globalization*. Philadelphia: Temple University Press, 2005.

Kristeva, Julia. *Black Sun: Depression and Melancholia*. (1987) Translated by Leon S. Roudiez. New York: Columbia University Press, 1989.

———. *Powers of Horror: An Essay on Abjection*. New York: Columbia University Press, 1982.

Kwami, Mark. *Adinkra: Symbolic Language of the Ashanti*. Berlin: Haus der Kulturen der Welt, 1993.

La Charanga Habanera. "La Gorda." *Soy Cubano Soy Popular* (2002).

Las Krudas Cubensi. "Krudas Cubensi–La Gorda" (music video). https://www.youtube.com/watch?v=Mlzf9BPHZYo.

———. "La Gorda." Krudas Mixtape (2009).

Latham, Marc. "Folding Mirror Poetry." *Folding Mirror Poetry: A Site for Reading and Publishing Folding Mirror and Related Poetry*. www.foldingmirrorpoetry.webs.com Nd. 2009. May 5, 2010.

LeBesco, Kathleen. *Revolting Bodies? The Struggle to Redefine Fat Identity*. Amherst: University of Massachusetts Press, 2003.

Lefebvre, Henri. *The Production of Space*. Translated by Donald Nicholson-Smith. Cambridge, MA: Blackwell Publishers, 1991.

Lenz, Brooke. "Postcolonial Fiction and the Outsider Within: Toward a Literary Practice of Standpoint Theory." *NWSA Journal* 16, no. 2 (Summer 2004): 98–120.

Lester, Neal A. "At the Heart of Shange's Feminism: An Interview." *Black American Literature Forum* 24, no. 4 (Winter 1990): 717–730.

Lévi-Strauss, Claude. *The Elementary Structures of Kinship*. Edited by Rodney Needham, translated by J. Harle Bell and John Richard von Sturmer. Boston: Beacon Press, 1969.

LGBT Hate Crimes Project. "Sakia Gunn," "Michael Sandy." www.lgbthatecrimes.org.

Lillvis, Kristen. *Posthuman Blackness and the Black Female Imagination*. Athens: University of Georgia Press, 2017.

Lima, Rosa Muñoz "Krudas Cubensi: 'En Posesión del Secreto de la Alegría'" *DW*. https://www.dw.com/es/krudas-cubeensi-en-posesion-del-secreto-de-la—alegr%C3%ADa/a-18807568. October 27, 2015.

*Looking for Langston*. Directed by Isaac Julien. Sankofa Film & Video Productions, 1989.

Lorde, Audre. "Age, Race, Class and Sex: Women Redefining Difference." In *Sister Outsider: Essays and Speeches*. Freedom, CA: The Crossing Press, 1984.

———. *The Black Unicorn*. New York: W.W. Norton, 1978.

———. *The Collected Poems of Audre Lorde*. New York: Norton, 1997.

———. "Learning from the 60s." In *Sister Outsider: Essays and Speeches*. Freedom, CA: The Crossing Press, 1984.

———. *Need: A Chorale for Black Woman Voices*. Albany: Communication Services, 1990.

———. *Sister Outsider: Essays and Speeches*. Freedom, CA: The Crossing Press, 1984.

———. "Uses of the Erotic: The Erotic as Power." In *Sister Outsider: Essays and Speeches*. Freedom, CA: The Crossing Press, 1984.

———. *Zami: A New Spelling of My Name*. Freedom, CA: The Crossing Press, 1982.

Love, Heather. *Feeling Backward: Loss and the Politics of Queer History*. Cambridge: Harvard University Press, 2007.

Lubiano, Wahneema. "Shuckin' Off the African-American Native Other: What's Po-Mo Got to Do with It?" *Cultural Critique* no. 18 (1991): 149–186.

Lunsford, Andrea, and Lahoucine Ouzgane, eds. *Crossing Borderlands: Composition and Postcolonial Studies*. Pittsburgh: University of Pittsburgh Press, 2004.

Lyndsay, "The Burlesque Booty Queen: Interview with Jan Tina." *Quail Bell Magazine* [Originally published in *Luna Mag*]. September 22, 2015.

Madison, D. Soyini. *Acts of Activism: Human Rights as Radical Performance. Cambridge*: Cambridge University Press, 2012.

Magget, Sonya. "Miss Elliott Gay Wedding 2013." *Enstars* September 26, 2013. https://www.enstarz.com/articles/25876/20130926/miss-elliott-gay-wedding-2013-wed-rapper-sharaya-j-friend-reacts.htm.

Mandri, Flora María González. *Guarding Cultural Memory: Afro-Cuban Women in Literature and the Arts*. Charlottesville: University of Virginia Press, 2006.

Manning, Patrick. *The African Diaspora: A History through Culture*. New York: Columbia University Press, 2009.

Marshall, Paule. *Praisesong for the Widow*. New York: Plume, 1983.

Matebeni, Zethu. "Sexing Women: Young Black Lesbians' Reflections on Sex and Responses to Safe(r) Sex." In *From Social Silence to Social Science: Same-sex Sexuality, HIV & AIDS and Gender in South Africa*. Conference proceedings edited by Vasu Reddy, Theo Sandfort, and Laetitia Rispel. Cape Town: Human Sciences Research Council Press, 2009.

Mathes, Carter. *Imagine the Sound: Experimental African American Literature after Civil Rights*. Minneapolis: University of Minnesota Press, 2015.

Mbembe, Achille. *On the Postcolony*. Oakland: University of California Press, 2001.

McCall, Leslie. "The Complexity of Intersectionality." *Signs: Journal of Women in Culture and Society* 30, no. 3 (2005): 1771–1800.

McCallum, Shara. "Remaking the Wor(l)d: A Poetics of Resistance and Transformation in Marlene Nourbese Philip's *she tries her tongue: her silence softly breaks.*" In *Postcolonial Perspectives on Women Writers from Africa, the Caribbean, and the U.S.*, edited by Martin Japtok. Trenton: Africa World Press, 2003.

McCollough, Kate. "'Marked by Genetics and Exile': Narrativizing Transcultural Sexualities in *Memory Mambo.*" *GLQ: A Journal of Lesbian and Gay Studies* 6, no. 4 (2000): 577–607.

McDaniel, Rena. "Photo Essay: Jeezy's Juke Joint: Confronting Queer Black Erasure One Article of Clothing at a Time," *Autostraddle*, May 11, 2015.

McKittrick, Katherine. *Demonic Grounds: Black Women and the Cartographies of Struggle.* Minneapolis: University of Minnesota Press, 2006.

———. *Sylvia Wynter: On Being Human as Praxis.* Durham: Duke University Press, 2015.

McLaren, Joseph. "From the New Diaspora and the Continent: African American Return Figurations." In *The New African Diaspora*, edited by Isidore Okpewho and Nkiru Nzegwu, 423–441. Bloomington: Indiana University Press, 2009.

Mehta, Brinda. *Notions of Identity, Diaspora, and Gender in Caribbean Women's Writing.* New York: Palgrave MacMillan, 2009.

Meier, Terry. "Stand Up and Speak Out: 'Oppositional Talk' in the Discourse of African American Girls." In *African American Women's Language. Discourse, Education, and Identity*, edited by Sonja L. Lanehart, 245–260. Newcastle, UK: Cambridge Scholars Publishing, 2009.

Mendible, Myra. "Growing Up Cuban in Miami: History, Storytelling and the Politics of Exile." *Jouvert: A Journal of Postcolonial Studies* 6 (2001). http://social.chass.ncsu.edu/jouvert/.

Mercer, Kobena. *Travel & See: Black Diaspora Art Practices since the 1980s.* Durham: Duke University Press, 2016.

Migraine-George, Thérèse. "Ama Ata Aidoo's Orphan Ghosts: African Literature and Aesthetic Postmodernity." *Research in African Literatures* 34, no. 4 (Winter 2003): 83–95.

"Mi Jibarita." *Johnny Rodriguez y su Orquesta. 1935–1940.* Harlequin Records, 1996.

Miller-Young, Mireille. *A Taste for Brown Sugar: Black Women in Pornography.* Durham: Duke University Press, 2014.

Mock, Janet. *Redefining Realness: My Path to Womanhood, Identity, Love & So Much More.* New York: Atria, 2014.

———. *Surpassing Certainty: What My Twenties Taught Me.* New York: Atria Books, 2017.

Moïse, Lenelle. *Cornered in the Dark: A Choreopoem.* (Unpublished performance), 2002.

Monáe, Janelle. *Dirty Computer.* Bad Boy/Wonderland, 2018.

———. "Dirty Computer [Emotion Picture]." YouTube, April 27, 2018.

Moon, Kamilah Aisha. *She Has a Name.* New York: Four Way Books, 2014.

Moore, Lisa C., and Tiona McClodden. "Untitled Black Lesbian Elders Project." www.ubleproject.tumblr.com.

Moraga, Cherríe, "Entering the Lives of Others: Theory in the Flesh." In Cherríe Moraga and Gloria Anzaldúa, eds. *This Bridge Called My Back: Writings by Radical Women of Color.* New York: Kitchen Table Women of Color Press, 1983.

Morand, Paul. *Black Magic.* New York: Viking Press, 1929.

Moretti, Franco. *The Way of the World: The Bildungsroman in European Culture* (1987). New York: Verso, 2000.

Morgan, Marcyliena. "Just Take Me as I Am." Foreword to *African American Women's Language: Discourse, Education and Identity*, edited by Sonja Lanehart, xiii. Newcastle, UK: Cambridge Scholars Publishing, 2009.

Morris, Susana M. "Black Girls Are from the Future: Afrofuturist Feminism in Octavia E. Butler's "Fledgling."" *Women's Studies Quarterly* 40, no. 3/4 (2012): 146–166.

Morrison, Toni. *Beloved*. New York: Plume, 1987.

———. *Jazz*. New York: Plume, 1992.

———. *Love*. New York: Plume, 2003.

———. "Recitatif." In *Confirmation: An Anthology of African American Women* by Amiri (Leroi Jones) Baraka and Amina Baraka. New York: Quill Press, 1983.

Moten, Fred. "The Case of Blackness." *Criticism* 50, no.2 (2008): 177–218.

———. *In the Break: The Aesthetics of the Black Radical Tradition*. Minneapolis: University of Minnesota Press, 2003.

Mudimbe, Valentin Y. *The Idea of Africa*. Bloomington: Indiana University Press, 1994.

Muholi, Zanele. *what do you see when you look at us?* 2011. ww.inkanyiso.org.

Mullen, Harryette. *Muse and Drudge*. San Diego: Singing Horse Press, 1995.

———. *Recyclopedia: Trimmings, S*PeRM**K*T, and Muse & Drudge*. St. Paul: Graywolf Press, 2006.

———. *Sleeping with the Dictionary*. Oakland: University of California Press, 2002.

Muñoz, José Esteban. *Cruising Utopia: The Then and There of Queer Futurity*. New York: New York University Press, 2009.

———. "Thinking beyond Anti Relationality and Anti Utopianism in Queer Critique." In "Forum: Conference Debates: The Anti-Social Thesis in Queer Theory," *PMLA* 121, no. 3 (2006): 825–826.

Musser, Amber Jamilla. *Sensual Excess: Queer Femininity and Brown Jouissance*. New York: New York University Press, 2018.

Nash, Jennifer Christine. *The Black Body in Ecstasy: Reading Race, Reading Pornography*. Durham: Duke University Press, 2014.

———. "Practicing Love: Black Feminism, Love-Politics, and Post-Intersectionality." *Meridians* 11, no. 2 (2011): 1–24.

Navarro, Elena Levy. "Fattening Queer History: Where Does Fat History Go from Here?" In *The Fat Studies Reader*, edited by Edna Rothblum and Sandra Solovay, 15–24. New York: New York University Press, 2009.

Naylor, Gloria. *The Women of Brewster Place*. New York: Penguin Contemporary, 1982.

Nfah-Abbenyi, Juliana Makuchi. *Gender in African Women's Writing: Identity, Sexuality, and Difference*. Bloomington: University of Indiana Press, 1997.

Nixon, Angelique. *Resisting Paradise: Tourism, Diaspora, and Sexuality in Caribbean Culture*. Jackson: University Press of Mississippi, 2015.

NOLOSE. "A Response to White Fat Activism from People of Color in the Fat Justice Movement." March 2012. https://nolose.org/about/policy/fat-white-activism-poc/.

"Ntozake Shange." In *Historical Dictionary of African American Theatre*, edited by Anthony D. Hill and Douglas Q. Barnett. Lanham, MD: Scarecrow Press, 2009.

Nyong'o, Tavia. Afro-Fabulations: The Queer Drama of Black Life. New York: New York University Press, 2018.

Obejas, Achy. *Memory Mambo*. Jersey City: Cleis Press, 1996.

O'Donnell, Shannon, Ilan H. Meyer, and Sharon Schwartz. "Increased Risk of Suicide Attempts among Black and Latino Lesbians, Gay Men, and Bisexuals." *American Journal of Public Health* 101, no. 6 (2011): 1055–1059.

Ogundipe-Leslie, 'Molara. "Introduction: Women in Africa and Her Diaspora" and "The Bilingual to Quatrilingual Poet in Africa." In *Moving beyond Boundaries: Volume 1 International Dimensions of Black Women's Writing*, edited by Carol E. Boyce-Davies and 'Molara Ogundipe-Leslie. New York: New York University Press, 1995.

Okara, Ben. "African Speech . . . English Words." In *Switching Languages: Translingual Writers Reflect on Their Craft*, edited by Steven G. Kellman, 169–182. Lincoln: University of Nebraska Press, 2003.

Okpewho, Isodore, Carole Boyce Davies, and Alo A. Mazrui, eds. *The African Diaspora: African Origins and New World Identities*. Bloomington: Indiana University Press, 2001.

Oliver, Akilah. *The She Said Dialogues: Flesh Memory*. New York: Snakeproof Press, 1998.

Olney, Christian. "Dionne Brand in Conversation." *Ariel* 33, no. 2 (2002): 87–102.

O'Neale, Sondra. "Race, Sex and Self: Aspects of Bildüng in Select Novels by Black American Women Novelists." *MELUS* 9, no. 4 (Winter 1982): 25–37.

Oram, Alison, and Annmarie Turnbull. *The Lesbian History Sourcebook: Love and Sex between Women in Britain from 1780 to 1970*. New York: Routledge, 2001.

Oxford English Dictionary. 2nd Edition, 1989.

Parker, JanTina. 2012. "Silhouettes" Master's Theses. *CUNY Academic Works*. https://academicworks.cuny.edu/cc_etds_theses/445.

Parks, Suzan-Lori. *The Red Letter Plays: In The Blood and Fucking A*. New York: Theatre Communications Group, 2001.

Patterson, Orlando. *Slavery and Social Death: A Comparative Study*. Cambridge: Harvard University Press, 2018.

Pavlič, Ed. *Crossroads Modernism: Descent and Emergence in African-American Literary Culture*. Minneapolis: University of Minnesota Press, 2002.

Perry, Donna Marie. "Jamaica Kincaid: An Interview." In *Backtalk: Women Writers Speak Out: Interviews by Donna Perry*. New Brunswick: Rutgers University Press, 1993.

Peterson, Dale E. "Response and Call: The African American Dialogue with Bakhtin." *American Literature* 65, no. 4 (1993): 761–775.

Philip, M. NourbeSe. "Dis Place the Space Between." In *Feminist Measures: Soundings in Poetry and Theory*, edited by Lynn Keller and Christanne Miller, 287–316. Ann Arbor: University of Michigan Press, 1994.

———. "Fugues, Fragments and Fissures: A Work in Progress." In *Music • Memory • Resistance: Calypso and the Caribbean Literary Imagination*, edited by Sandra Pouchet Paquet, Patricia Saunders, and Stephen Stuempfle. Jamaica: Ian Randle Publications, 2007.

———. *A Genealogy of Resistance: And Other Essays*. Toronto: Mercury Press, 1997.

———. *She Tries Her Tongue, Her Silence Softly Breaks*. Middletown, CT: Wesleyan University Press, 2015.

Phillips, Maggi. "Engaging Dreams: Alternative Perspectives on Flora Nwapa, Buchi Emecheta, Ama Ata Aidoo, Bessie Head, and Tsitsi Dangarembga's Writing." *Research in African Literatures* 25, no. 4 (Winter 1994): 89–103.

Pinto, Samantha. *Difficult Diasporas: The Transnational Feminist Aesthetic of the Black Atlantic.* New York: New York University Press, 2013.

Popoola, Olumide. *this is not about sadness.* Münster, Germany: Unrast Verlag, 2010.

Prince, Mary. *The History of Mary Prince, A West Indian Slave, Related by Herself.* London: F. Wesley and AH Davis, 1831.

Puar, Jasbir K. "'I would rather be a cyborg than a goddess': Becoming-Intersectional in Assemblage Theory." *philoSOPHIA* 2 (2012): 49–66.

Pujolràs Noguer, Esther. *An African (Auto)biography: Ama Ata Aidoo's Literary Quest.* Dissertation, Department de Filologia Anglesa I Germanisitca, Facultat de Filosofia I Lletres, Universitat Autonoma de Barcelona (2010).

Quashie, Kevin. *The Sovereignty of Quiet: Beyond Resistance in Black Culture.* New Brunswick: Rutgers University Press, 2012.

———. "The Trouble with Publicness: Toward a Theory of Black Quiet." *African American Review* 43, no. 2/3 (2009): 329–343.

Quayson, Ato. *Calibrations: Reading for the Social.* Minneapolis: University of Minnesota Press, 2003.

———. "Incessant Particularities: 'Calibrations' as Close Reading." *Research in African Literatures* 36, no. 2 (Summer 2005): 122–131.

Ramazani, Jahan. "A Transnational Poetics." *American Literary History* 18, no. 2 (2006): 332–359.

———. *A Transnational Poetics.* Chicago: University of Chicago Press, 2014.

Ranta, Jerrald. "Palindromes, Poems, and Geometric Form." *College English* 36, no. 2 (October 1974): 161–172.

"Recitative." *New Grove Dictionary of Opera.* Via PennText, November 10, 2009.

Reddock, Rhoda. "Gender Equality, Pan-Africanism, and the Diaspora." *International Journal of African Renaissance Studies* 2, no. 2 (2007): 255–267.

Reed, Anthony. *Freedom Time: The Poetics and Politics of Black Experimental Writing.* Baltimore: Johns Hopkins University Press, 2014.

Réjouis, Rose-Myriam. "Caribbean Writers and Language: Autobiographical Poetics of Jamaica Kincaid and Patrick Chamoiseau." *Massachusetts Review* 44, no. 1/2 (Summer 2003): 213–232.

Richardson, Matt. *The Queer Limit of Black Memory: Black Lesbian Literature and Irresolution.* Columbus: Ohio State University Press, 2013.

Rojas, Maythee. *Women of Color and Feminism.* New York: Seal Press, 2009.

Roman, Miriam Jiménez, and Juan Flores, eds. *The Afro-Latin@ Reader: History and Culture in the United States.* Durham: Duke University Press, 2010.

Ross, Marlon B. "Beyond the Closet as Raceless Paradigm." In *Black Queer Studies: A Critical Anthology*, edited by E. Patrick Johnson and Mae G. Henderson, 161–189. Durham: Duke University Press, 2005.

———. "Pleasuring Identity, or the Delicious Politics of Belonging." *New Literary History* 31, no. 4 (2000): 827–850.

Ruddick, Sara. "Maternal Thinking as a Feminist Standpoint." In *The Feminist Standpoint Theory Reader: Intellectual and Political Controversies*, edited by Sandra G. Harding, 161–168. New York: Routledge, 2004.

Rugoff, Kathy. "The Historical and Social Context of Gwendolyn Brooks's Poetry." In *Critical Insights: Gwendolyn Brooks*. Pasadena: Salem Press, 2009.

Russell, Heather. *Legba's Crossing: Narratology in the African Atlantic*. Athens: University of Georgia Press, 2009.

Russell, Michelle. "Slave Codes and Liner Notes." In *All the Women Are White, All the Blacks Are Men, But Some of Us Are Brave: Black Women's Studies*, edited by Gloria T. Hull, Patricia Bell Scott, and Barbara Smith, 129–143. Old Westbury, NY: The Feminist Press, 1982.

Salkey, Andrew. "Review [Untitled Review of Jamaica Kincaid's *At the Bottom of the River*]." *World Literature Today* 58, no. 2 (Spring 1984): 316.

Sapphire. *Push*. New York: Alfred A. Knopf, 1996.

Saussure, Ferdinand de. *Course in General Linguistics*. Edited by Charles Bally and Albert Sechehaye. Translation from the French by Wade Baskin. New York: McGraw-Hill, 1966.

Scott, Darieck. *Extravagant Abjection: Blackness, Power, and Sexuality in the African American Literary Imagination*. New York: New York University Press, 2010.

Scott, Karla D. "Crossing Cultural Borders: 'Girl' and 'Look' as Markers of Identity in Black Women's Language Use." *Discourse & Society* 11, no. 2 (2000): 237–248.

Sedgwick, Eve. *Epistemology of the Closet*. Berkeley: University of California Press, 1991.

Senghor, Léopold. "French, Language of Culture." In *Switching Languages: Translingual Writers Reflect on Their Craft*, edited by Steven G. Kellman, 35–42. Lincoln: University of Nebraska Press, 2003.

Sexton, Jared. "The Social Life of Social Death: On Afro-Pessimism and Black Optimism." *InTensions* 5 (Fall/Winter 2011): 28–29.

Shange, Ntozake. *Betsey Brown*. New York: St. Martin's Press, 1985.

———. *A Daughter's Geography*. New York: St. Martin's Press, 1983.

———. *for colored girls who have considered suicide/ when the rainbow is enuf*. First Printing. Berkeley: Shameless Hussy Press, 1975.

———. *for colored girls who have considered suicide/ when the rainbow is enuf*. Second Printing. Berkeley: Shameless Hussy Press, 1976.

———. *for colored girls who have considered suicide/ when the rainbow is enough*. Revised edition. New York: Collier, 1977.

———. *From Okra to Greens: A Different Kinda Love Story*. New York: Samuel French, 1983.

———. *lost in language & sound: or how i found my way to the arts: essays*. New York: St. Martin's Press, 2011.

———. *Nappy Edges*. New York: St. Martin's Press, 1991.

———. *Sassafrass, Cypress & Indigo*. New York: St. Martin's Press, 1982.

———. *See No Evil: Prefaces, Essays & Accounts, 1976–1983*. San Francisco: Momos Press, 1984.

———. *three pieces: spell #7, a photograph: lovers in motion, boogie woogie landscapes*. New York: St. Martin's Press, 1992.

Shklovsky, Victor. *Theory of Prose*. (1925) Translated by Benjamin Sher. Elmwood Park, IL: Dalkey Archive Press, 1990.

Shockley, Evie. "Going Overboard: African American Poetic Innovation and the Middle Passage." *Contemporary Literature* 52, no. 4 (Winter 2011): 791–817.

———. *Renegade Poetics: Black Aesthetics and Formal Innovation in African-American Poetry*. Iowa City: University of Iowa Press, 2011.

Simmons, Aishah Shahidah. "A State of Rage (for Toni Cade Bambara)." In *Shout Out: Women of Color Respond to Violence*, edited by Maria Ochoa and Barbara K. Ige, 221–224. Emeryville: The Seal Press, 2007.

Simone, Nina. "Four Women." *Wild Is the Wind*. Phillips Records, 1966.

Smiley, Lauren. "LGBT Suicides: Ayisha Hassan, Daughter of Marin Non-Profit Executive Director, Takes Life," *San Francisco Weekly*. October 12, 2010. https://www.sfweekly .com/news/lgbt-suicides-aiyisha-hassan-daughter-of-marin-non-profit-executive -director-takes-life.

Smith, Valerie. "Reading the Intersections of Race and Gender in Narratives of Passing." *Diacritics* 24, no. 2–3 (1993): 43–57.

Smith, Zadie. *On Beauty*. New York: Penguin Books, 2005.

Smitherman, Geneva. *Talkin that Talk: Language, Culture, and Education in African America*. New York: Routledge, 1999.

Snorton, C. Riley. *Nobody Is Supposed to Know: Black Sexuality on the Down Low*. Minneapolis: University of Minnesota Press, 2014.

Somerville, Siobhan. *Queering the Color Line: Race and the Invention of Homosexuality in American Culture*. Durham: Duke University Press, 2000.

Spillers, Hortense J. *Black, White, and in Color: Essays on American Literature and Culture*. Chicago: University of Chicago Press, 2003.

———. "Interstices: A Small Drama of Words." In *Black, White, and in Color: Essays on American Literature and Culture*. Chicago: University of Chicago Press, 2003. First published in *Pleasure and Danger: Exploring Female Sexuality*, edited by Carol Vance. New York: Pandora/HarperCollins, 1984.

———. "Introduction: Peter's Pans: Eating in the Diaspora." In *Black, White, and in Color: Essays on American Literature and Culture*, 1–64. Chicago: University of Chicago Press, 2003.

———. "Mama's Baby, Papa's Maybe: An American Grammar Book." In *Black, White, and in Color: Essays on American Literature and Culture*. Chicago: University of Chicago Press, 2003. First published in *Diacritics* (Summer 1987).

Stallings, L. H. *A Dirty South Manifesto: Sexual Resistance and Imagination in the New South*. Durham: University of North Carolina Press, 2019.

———. "Funking Machine: A Choreostory." Presentation at the American Studies Association Annual Meeting, Los Angeles 2014.

———. *Funk the Erotic: Transaesthetics and Black Sexual Cultures*. Urbana: University of Illinois Press, 2015.

———. *Mutha' Is Half a Word: Intersections of Folklore, Vernacular, Myth, and Queerness in Black Female Culture.* Columbus: Ohio State University Press, 2007.

Staples, Robert. "The Myth of Black Macho: A Response to Angry Black Feminists." *Black Scholar* 10, no. 6/7 (March/April 1979): 24–33.

Starbury, Allen, "Keri Hilson, Missy Elliott Rebuke Lesbian Relationship Rumor." *BallerStatus*, March 16, 2014.

Stras, Laurie. "White Face, Black Voice: Race, Gender, and Region in the Music of the Boswell Sisters." *Journal of the Society for American Music* 1, no. 2 (2007): 207–255.

Sugg, Katherine. "Migratory Sexualities, Diasporic Histories, and Memory in Queer Cuban-American Cultural Production." *Society and Space* 21, no. 4 (2003): 461–477.

Sullivan, Joanna. "Redefining the Novel in Africa." *Research in African Literatures* 37, no. 4 (2006): 177–188.

Tadiar, Neferti Xina M. "Personal Diaspora." *Diaspora and Immigration*, edited by V. Y. Mudimbe and Sabine Engel. A Special Issue of *South Atlantic Quarterly* 98, no. 1 (Winter 1999).

Tate, Chicava "HoneyChild." "Evil Beautiful Sunshine." Performance at Jazzy's Juke Joint. June 2, 2008. Video.

Tate, Claudia. *Black Women Writers at Work.* New York: Continuum, 1983.

Tiffin, Helen. "Cold Hearts and (Foreign) Tongues: Recitation and the Reclamation of the Female Body in the Works of Erna Brodber and Jamaica Kincaid." *Callaloo* 16, no. 4 (1993): 909–921.

Tinsley, Omise'eke Natasha. *Ezili's Mirrors: Imagining Black Queer Genders.* Durham: Duke University Press, 2018.

Umeh, Marie A. "The Joys of Motherhood: Myth or Reality?" *Colby Library Quarterly* 18, no. 1 (March 1982): 39–46.

Vernon, Olympia. *Eden.* New York: Grove Press, 2002.

Walcott, Rinaldo. "Outside in Black Studies: Reading from a Queer Place in the Diaspora." In *Black Queer Studies*, edited by E. Patrick Johnson and Mae Henderson, 90–105. Durham: Duke University Press, 2005.

Walker, Alice. *The Color Purple.* New York: Harcourt Brace Jovanovich, 1982.

———. *In Search of Our Mothers' Gardens: Womanist Prose.* New York: Houghton Mifflin, 1983.

———. *Possessing the Secret of Joy.* New York: Harcourt Brace Jovanovich, 1992.

———. *The Temple of My Familiar.* New York: Harcourt Brace Jovanovich, 1989.

Wann, Marilyn. 2012. "I Stand" project. marilynwann.com.

Warner, Michael. *The Trouble with Normal: Sex, Politics, and the Ethics of Queer Life.* Cambridge: Harvard University Press, 1999.

Warren, Kenneth W. *What Was African American Literature?* Cambridge: Harvard University Press, 2012.

Washington, Mary Helen. "'Taming All That Anger Down': Rage and Silence in Gwendolyn Brooks' *Maud Martha.*" *Massachusetts Review* 24, no. 2 (1983): 453–466.

*Watermelon Woman.* Directed by Cheryl Dunye. Dancing Girl Productions, 1996.

Wa Thiong'o, Ngũgĩ. "Imperialism of Language: English, a Language for the World?" In

*Switching Languages: Translingual Writers Reflect on Their Craft*, edited by Steven G. Kellman, 167–168. Lincoln: University of Nebraska Press, 2003.

Weeks, Jeffery. *What Is Sexual History?* Cambridge: Polity Press, 2016.

Weheliye, Alexander G. *Habeas Viscus: Racializing Assemblages, Biopolitics, and Black Feminist Theories of the Human.* Durham: Duke University Press, 2014.

———. *Phonographies: Grooves in Sonic Afro-Modernity.* Durham: Duke University Press, 2008.

Wekker, Gloria. *The Politics of Passion: Women's Sexual Culture in the Afro-Surinamese Diaspora.* New York: Columbia University Press, 2006.

West, Cornell. "The New Cultural Politics of Difference." *Humanities as Social Technology* 53 (Summer 1990): 93–109.

West, Kanye. "Monster," featuring Rick Ross, Nicki Minaj, and Jay-Z. *My Beautiful Dark Twisted Fantasy.* Roc-A-Fella Records, 2010.

Wilderson, Frank. *Red, White & Black: Cinema and the Structure of US Antagonisms.* Durham: Duke University Press, 2010.

Williams, Dana A. *Contemporary African American Women Playwrights: An Annotated Bibliography.* Westport, CT: Greenwood Press, 1998.

Willis, Deborah, and Carla Williams, editors. *The Black Female Body: A Photographic History.* Philadelphia: Temple University Press, 2002.

Wilson, Bianca D. M. "Widening the Dialogue to Narrow the Gap in Health Disparities: Approaches to Fat Black Lesbian and Bisexual Women's Health Promotion." *Fat Studies Reader*, edited by Edna Rothblum and Sondra Solovay, 54–64. New York: New York University Press, 2009.

Wright, Michelle M. *Physics of Blackness: Beyond the Middle Passage.* Minneapolis: University of Minnesota Press, 2015.

Wright, Michelle M., and Antje Schuhmann, eds. *Blackness and Sexualities.* Berlin: LIT Verlag, 2007.

Xekatwane, Vuyiswa. "Conquering Fears of Queerness: Zanele Muholi's 'Somnyama Ngonyama.'" *Between 10 and 5: The Creative Showcase*, November 20, 2015.

Young, Jean. "Ritual Poetics and Rites of Passage in Ntozake Shange's *for colored girls who have considered suicide/ when the rainbow is enuf.*" In *Black Theatre: Ritual Performance in the African Diaspora*, edited by Paul Carter Harrison, Victor Leo Walker II, and Gus Edwards, 296–310. Philadelphia: Temple University Press, 2002.

Zeleza, Paul Tiyambe. "Rewriting the African Diaspora: Beyond the Black Atlantic." *African Affairs* 104, no. 414 (2005): 35–68.

# Index

MECCA JAMILAH SULLIVAN is an assistant professor of English at Bryn Mawr and the author of *Blue Talk and Love*.

## The New Black Studies Series

Beyond Bondage: Free Women of Color in the Americas    *Edited by
David Barry Gaspar and Darlene Clark Hine*

The Early Black History Movement, Carter G. Woodson, and Lorenzo
Johnston Greene    *Pero Gaglo Dagbovie*

"Baad Bitches" and Sassy Supermamas: Black Power Action Films    *Stephane Dunn*

Black Maverick: T. R. M. Howard's Fight for Civil Rights and Economic Power
*David T. Beito and Linda Royster Beito*

Beyond the Black Lady: Sexuality and the New African American Middle Class
*Lisa B. Thompson*

Extending the Diaspora: New Histories of Black People    *Dawne Y. Curry,
Eric D. Duke, and Marshanda A. Smith*

Activist Sentiments: Reading Black Women in the Nineteenth Century
*P. Gabrielle Foreman*

Black Europe and the African Diaspora    *Edited by Darlene Clark Hine,
Trica Danielle Keaton, and Stephen Small*

Freeing Charles: The Struggle to Free a Slave on the Eve of the Civil War
*Scott Christianson*

African American History Reconsidered    *Pero Gaglo Dagbovie*

Freud Upside Down: African American Literature and Psychoanalytic Culture
*Badia Sahar Ahad*

A. Philip Randolph and the Struggle for Civil Rights    *Cornelius L. Bynum*

Queer Pollen: White Seduction, Black Male Homosexuality, and the Cinematic
*David A. Gerstner*

The Rise of Chicago's Black Metropolis, 1920–1929    *Christopher Robert Reed*

The Muse Is Music: Jazz Poetry from the Harlem Renaissance to Spoken Word
*Meta DuEwa Jones*

Living with Lynching: African American Lynching Plays, Performance, and
Citizenship, 1890–1930    *Koritha Mitchell*

Africans to Spanish America: Expanding the Diaspora    *Edited by Sherwin K. Bryant,
Rachel Sarah O'Toole, and Ben Vinson III*

Rebels and Runaways: Slave Resistance in Nineteenth-Century Florida
*Larry Eugene Rivers*

The Black Chicago Renaissance    *Edited by Darlene Clark Hine and John McCluskey Jr.*

The Negro in Illinois: The WPA Papers    *Edited by Brian Dolinar*

Along the Streets of Bronzeville: Black Chicago's Literary Landscape
*Elizabeth Schroeder Schlabach*

Gendered Resistance: Women, Slavery, and the Legacy of Margaret Garner
*Edited by Mary E. Frederickson and Delores M. Walters*

Racial Blackness and the Discontinuity of Western Modernity    *Lindon Barrett,
edited by Justin A. Joyce, Dwight A. McBride, and John Carlos Rowe*

Fannie Barrier Williams: Crossing the Borders of Region and Race
*Wanda A. Hendricks*

The University of Illinois Press
is a founding member of the
Association of University Presses.

———————————————

Composed in 10.5/13 Adobe Minion Pro
with Triplex display
by Jim Proefrock
at the University of Illinois Press
Manufactured by Versa Press, Inc.

University of Illinois Press
1325 South Oak Street
Champaign, IL 61820-6903
www.press.uillinois.edu